T0301510

THE GROWING CHALLENGE OF YOUTH UNEMPLOYMENT IN EUROPE AND AMERICA

A Cross-Cultural Perspective

Radha Jagannathan

With the assistance of Michael J. Camasso and other country experts

BRISTOL
UNIVERSITY
PRESS

First published in Great Britain in 2021 by

Bristol University Press
University of Bristol
1-9 Old Park Hill
Bristol
BS2 8BB
UK
t: +44 (0)117 954 5940
e: bup-info@bristol.ac.uk

Details of international sales and distribution partners are available at
bristoluniversitypress.co.uk

© Bristol University Press 2021

British Library Cataloguing in Publication Data
A catalogue record for this book is available from the British Library

ISBN 978-1-5292-0010-2 hardcover
ISBN 978-1-5292-0012-6 ePub
ISBN 978-1-5292-0011-9 ePdf

The right of Radha Jagannathan to be identified as author of this work has been asserted by
her in accordance with the Copyright, Designs and Patents Act 1988.

Cover design: blu inc, Bristol
Front cover image: iStock/MikhailMishchenko
Bristol University Press uses environmentally responsible
print partners.
Printed in and bound in Great Britain by CPI Group (UK) Ltd,
Croydon, CR0 4YY

To Jagan, Krishna and Meera – you are
everything to me

Contents

List of Figures, Tables and Boxes   vii
Notes on Contributors   ix
Preface   xii

1   Introduction   1
     Radha Jagannathan
2   Acceptable Jobs and the Epidemic of Youth   21
     Unemployment in Southern Italy
     Maurizio Caserta, Livio Ferrante, Radha Jagannathan
     and Simona Monteleone
3   No Jobs, No Hope: The Future of Youth Employment   51
     in Spain
     José L. Arco-Tirado, Francisco D. Fernández-Martín
     and Radha Jagannathan
4   *Dirigisme Pour L'Ordinaire:* Vocational Training in   79
     21st Century France
     Michael J. Camasso, Guillaume Moissonnier
     and Radha Jagannathan
5   Educating Youth for Future Unemployment in Greece   101
     Radha Jagannathan and Ioanna Tsoulou
6   Labor Market Policies to Fight Youth Unemployment   127
     in Portugal: Between Statism and Experimentalism
     Paulo Marques and Pedro Videira
7   Adaptability of the German Vocational Model to   165
     Mediterranean Countries
     Jale Tosun, Julia Weiß, Alexa Meyer-Hamme and
     Marcel Katzlinger

8   US Style Entrepreneurship as a Pathway to Youth   203
     Employment: Exporting the Promise
     Radha Jagannathan and Michael J. Camasso
9   Grading the Implementation Prospects: Where Do   233
     We Go from Here?
     Radha Jagannathan

Index   251

List of Figures, Tables and Boxes

Figures

1.1   Historical record of entrepreneurship in Europe   11
      and the US
2.1   Regional variation in survey responses   42
3.1   Unemployment rate by age groups in Spain and EU-28   53
3.2   Youth unemployment (15–29) by regions in Spain   54
4.1   The French education system   87
5.1   Education system in Greece   107
6.1   Youth unemployment in Portugal (2000–2018)   129
6.2   Share of involuntary temporary contracts: Portugal and 132
      EU-28 (2000–2018), 15–24-year-olds
6.3   Youth unemployment among graduates: Portugal   133
      and EU-28 (2005–2018)
6.4   Youth unemployment among those holding   133
      upper secondary and post-secondary non-tertiary
      education: Portugal and EU-28 (2005–2018)
7.1   Youth unemployment rates as a percentage of the active 168
      population aged 15–24 (1995–2018)
7.2   Response patterns to the question of whether skills   172
      mismatch is a driver of youth unemployment (2016)
7.3   German Foreign Direct Investment stock abroad (in   173
      millions of US dollars) (2001–2011)
8.1   Education system in the United States   208

Tables

2.1   Youth unemployment rate in EU countries   26
      (August 2019) (seasonally adjusted %)
2.2   Young people not in employment, education and   28
      training (NEET) rates (%)

2.3	CUPESSE survey results: all youth	39
2.4	CUPESSE survey results: unemployed youth	40
3.1	Policy interventions in general education in Spain	61
3.2	Policy interventions in vocational education and training (VET) in Spain	62
3.3	Participation of students, schools and enterprises on dual VET in Spain	67
3.4	Active labor market policies (ALMPs) in Spain	68
4.1	Demography, economy and labor in France (2001–2017)	92
5.1	Survey responses to closed-ended questions	116
6.1	Youth-oriented ALMPs (2000–2017)	143
6.2	Youth-oriented ALMPs during three distinct periods	150
6.3	Measures implemented in the scope of the Youth Guarantee	153
8.1	Entrepreneurship – a comparison of perception, motivation and action across study countries	217
8.2	Entrepreneurial framework conditions – a comparison across study countries	219
9.1	Scorecard on feasibility of German dual model and American entrepreneurship model	238

Boxes

6.1	Effectiveness of ALMPs in Portugal	154
9.1	Caserta – Italy	238
9.2	Arco Tirado – Spain	240
9.3	Camasso and Moissonier – France	241
9.4	Tsoulou – Greece	242
9.5	Marques – Portugal	243
9.6	Tosun – Germany	244
9.7	Jagannathan and Camasso – United States	245

Notes on Contributors

José L. Arco-Tirado is Professor at the Department of Developmental and Educational Psychology at the University of Granada, Spain. He has also worked at the Provincial Center for Drug Addiction and the Andalusian School of Public Health. At the University of Granada, Arco-Tirado teaches courses on developmental psychology and learning difficulties on a bilingual group in Primary Education Teacher Training and coordinates the Practicas in the Master Program. Arco-Tirado has published several books, chapters and papers on national and international congresses and over thirty articles in nationally and internationally indexed, peer-reviewed journals.

Michael J. Camasso is Professor of Resource Economics at Rutgers University, USA. He is a Fulbright Scholar, a DAAD Fellow, and a Bruel Prize Winner. He is also the recipient of the Laity Academic Leadership Award (American Association of University Professors) and the Academic Integrity Award (New Jersey Public Policy Association). Professor Camasso has written four books and numerous articles. His research has appeared in such journals as *Risk Analysis, Research in Labor Economics, Journal of Labor Economics, Contemporary Economic Policy, Journal of Policy Analysis and Management, Journal of Economic Perspectives, Research on Economic Inequality* and others.

Maurizio Caserta is Professor at the Department of Economics and Business at the University of Catania. Educated in Italy (Catania and Naples) and the UK (Cambridge and London), he has published in various fields ranging from growth theory and local development to the economics of culture and the economics of institutions. He is active in the political and social arena.

Francisco D. Fernández-Martín is Professor at the Department of Developmental and Educational Psychology, University of Granada, Spain. Fernández-Martín has vast experience in implementing public program evaluations, research studies and assessments in the education field with particular focus on entrepreneurship skills, plurilingual education, civic-community engagement, counseling and guidance services, inclusive education and elderly education. Fernández-Martín has published over thirty articles in nationally and internationally indexed, peer-reviewed journals and several books, book chapters and papers at international and national congresses and conferences.

Livio Ferrante is Researcher in Economics at the University of Catania, where he received his PhD in Economics and Management. His research interests are broad, and he is particularly interested in regional policies, econometrics, criminal behavior and local development.

Radha Jagannathan is Professor of Statistics at Rutgers University, USA. She received her PhD from Princeton University. She is a Fulbright Scholar whose research on poverty, child welfare and human capital development has received international attention. Her teaching and research at Rutgers have been recognized by numerous awards and prizes. She has authored three books and her research has appeared in top peer-reviewed journals in economics, policy analysis and evaluation. She has authored over 150 reports on the evaluation of publicly and privately funded human and social capital investment programs in the US; and has founded a human capital development program for public school students entitled *Nurture thru Nature,* that has received critical acclaim.

Marcel Katzlinger is a journalist and works with the Austrian Broadcasting Corporation (ORF). He completed his Bachelor's and Master's degrees at Heidelberg University and worked as a research assistant in the project *Cultural Pathways to Economic Self-Sufficiency and Entrepreneurship* (CUPESSE).

Paulo Marques is Assistant Professor in the Department of Political Economy, ISCTE – University Institute of Lisbon. He is also a researcher at DINÂMIA'CET. He contributes to the field of Comparative Political Economy and his research interests include labor market policies and labor market segmentation. He has published his research in the *Socio-Economic Review, Comparative European Politics* and the *International Journal of Social Welfare.*

Alexa Meyer-Hamme is a project manager at the Bertelsmann Foundation who works on issues related to education and training, and has profound knowledge of the youth labor market situation in

Spain. She received her Magister Degree from the Leuphana University at Lüneburg (2008) and completed her doctorate at the Bremen International Graduate School of Social Sciences (2014).

Simona Monteleone is Researcher in Political Economy and Professor in the Department of Education at the University of Catania. Her research topics include informal economy, brain drain, youth unemployment and crowdfunding.

Guillaume Moissonnier is an undergraduate student at Rutgers University, majoring in business economics and entrepreneurship. He also serves as a research assistant with interests in youth employment policies and programs directed at school-to-work transitions.

Jale Tosun is Professor of Political Science at Heidelberg University. Her research areas include comparative public policy, international political economy, public administration and European studies. She coordinated the EU-funded collaborative research project *Cultural Pathways to Economic Self-Sufficiency and Entrepreneurship* (CUPESSE; grant agreement ID: 613257).

Ioanna Tsoulou is Research Fellow at UCL, Institute for Environmental Design and Engineering. She has a Master's and a PhD from Rutgers University, USA, and a Master's in Civil Engineering from the University of Patras, Greece. Her research focuses on climate adaptation and resilience, in particular thermal and air quality performance of buildings and neighborhoods, occupant behavior modeling, and green infrastructure.

Pedro Videira is Researcher at DINÂMIA'CET (Centre for Socioeconomic and Territorial Studies) and at CIPES (Centre for Research in Higher Education Policies). His main research interests lie in the field of higher education policies, namely changes to the academic profession and graduates' employability and skills development. He has published several articles and book chapters on those subjects.

Julia Weiß is a doctoral student at the Institute for Political Science at Heidelberg University. Her work concentrates on the integration of young people into labor markets and the society more generally as part of the research project *Change through Crisis? Solidarity and Desolidarization in Germany and Europe* (Solikris), funded by the German Federal Ministry of Education and Research.

Preface

Having grown up in an environment where just about everything – school and college admissions, getting and securing a job, or even receiving a driver's license – turned on knowing the right people or having money, my immigration to the US has been nothing short of an amazing eye-opener on what free market capitalism operating with a substantial decrease in corruption can accomplish. That the US valued individualism and a strong belief that if individuals acted in their own self-interest in a righteous way it would automatically result in societal good, a very Adam Smith-ian approach, both thrilled and scared me. This particular pathway to economic success, moreover, is generally open to one and all – one needed however to embrace the philosophy or the value formula. I also believe that there is an honest attempt here at equalizing opportunities and at becoming better economically as a people. My frequent visits to Germany for teaching and research allowed a personal glimpse into another, quite different pathway to productive citizenship, one where an individual's economic success was more scripted and coordinated by labor supply and labor demand institutions in concert with the government.

With an aging population in the western world and a concomitant increase in dependency ratios, much of the labor market research spotlight has refocused on studying problems in the youth labor market and a search for solutions in the many countries where this problem has become acute. My personal experiences in the US and Germany and my extensive travels across Europe made me think aloud whether (a) the American free-spirit enterprise characterized by risk taking or the coordinated German labor market approach distinguished by trust and cooperation can serve as exemplars for other countries, for example, countries in the Mediterranean region, where youth unemployment rates are well above European averages; and (b) if what I perceive as the national cultures will be accommodative of these approaches.

I realized that this kind of exploration is best done as a joint venture with experts who can provide in situ assessments of their country's youth unemployment problems and the potential for emulating the American or German model. My key role in designing a recently completed cross-country European study on the subject of youth unemployment opened up access to a rich network of colleagues across Europe, colleagues who were enthusiastic in undertaking this explorative journey with me. I invite the reader to embark on this journey with us through Europe and North America to examine the youth unemployment problem. I hope that you gain insight on this journey as much as I have when selecting its destinations and structuring and populating the content of the travel itinerary.

Radha Jagannathan

1

Introduction

Radha Jagannathan

I would like to begin this book on youth unemployment in Europe and America with a personal story. I emigrated from India to the US in the early 1980s as a young bride, barely out of my teens, with an undergraduate degree in economics; I also had developed skills in shorthand and typing. Within weeks of coming to America, I was able to find employment as a project secretary in a major research university, a place where I subsequently rose to the level of full professor. While I no doubt worked hard earning an undergraduate degree in business, a graduate degree in statistics and a doctoral degree in demography and public affairs along the way – and all while raising a family, I credit a good bit of my upward career mobility to an opportunity structure that gave primacy to merit. I do not have a proper counterfactual of course, but I do firmly believe that my career progression would not have followed the same path had I remained in India – and I say this with the utmost respect and love for my birth country. Despite the risk of sounding cliché-ish, I have indeed come to see America as a 'land of opportunity' and have personally experienced the results of what Alexis de Tocqueville labeled 'America's self-interest rightly understood'.

Another characteristic that is quintessentially American, risk-taking, has also seeped into my psychological makeup and has manifested itself in the many decisions I have made for myself and my family. One professional example of this free-wheeling entrepreneurial spirit is my founding with my longtime colleague and mentor, Michael J. Camasso, of a successful STEM education program called *Nurture thru Nature* (NtN), designed to benefit disadvantaged students. Self-interest rightly understood, risk-taking and personal achievement also took me to Germany, aided by a Fulbright scholarship. In retrospect, I find it very hard to believe that after leading a rather sheltered life well into my 30s I ventured out to a country where I knew no one, didn't speak the language, nor knew its customs and practices. Nevertheless, the experience was splendidly rewarding, and I saw firsthand how the German dual education system connected relatively seamlessly with the labor market producing young school leavers with highly marketable skills.

I hope to use the preceding highly personal narration to set the context for the study of youth unemployment this book aims to undertake. As the reader will observe, a recurring theme in this book is the exploration of the importability of the American entrepreneurship model and/or the German dual education system to countries with very high levels of youth unemployment in Southern Europe. I invited experts from Germany, Portugal, Spain, Greece, France, Italy and the US to explore this possibility from both strategy-demand and strategy-supply perspectives, urging them to draw upon the cultural and historical contexts that make each nation a unique venue for system transfer and adoption.

The youth labor market

Why study youth unemployment at this juncture? When François Hollande, the previous President of France, asserted that the two major social issues facing his country were terrorism and youth unemployment, he gave voice to an assessment shared by public and private sector leaders from across Europe and the US. And while terrorism may make for more sensational headlines, youth unemployment, if left unabated, promises to yield consequences for the economic and political fabric that are at least as damaging as a major terrorist event. Today's labels for unemployed youth – the 'scarred' or 'time pass' generation, and NEET (Not in Employment, Education or Training) or NLFET (Not in Labor Force, Education or Training) paint a portrait of discouragement, skills deterioration and disaffection, fostering a new age where many youth do not believe they can measure up to the achievements of their parents.

The COVID-19 pandemic has resulted in unemployment reminiscent of the Great Depression in 1929. In the US, record low overall and youth unemployment rates of the recent past became record high rates in a matter of three months. GDP growth shrank 4.8% in the first quarter of 2020; and one estimate from the Federal Reserve puts job losses at 47 million, with the unemployment rate climbing past 30%, a rate much higher than was experienced during the Great Depression (Faria-e-Castro, 2020). These grim estimates are tempered with optimistic news, and in the words of the St. Louis Federal Reserve Bank Chairman, "everything will snap back to normal once this is over ... if we play our cards right" (Cox, 2020). To some extent such optimism seems to have been well placed, as evidenced by the third quarter GDP increasing at an annual rate of 33.1% (Bureau of Economic Analysis, 2020), and the unemployment rate falling to under 7% in October, 2020, less than half of what it was just six months prior (US Bureau of Labor Statistics, 2020). The other countries represented in this book have also experienced devastating economic effects from the COVID-19 pandemic, and in Italy and Spain the health effects have been equally devastating. In countries where the youth population was already severely affected (for example, Greece, Spain, Italy) there will be further deterioration of their plight and in the attendant economic and social consequences. What is more, these consequences may be more persistent and longer lasting, particularly affecting their employment and wage mobility (Puerto and Kim, 2020).

A sharpened focus on the youth unemployment problem will no doubt occur post-COVID-19, one that will be globally shared. Concerns about the youth labor market were already well reflected in the United Nation's Sustainable Development Goal #4 ('Ensure inclusive and equitable quality education and promote lifelong learning opportunities for all'). Although there are wide regional variations, the most recent data available prior to COVID-19 puts the global youth unemployment rate at 13.6% , with their labor force participation rate also declining substantially between 1999 and 2019, by 12%, even as the number of young people eligible for the labor force grew (ILO, 2020). The NEET rates for youth 25–29 years old were 30.9% in Italy, closely followed by Greece at 29.5%, with relatively high rates also observed in Spain (20.6%) and France (18.7%) (Eurostat, 2019). Nordic countries, the Netherlands, Austria and Germany recorded much lower rates, in the 8–12% range. COVID-19 can be expected to raise these levels and exacerbate the regional differentials.

In past generations youth unemployment was more often than not seen as a natural outcome of labor market dynamics, that is, a demand and supply problem, as well as life cycle transitions. Changing technology or changing societal preferences reduced the demand for some skill/education sets and, conversely, stimulated the demand for others. Expanding economies in Western Europe and the US served as the catalyst that encouraged job seekers to seek retraining or to engage in geographic or sectoral mobility with a high prospect for success.

Today's more or less stagnant economies in some sections of the US and much of Mediterranean Europe limit the employment prospects of retraining and mobility. In addition, a diminution in the interest among millennials in taking low-paying, manufacturing/service jobs has produced a youth labor force with limited work experiences and soft-skill deficits. Youth unemployment has also taken on a decidedly menacing and destructive countenance, mixing rather easily with drug abuse, crime, social unrest, and political extremism, and is exacerbated by the economic consequences of very real losses in earnings potential and, the erosion of a solid good work ethic (Piecha and Wescott, 2014; ILO, 2001; O'Higgins, 2001).

The typical culprits implicated in the problem of unemployment include supply-side factors like skill obsolescence, lower returns to employment than unemployment, skills mismatch, that is, situations where skill supply and demand diverge due to economic shocks, business cycles, and so on (Layard, 1982; Borjas, 2008; Cedefop, 2019), or insufficient labor demand because of a slow or no growth economy, excessive taxes or regulations leading to labor market rigidity, and global trade and job exportation (Bartlett and Steele, 1996; Crisp and Powell, 2017; Borjas, 2008). Minimum wage policies have also been implicated in employers' decisions to hire youth (Card and Kruger, 1995; Layard, 1982; Piketty, 2014) with higher wages thought to lower demand. Germany and America have been able to in large measure sidestep these employment problems, giving rise to the important question – the one I ask in the book – can the approaches practiced in Germany or the US help other countries, specifically the Southern Mediterranean countries, shape their youth employment initiatives? Obviously there are a great many features of the American and German systems on both the demand and supply sides of the issue that make those economic systems work so well in keeping youth unemployment low. I have asked all of our contributors to focus on just two supply side adjustments, viz., the German dual education system and entrepreneurship training in the US.

The selection of countries

As the book's title suggests, the problem of youth unemployment is broached from the vantage point of cultural similarities and differences. The idea that culture, that is, shared values and preferences with intergenerational sustainability (Becker, 1996), has economic consequences is, of course, not new and can be traced back to the pioneering work of Max Weber (1904), Tawney (1922) and Sombart

(1911). In a much more current literature, the idea is on vigorous display in the work of Mokyr (2019), Guisa, Sapienza and Zingales (2006), Fernandez (2008), Bisin and Verdier (2001) and Camasso and Jagannathan (2021), to name a few prominent examples.

While a cross-cultural perspective provides a useful frame of reference for examining national economies, their structure and functioning, and their successes and failures, it is but one of a number that are available. A popular conceptual approach with close links to political science can be found in the varieties of capitalism (VoC) typology promulgated by Hall and Soskice (2001). Countries are classified by how business and industry coordinate their market activities with other key societal institutions, viz., government, education and training, labor and finance to hopefully create production regimes that are prosperous and expanding. Central to this classification is the formation of 'institutional complementarities' that arise between economic and non-market sectors, especially the private business sector and the government.

In the original formulation of the typology, countries were assigned to a category termed liberal market economies (LMEs) if production regimes were the consequence of supply and demand conditions in competitive markets with other institutional actors more or less passive spectators, or to the category of coordinated market economies (CMEs) if firms depended on non-market mechanisms to coordinate their economic actions and conduct business. Examples of the former included the US, Great Britain and some members of the British Commonwealth. Typical CMEs included countries as culturally diverse as Germany, France, Sweden and Italy.

Criticism of the VoC typology has taken many forms and many of these have been catalogued by Hancké et al (2007). Perhaps the most serious of these is what they call a 'mechanistic conception of institutional complementarities' (Hancké et al, 2007: 7). These same authors advocate a revised VoC typology that contains four categories. Membership in the LME remains largely unchanged but CME countries are now divided into three subcategories: pure CMEs that comprise Germany, Austria, Denmark and several other northern European countries; nations with deep state government penetration into the market like France; and countries with compensating state penetration where deep penetration is frustrated by a well-organized business sector (Hancké et al, 2007: 24–28). This last category includes the Southern Mediterranean countries of Italy, Spain, Portugal and Greece.

Within the VoC framework, human capital formation and deployment is discussed as an institution coordination problem, that is, as a problem of securing a workforce with suitable skills (Hall and Soskice, 2001). Hall and Soskice (2001) maintain that nations with CMEs and not LMEs provide guarantees against the erosion of skill specificity with a set of wage, employment and unemployment protections. Left unexplained is the rationale for nations characterized by deep or compensating government penetration in their development of human capital that favors general education over specific skills.

To be fair, VoC was developed primarily as a vehicle to explain production arrangements in a country, and the issues around human capital development and labor supply play a peripheral role in typology formulation and modification. An alternative classification of national economies proposed by Esping-Andersen (1990, 2002) employs the concept of 'welfare state' to distinguish how individual nation-states choose to practice capitalism and prepare their citizens for participation in that enterprise.

In his initial attempt at classifying 'welfare capitalism' Esping-Andersen (1990) identified three distinctive 'worlds': (1) Nordic countries where the government takes the lead in forming active labor market (integration) policies (ALMPs); (2) Continental European countries where the governmental hegemony is lacking but nevertheless the state plays an active role in facilitating economic policy in general, and human capital creation specifically; and (3) Anglophone countries where government is deferential to the vagaries of the market and human capital is created through flexible labor markets, general education and the largely unregulated transition between the two. Esping-Andersen (2002) subsequently revised his typology, recognizing that his Continental European category was too broad, and grouped countries like Germany and Italy that manifested vastly different expressions of 'welfare state'. A fourth category, 'Southern European', was added to distinguish those continental countries where income redistribution is negligible, family assistance is promoted, cooperation between business, labor and the state is disjointed and halting, and where general education is the accepted pathway to labor market participation.

The Esping-Andersen typology in both its original and amended forms has been accused of conceptual fuzziness (see, for example, Arts and Gelissen, 2002) which can in part be traced to a reliance on formal institutional relationships. Informal norms and historical understandings, both critical components in the creation of social and economic institutions are, at best, muffled in an effort to magnify regional differences. It is interesting to note that in earlier work Esping-Andersen (1985) identifies the distinctive forms of democratic capitalism which evolved in Sweden, Norway and Denmark, convincingly linking these differences to cultural and historic variations. Hall and Soskice (2001), too, recognize the important role played by culture in the creation of contrasting forms of capitalism; however, this recognition is only partially realized in contributions to either their original typology (Hall and Soskice, 2001) or to the revision (Hancké et al, 2007). The creation of mixed-market economies (MMEs) (see, for example, Molina and Rhodes, 2007) is largely a modification premised on the refinement of the institutional complementarities concept, allowing the authors, for example, to discuss Italy and Spain as simply nuanced versions of MMEs.

While this book acknowledges the contributions of these typologies to the literature on capitalism and its many strengths and frailties, an effort is made here to address a critical economic problem, that is, youth unemployment, through the recognition of the lack of uniformity that characterizes capitalism in western democracies. This selection of high efficiency and expanding economies – Germany and the US – as potential solutions to the youth unemployment problem comports well with CME and LME ideal types in VoC and the corporatist and liberal market pillars of Esping-Andersen. The criterion for their selection, however, is not the level of institutional cooperation, extent of state intrusion, or income redistribution mechanisms, but rather the distinctive value orientations in these countries that facilitate school-to-work transitions and, more generally, the conditions for labor supply and demand equilibria that sustain high levels of efficiency and economic growth. Likewise, the selection of Mediterranean countries is not based on their status as MMEs or the primacy of the family, but on their unique cultural and historic approaches to capitalism – approaches that have contributed to equilibria that are less efficient and produce slower growth. Moreover, a reliance on within-country observers of the youth employment scene to contribute to country chapters taps into the cultural diversity that distinguishes these nations. It facilitates a richness of description and in situ judgements of transfer feasibility that are likely to elude more aggregated assessments of the youth unemployment problem.

A fair question asked by a reviewer after reading a draft of this book is why wasn't the Scandinavian approach to combating youth unemployment included? Sweden and other Nordic countries certainly have low youth unemployment rates with vibrant and growing economies. Nordic and Mediterranean countries have both relied heavily on active labor market policies (ALMPs) to mitigate the youth unemployment produced by rigid labor markets, and have done so with spectacular success in the former instance and a set of striking failures in the latter. This tale of two ALMPs figured prominently in the decision to exclude a Scandinavian alternative.

The levels of success emerging from the Nordic ALMP strategy can be traced to a value orientation of cooperation and trust that has not been duplicated in other western democracies. Adoption of such a business culture in the Mediterranean world would require not simply changes in the institutional arrangements between business, labor, education and family, but a dramatic transformation in the national enculturation process. Without seeking to sound glib, the book's other contributors and I share Schumpeter's (1950) aphoristic attribution to nations that are keen on copying Swedish examples: 'the only effective way of doing so would be to import Swedes and to put them in charge' (Schumpeter, 1950: 325).

The German dual system

Ulijn and Fayolle (2004), in an interesting study, examined work cultures in French, Dutch and German engineering firms, and based on their observations the authors delineate widely variant motivations for engaging in work. The French engineers were drawn to the intellectual challenges that were immanent in product design; the Germans were motivated by the processes of competent fabrication and implementation; and the Dutch were stimulated by product sales and marketability. The study revealed what many others have described previously, that is, the French favor education that can be termed a 'theory to practice model', while the Germans recognized the importance of 'practice to theory' (Fazekas and Field, 2013; McClelland, 1964; Murphy, 2017).

The Ulijn and Fayolle (2004) study is useful in highlighting one of the central features of human capital creation in Germany, which is that operational definitions necessitate both general (conceptual) and specific knowledge and skills. A second, and perhaps not so obvious lesson, comes from what McClelland (1964) has labeled the German Value Formula – 'I must be able to believe and do what I should do for the good of the whole' (McClelland, 1964: 80).

At a time in the US and in a large part of Europe when human capital investments appear preoccupied with tertiary[1] level university degrees, Germany and several of its geographic neighbors – Switzerland, Denmark, and Austria – have pursued a strategy that is designed around flexible meritocracy, innovative and high-quality production and stakeholder collaboration. An integral component of this strategy is the dual education system or simply the dual system.

In 2006, 47% of German students entered into vocational education either through the Realschule track which can prepare the student for either general or vocational educational opportunities or Hauptschule which is much more narrowly focused on preparation for manual skills work (Hoeckel and Schwartz, 2010). By 2016 this proportion had dropped to about 43% (OECD, 2018). Of students who continue on the vocational track beyond 10 years of schooling (upper secondary level), about 25–30% attend full-time vocational education training (VET) schools known variously as Fachschulen, Fachoberschule or Berufsfachschulen, with the vast majority, mostly young men, enrolling in an apprenticeship (dual system) program.

While entry into the secondary level vocational school like Fachoberschule requires a lower secondary school diploma, students who enter dual VET programs which feature apprenticeships, do not. Many young men, in fact, enter with only a Hauptschule certificate and a small percentage have no credential at all (Haeckel and Schwartz, 2010; German Federal Ministry of Education and Research, 2014). Typical apprenticeships require that 80% of training take place in the business/industry firm with the balance of time spent in part-time VET schools where conceptual skills are taught. Nearly all dual programs last for three to three-and-a-half years with apprentices spending three or four days each week on the job at a business site. He/she is paid a salary that is on average a third that of a full-time skilled worker and upon completion of training receives a license to practice one of over 350 skilled crafts or trades, ranging from chimney sweep and diamond cutter or welder to millwright and auto mechanic (Zimmermann et al, 2013; Cedefop, 2019). As Pastore (2018) notes, the goal of VET and the dual system in Germany is to develop highly-qualified workers with exceptional specific knowledge. The evidence that the program is successful can be drawn from the statistic that the conversion rate of apprenticeship contracts into full-time employment has averaged around 55% over the last two decades (Zimmermann et al, 2013; German Federal Ministry of Education and Research, 2014).

The success of the German manufacturing sector powered by highly-skilled technicians with a high school diploma or a two-year associates degree has caused many economists, politicians and government officials from across the globe to recommend the adoption of a German-style education system in their countries. Efforts to copy the 'German model' have encountered a number of obstacles, however. The implementation of a functioning dual system or even a full-time vocational school program with application-oriented curriculum mandates a level of coordination among business, labor unions and the government that has proven to be illusive in most capitalist democracies. German Chambers of Crafts and Commerce monitor whether working and training standards are met by participating firms; they also work with unions and government offices like the Federal Institute for Vocational Education and Training to reform or replace existing regulations, certifications or training modules. They coordinate with VET schools and employers to ensure that students receive sufficient general education, allowing them to move and take advantage of different or emerging trades, crafts or professions (Vogel, 2015; OECD, 2016; Cedefop, 2019).

The 'free-wheeling' American entrepreneurship model

Youth unemployment in the US stood at 7.7% in December 2019, quite low in comparison to the European average of 14.2%, and only behind Germany which had a slightly lower rate of 5.6%, according to the most recent data from the International Labor Organization (ILO). But how much of America's success in having a much higher proportion of its youth engaged in the labor market as workers and job creators can be attributed to her entrepreneurial ethos? The US has around 30 million firms, virtually all (99.9%) of which are of the small/medium business variety, and account for about 45% of its GDP (US Chamber of Commerce, 2019).

Many world rankings on entrepreneurial capacity, inclination, and behavior rank Americans at or near the top, and there is little debate that Americans 'play for keeps' with high propensity for risk and even higher expectations of rewards. Unlike many European labor markets that are characterized by rigidity and employee protectionism, American workers encounter a fairly flexible labor market, and exhibit greater sectoral and geographical mobility in search of jobs or to begin their own enterprise. And while entrepreneurship is considered as an eminently reasonable pathway to solving the youth unemployment problem in the US, given its deep-seated cultural proclivity for taking risks and pursuit of individual personal achievement, can this approach work in other cultures/countries where risk-taking and individual achievement are not so readily accepted?

It is not that the US has always had the edge when it comes to business ventures. The following graphic (Figure 1.1) published in *The Economist* (2012) is quite revealing. In the 19th century, Europe was witness to flourishing entrepreneurship that followed the British industrial revolution when 'ambition and access to capital could take a young man far'. However, after the world wars, Europe had far less

Figure 1.1: Historical record of entrepreneurship in Europe and the US

A long time ago

Number of big* companies founded at given dates

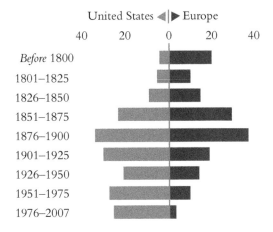

Note: *Included in the FT Global 500, September 30th 2007
Source: Bruegel (2008)

appetite for innovation, and had become much less tolerant of risk, perhaps because of the war fatigue. During 1950–2007, Europe had spawned just 12 new big firms whereas America produced 52 in the same period.

Successive years of data from the Global Entrepreneurship Monitor (GEM) show that early-stage entrepreneurial activities in Europe are much lower than in the US, with Europe experiencing significantly more trouble creating new businesses with substantial growth potential. A survey of more than 1,500 young entrepreneurs across the G20 countries conducted in 2013 by Ernst and Young showed that German, Italian and French entrepreneurs expressed far less confidence in their country's ability to foster start-ups compared to those from America, Canada or Brazil, and when asked which cities have the best chance of producing the next Microsoft or Google, the respondents overwhelmingly chose Shanghai, San Francisco and Mumbai (Ernst and Young, 2013).

The most prominent reasons for the differences in entrepreneurial output between the US and Europe are the latter's: (a) more cumbersome and protectionist labor laws; (b) more fragmented markets that make it harder for start-ups to reach; (c) less availability of venture capital; (d) fewer start-up 'hubs' like Silicon Valley; and finally (e) less tolerance of failure and more time to recover from a bankruptcy – for example, it takes a Frenchman about nine years to recover, compared to less than one for an American (*The Economist*, 2012). These limitations have 'left the continent with a dearth of the sort of entrepreneurial successes which would serve to inspire others; very few people think that going to work for a visionary in a garage offers a long-shot at millionairedom. Parisian opinion is convinced that if Sergey Brin's father had picked France instead of America after leaving Russia, the son would have become an ivory-tower computer scientist instead of co-founding Google' (*The Economist*, 2012).

Organization of the book

In Chapter 2, 'Acceptable Jobs and the Epidemic of Youth Unemployment in Southern Italy', Maurizio Caserta, Livio Ferrante, Radha Jagannathan and Simona Monteleone take a labor economics perspective to paint a portrait of Italian youth, especially in the *Mezzogiorno*, detailing their labor market preparation, prospects, and outcomes. After providing an in-depth look at the nature and magnitude of youth unemployment in the southern region of Italy in comparison to the rest of the country and the continent, the authors explore the contributions of (a) the great recession; (b) human capital development; and (c) labor market coordination with the educational sector and resultant skills (mis)match, to existing high levels of youth disengagement. They describe the education system in some detail and the efforts to improve their vocational education and training (VET) model. The authors argue that while the free-market principle uses the price mechanism to bring labor supply and demand to equilibrium levels, the segmentation of the Italian labor market, segregated along skill lines and by region, works against the efficiency of price-driven principles. If the free-market principle worked perfectly, the authors claim, it will lead to desertification of the southern parts of Italy, with young labor moving up north following high wages; its imperfect working permits (some of) the youth population to still remain in the south, although the ones who remain may be lacking in marketable skills. The authors then provide some evidence from a youth survey conducted as part of the 11-country EU project called Cultural Pathways to Economic Self-sufficiency and Entrepreneurship (CUPESSE) about prevailing values regarding work among youth in general and among unemployed youth in particular and how these values also vary regionally. They conclude with a discussion of the implication of (a) low levels of trust and cooperation that have historically characterized the country for the success of an authentically fashioned German dual education system; and (b) the sufficiency of the cultural norms that promote risk tolerance and entrepreneurship.

In Chapter 3, 'No Jobs, No Hope: The Future of Youth Employment in Spain', José Luis Arco-Tirado, Francisco D. Fernández-Martín, and Radha Jagannathan take an empirical perspective to the chronically high youth unemployment in Spain and provide details on its correlates, viz., economic growth rates, human capital factors and active labor market policies targeted at youth. After a review of comparative unemployment statistics for youth in Spain and in the EU, the authors present a historical record of the reforms undertaken by the Spanish government to restructure its general education and vocational education systems, the uneven public spending on human capital development and the attendant performance differentials in the various autonomous communities. They go on to present available evidence on whether these general education and VET system reforms have been effective in improving young people's employment probabilities and strengthening their connection to the labor market. The authors proceed to a review of the active labor market policies aimed at skills activation and skills matching that Spain implemented immediately following the great recession under the Youth Guarantee program, and provide a discussion on whether these efforts have been productive. They conclude with (a) a comparison of the existing VET system with the German apprenticeship model and the barriers that need to be overcome before the latter can fully be transplanted in Spain; and (b) some final thoughts on the paradoxical nature of the data on entrepreneurship gleaned from the Global Entrepreneurship Monitor (GEM).

In Chapter 4, '*Dirigisme Pour L'Ordinaire*: Vocational Training in 21st Century France', Michael J. Camasso, Guillaume Moissonnier and Radha Jagannathan begin with a description of some of the policy measures that France has attempted in order to blunt the growth of youth unemployment, with specific reference to their VET system. The authors discuss the nearly uniform disdain attached to VET by French parents, youth and employers and aver that to understand this, one must recognize the roles of *dirigisme* or the primacy of the role of the state over that of industry, and *Étatisme*, or state control over the citizens. They go on to explain the French preference for intellectual or symbolic capital over market-generated profits, the former driven by academic qualifications, and the latter by routine labor market engagement. The authors trace the foundations of this intellectual superiority and its maintenance to the unique system of Grandes Écoles (the highly selective educational establishments that provide a training ground for heads of state, future captains of business and industry, engineering professionals, and the intelligentsia) that spawns future 'state nobility' equipped to wield enormous power and control over the economy and other affairs of the state. Moreover, the cultivation of this nobility comes at the cost of underfunding public universities and VET, limiting the skills and responsibilities of workers, and engendering a highly segmented labor market. By interweaving historical and comparative information on the functioning of the French, American and German labor markets, the authors provide insight into the French reverence for the Grandes Écoles system and undervaluation of VET. The authors also address the fit between *dirigisme*, the French cultural proclivity for risk avoidance, and the preference for the abstract over the applied knowledge. They conclude with a presentation of youth opinions on the educational system, its relevance for today's labor market, and the institution(s) on which the youth place the responsibility for unemployment and underemployment issues. These opinions were collected through personal interviews from a small, non-random sample of French youth from Marseilles, Paris and Nice.

In Chapter 5, 'Educating Youth for Future Unemployment in Greece', Radha Jagannathan and Ioanna Tsoulou begin with a discussion of the economic turmoil Greece has experienced in recent history, taking us through the debt crisis, the austerity measures that followed, and the cash-for-reform deal with the EU. Focusing principally on the supply side, and on Greek society's tendency for over-educating its young, the authors then go to describe the rise of the precariat (a class of young people not anchored by economic stability) as a direct consequence of the labor market's inability to absorb the highly-educated/highly-skilled labor. The authors focus considerable attention on the prevailing norms of clientelism, nepotism and non-meritocracy that have earned Greece a rather dubious distinction as one of the most corrupt western democracies. The authors provide an overview of the Greek education system, including its VET, VET's poor reputation, reasons why VET is undervalued and underfunded, and VET's tenuous connection to the labor market. They then move on to a comparative discussion of the active labor market policies that Greece and Portugal adopted following the EU bailout, and how and why similar reforms in the two countries led to divergent results. This is followed by a reprisal of a European Commission evaluation of the German-like dual system implemented in Greece in 2014 through voucher schemes. After a brief consideration of Greece's capacity to adopt an entrepreneurship pathway to curbing youth unemployment, the authors present results from a survey of 30 Greek youth who opined on the issues of Greek over-education, an education system that is mostly divorced from needs of the labor market, and a culture of corruption.

In Chapter 6, 'Labor Market Policies to Fight Youth Unemployment in Portugal: Between Statism and Experimentalism', Paulo Marques and Pedro Videira use a comparative political economy framework and employ the varieties of capitalism typology to organize their work. The authors explain that Portugal does not fall neatly into the categorization of either a liberal market economy or a coordinated market economy, and talk about the differences in institutional complementarities that follow. Arguing the absence of perfect free-market capitalism or perfect coordination of employment efforts by the government, businesses and the educational institutions, the authors hypothesize that (a) *statism* played a key role in tackling youth unemployment through programs that did not rely completely on either liberalized or coordinated markets; (b) the Portuguese government may have implicitly relied on an American entrepreneurship model to transition to a knowledge-based economy to stimulate economic growth; and (c) the state has had to rely on a mix of active labor market policies for youth advocated by the EU both on the supply and the demand sides of the market (for example, apprenticeships and internships, wage subsidies), but not in a very consistent fashion (*experimentalism*). The authors use historic data on youth-oriented active labor market policies implemented in Portugal between 2000 and 2017 to test their hypotheses, and present their results on the congruence of their hypotheses with empirical data. They conclude with a discussion of their expectations on the kinds of policies the government is likely to pursue in the next few years to address continuing concerns of absorbing young graduates into the productive workforce.

In Chapter 7, 'Adaptability of the German Vocational Model to Mediterranean Countries', Jale Tosun, Julia Weiß, Alexa Meyer-Hamme and Marcel Katzlinger undertake the important task of evaluating – from the German perspective – if the German dual model can be successfully transported to some of the Southern European countries where youth unemployment has traditionally been, and continues to be, at crisis levels. In this chapter, the authors examine the adaptability of the German model to Italy and Spain. Focusing on the involvement of German multinational companies and their subsidiaries abroad, Tosun and her colleagues assess the efforts Italy and Spain have expended in implementing the German dual vocational education and training model and the extent to which ground realities have had to be taken into account to make the model work locally. In so doing, the authors treat us to a historical recounting of the educational and labor market systems, their (non)coordination in the two countries, and their current efforts on reform. The authors argue that organizational networks can help to facilitate the role of German companies as successful transfer agents for dual vocational education and training. They express optimism that if such networks can be created, German companies can inspire other companies to join in their effort, negotiate with vocational schools curricula and learning conditions that fit their needs, and eventually produce policy demand for apprenticeship programs.

In Chapter 8, 'US Style Entrepreneurship as a Pathway to Youth Employment: Exporting the Promise', Radha Jagannathan and Michael Camasso examine the feasibility of exporting the spirit of entrepreneurship, a mindset that has traditionally existed in the mix of policies to promote youth economic development in the US. The authors use de Tocqueville's description of Americans as following 'the principle of self-interest rightly understood' as a vehicle that portrays how Americans approach economic activity generally. They provide an overview of policy tools adopted by the US from both the demand and supply side of the labor market, and the flexible character of the economy that accommodates worker mobility along geographic and sectoral lines. The discouraging results the country has had in implementing VET programs through the Comprehensive Employment and Training Act of 1973, the Job Training Partnership Act of 1982, the Workforce Investment Act of 1998, and the more recent Workforce Innovation and Opportunity Act of 2013 are recounted, as are some demand–side fixes such as wage subsidies to employers and minimum wage changes. These discussions are a prologue to a longer treatment of American entrepreneurship and how it has been used as a pivotal youth employment strategy. Lastly, the authors examine the transferability of American-style entrepreneurship to Greece, France, Italy, Portugal and Spain and provide some suggestions for success in this regard.

In this final chapter, 'Grading the Implementation Prospects: Where Do We Go From Here?' Radha Jagannathan begins with an examination of the disconnect that exists between knowledge/data on the employment policies with an empirical record of success and the motivation to implement these policies that could dramatically reduce the youth unemployment rates in Southern Mediterranean countries. This apparent disconnect is explored through a cultural lens with the help of five, not necessarily mutually exclusive, hypotheses. The chapter then goes on to provide the reader with a scorecard of the feasibility of the German and American models for the Southern Mediterranean countries featured in this book. This scorecard contrasts the rankings of chapter experts with assessments of each country's (Spain, Portugal, Greece, France, Italy) prospects by the authors of the German and American chapters (Chapters 7 and 8). Each chapter expert was asked to provide a brief rationale for his/her ranking based on the data and discussion which appear in the chapter contributions. These rationales are presented unfiltered. The chapter concludes with a final word on technology transfer in an environment of renewed nationalism.

Note

[1]   A tertiary level of education is defined by the International Standard Classification of Education (ISCED) as education that occurs at a university, college or trade school level typically after an upper secondary level diploma or certificate has been received. The ISCED descriptions of primary, secondary and tertiary education are promulgated by the United Nations Education, Scientific and Cultural Organization (UNESCO).

References

Arts, W. and Gelissen, J. (2002) Three worlds of capitalism or more? A state-of-the-art report, *Journal of European Social Policy*, 12: 137–58.

Bartlett, D.L. and Steele, J.B. (1996) *America: Who Stole the Dream?* Kansas City, MO: Andrews McMeel Publishing.

Becker, G. (1996) *Accounting for Taste*, Cambridge, MA: Harvard University Press.

Bisin, A. and Verdier, T. (2011) The economics of cultural transmission and socialization, *Handbook of Social Economics*, IA: 339–416.

Borjas, G.J. (2008) *Labor Economics*, New York: McGraw Hill.

Bureau of Economic Analysis (2020) Gross domestic product, third quarter, 2020, https://www.bea.gov/news/2020/gross-domestic-product-third-quarter-2020-advance-estimate

Camasso, M.J. and Jagannathan, R. (2021) *Caught in the Cultural Preference Net: Three Generations of Employment Choices in Six Capitalist Democracies*, New York: Oxford University Press.

Card, D. and Krueger, A.B. (1995) *Myth and Measurement: The New Economics of the Minimum Wage*, Princeton, NJ: Princeton University Press.

Cedefop (European Center for the Development of Vocational Training) (2019) *2018 European Skills Index*, Cedefop reference series; No 111, Luxembourg: Publications Office of the European Union, http://data.europa.eu/doi/10.2801/564143

Cox, J. (2020) Fed's James Bullard says after a short-term 'unparalleled' shock, economy will boom again, https://www.cnbc.com/2020/03/25/feds-james-bullard-says-after-a-short-term-unparalleled-shock-economy-will-boom-again.html

Crisp, R. and Powell, R. (2017) Young people and UK labor market policy: a critique of 'employability' as a tool for understanding youth unemployment, *Urban Studies*, 54: 1784–807.

Ernst and Young (2013) Avoiding a lost generation: young entrepreneurs identify five imperatives for action. Produced for the G20 Young Entrepreneurs' Alliance Summit. https://www.ey.com/publication/vwluassets/avoiding_a_lost_generation_june_2013/$file/avoiding_a_lost_generation_lores_final.pdf

Esping-Andersen, G. (1985) *Politics against Markets: The Social Democratic Road to Power*, Princeton, NJ: Princeton University Press.

Esping-Andersen, G. (1990) *The Three Worlds of Welfare Capitalism*, Princeton, NJ: Princeton University Press.

Esping-Andersen, G. (2002) Towards the good society, once again? in G. Esping-Andersen (ed) *Why We Need a New Welfare State*, New York: Oxford University Press, pp 1–25.

Eurostat (2019) Statistics on young people neither in employment nor in education or training, https://ec.europa.eu/eurostat/statistics-explained/index.php/Statistics_on_young_people_neither_in_employment_nor_in_education_or_training

Faria-e-Castro, M. (2020) Back-of-the-envelope estimates of next quarter's unemployment rate, Federal Reserve Bank of St. Louis, https://www.stlouisfed.org/on-the-economy/2020/march/back-envelope-estimates-next-quarters-unemployment-rate

Fazekas, M. and Field, S. (2013) *A Skills beyond School Review of Germany*, OECD Reviews of Vocational Education and Training, Paris: OECD Publishing, http://dx.doi.org/10.1787/9789264202146-en

Fernández R. (2008) Culture and economics, in *The New Palgrave Dictionary of Economics*, London: Palgrave Macmillan, pp 1229–36.

German Federal Ministry of Education and Research (2014) One stop international cooperation in vocational training, https://www.bmbf.de/upload_filestore/pub/One_stop_International_Cooperation_in_Vocational_Training.pdf

Guiso, L., Sapienza, P. and Zingales, L. (2006) Does culture affect economic outcomes? *Journal of Economic Perspectives*, 20: 23–48.

Hall, P.A. and Soskice, D. (eds) (2001) *Varieties of Capitalism*, New York: Oxford University Press.

Hancké, B., Rhodes, M. and Thatcher, M. (2007) Introduction: beyond varieties of capitalism, in B. Hancké, M. Rhodes and M. Thatcher (eds) *Beyond Varieties of Capitalism*, New York: Oxford University Press, pp 3–38.

Hoeckel, K. and Schwartz, R. (2010) *OECD Reviews of Vocational Education and Training: A Learning for Jobs Review of Germany 2010*, Paris: OECD Publishing.

ILO (International Labor Organization) (2001) Starting right: decent work for young people, https://www.ilo.org/youthmakingithappen/PDF/tmyewf-04_en.pdf

ILO (International Labor Organization) (2020) http://www.youthstatistics.org/database.aspx

Layard, R. (1982) Special issue on unemployment, *Review of Economic Studies*, 49: 675–7.

McClelland, D.C. (1964) *The Roots of Consciousness*, Princeton, NJ: Van Nostrand.

Mokyr, J. (2019) *A Culture of Growth: The Origins of the Modern Economy*, Princeton, NJ: Princeton University Press.

Molina, O. and Rhodes, M. (2007) The political economy of adjustment in mixed market economies: a study of Spain and Italy, in B. Hancké, M. Rhodes and M. Thatcher (eds) *Beyond Varieties of Capitalism*, New York: Oxford University Press, pp 223–52.

Murphy, J. (2017) *Yearning to Labor: Youth, Unemployment, and Social Destiny in Urban France*, Lincoln, NE: University of Nebraska Press.

OECD (2016) *Job Creation and Local Economic Development*, Paris: OECD Publishing.

OECD (2018) *Getting Skills Right*, Paris: OECD Publishing.

O'Higgins, S.N. (2001) *Youth Unemployment and Employment Policy: A Global Perspective*, Geneva: ILO, https://ssrn.com/abstract=3019316

Pastore, F. (2018) Why is youth unemployment so high and different across countries? *IZA World of Labor*, 10.15185/izawol.420.

Piecha, J. and Wescott, C.G. (2014) The challenges for European governments in addressing youth unemployment, *International Public Management Review*, 15: 45–82.

Piketty, T. (2014) *Capital in the Twenty-First Century*, Cambridge, MA: Harvard University Press.

Puerto, S. and Kim, K. (2020) Young workers will be hit hard by COVID-19's economic fallout, The International Labor Organization (ILO), https://iloblog.org/2020/04/15/young-workers-will-be-hit-hard-by-covid-19s-economic-fallout/

Schumpeter, J.A. (1950) *Capitalism, Socialism, and Democracy*, New York: Harper & Row.

Sombart, W. (1911) *The Jews and Modern Capitalism*, New York: Collier Books.

Tawney, R.H. (1922) *Religion and the Rise of Capitalism*, New York: Penguin Books.

The Economist (2012) European entrepreneurs: les misérables, briefing, July 28, https://www.economist.com/briefing/2012/07/28/les-miserables

Ulijn, J. and Fayolle, A. (2004) Towards cooperation between European start-ups: The position of the French, Dutch, and German entrepreneurial and innovative engineer, in T.E. Brown and J. Ulijn (eds) *Innovation, Entrepreneurship and Culture: The Interaction Between Technology, Progress and Economic Growth*, Cheltenham: Edward Elgar, pp 204–32.

US Bureau of Labor Statistics (2020) The employment situation, October 2020, https://www.bls.gov/news.release/pdf/empsit.pdf

US Chamber of Commerce (2019) Small business statistics, https://www.chamberofcommerce.org/small-business-statistics/

Vogel, P. (2015) *Generation Jobless?* London: Palgrave Macmillan.

Weber, M. (1904) *The Protestant Ethic and Spirit of Capitalism*, New York: Charles Scribner's Sons.

Zimmermann, K.F., Biavaschi, C., Eichhorst, W., Giulietti, C., Kendzia, M.J., Muravyev, A., Pieters, J., Rodriguez-Planas, N. and Schmidl, R. (2013) Youth unemployment and vocational training, *Foundations and Trends in Microeconomics*, 9: 1–157.

2

Acceptable Jobs and the Epidemic of Youth Unemployment in Southern Italy

Maurizio Caserta, Livio Ferrante, Radha Jagannathan and Simona Monteleone

Introduction

Labor market economics is about the effectiveness of the market in allocating people's own time and abilities. The job of the labor market is matching supply and demand. In an ideal economy, supply of labor continuously rearranges itself to meet the demand for labor, moving from one set of skills to another and from one region to another to clear the global labor market. Demand for labor, too, may move across countries and across sectors to search for cheap and appropriate labor. This global process should be driven by prices, in that the price system brings supply where demand is abundant and, similarly, demand where supply is abundant. There may be situations, however, where the price system fails to deliver that outcome, at least in the short and medium run, and results in unemployment of labor and underutilization of capital. In this case institutional mechanisms may step in to make up for the failings of the market system, driving demand and supply towards each other. This is not an unimportant or easy task; what is at stake are the lives of individuals and firms. Policy makers and legislators, therefore, may need to intervene and devise the best institutional setting to prevent people from remaining unemployed and firms from remaining unstaffed. Quite clearly, the question hinges on the degree of confidence in the price system. The higher the confidence, the weaker the action required; the lower the confidence, the stronger the action required to compensate for the failings of that system.

In this chapter, we examine the nature and extent of this market failure in one segment of the Italian labor market, that of youth. We delve a bit into the reasons for high rates of unemployment among youth, some institutional responses to curb the problem, and also propose some solutions. We focus particularly in the southern part of the country where youth unemployment is severe.

Youth unemployment concerns people who, in most cases, approach the labor market for the first time. Such individuals have very little experience of the labor market; likewise, firms know very little about them. It is no surprise, therefore, that the market fails more with young people than it does with adults. Having little or no experience of the labor market, young people may badly perceive the signals of the labor market and may end up investing wrongly in education and training. Therefore, it might take a long time to identify the right trends of the market. What is worse is that they may have invested in acquiring competencies in the wrong field, resulting in being 'stuck' in that field for a long time.

The reasons why the south of Italy has lagged behind the rest of the country have been extensively investigated in the literature. It would be a tall order here to mention even just the most important strands of that investigation. Lack of proper infrastructure, inadequate human capital, low quality of government, crime, and levels of low trust have been repeatedly singled out to account for the bad economic performance of Southern Italy, the *Mezzogiorno*.[1] High youth unemployment has figured prominently among the various indicators of that bad performance. The Southern Italian labor market has, by all accounts, failed to secure a job for all the young people ready to work.

Such a state of affairs may emerge from a number of circumstances (Hadjivassiliou et al, 2015). Employers may reduce their demand for labor because of insufficient demand in the goods market, which leads them to underutilize their capital equipment thus slowing down their hiring process, starting in the youth labor market. Given the available techniques, employers may not have enough capital to employ all the available workers who gradually come of age. Finally, despite having a number of jobs to offer, employers may find it difficult to reach those willing to work, either because they are located at a distance from the productive site or because they are technologically distant from their specific market. In such cases, employers will shift their preferences to older workers, whom they know better and who may also have far more experience than the younger workers.

An effective price system would fix all these imbalances by inducing young people to relocate or to retrain and employers to relocate themselves or to change their investment policy. In actual fact this rarely happens, so there is room for effective labor market policies designed to mimic the working of the price system. These interventions may let employers know the skills composition of the available young labor force, on the one hand, and may allow young people to find the current trends of the productive system, on the other. Hence, what is needed is an effective policy designed to reduce the knowledge gap between the educational system, where young prospective workers develop their professional abilities, and the productive system that is in need of all those abilities.

In what follows, we discuss the severity of the youth unemployment problem in the south of the country and the policies adopted so far, and then address the question of the reform of the labor market in Italy and its southern regions. The focus will be on school-to-work transition and one of its principal inputs, the vocational education system. The level of coordination between education/training systems and labor markets determines levels of youth unemployment in many OECD countries (Breen, 2005). Furthermore, the way the vocational education systems are organized in a country, that is, whether they provide only theoretical vocational education in schools or provide hands-on work experience through apprenticeships, may have differential effects on the labor market entry process.

There is general agreement (Eichhorst et al, 2012), that vocational education and training is able to smooth the transition from school to work. Training, combined with practical work experience, is the most efficient way to ensure sustainable employment. Generally, it is possible to distinguish between the school-based system in France from the company-based dual apprenticeship system in Germany, or from mixed systems like those in the Netherlands (Walther, 2006). They are all interventionist models, different from the British/ American free-market system, which relies predominantly on the price system. We argue that the particular nature of the Italian economic system rules out any free-market option. Instead, recent reforms have tried to mimic the German dual model. However, a number of obstacles still get in the way of a full transformation of the Italian vocational education and training system into a truly German dual model.

Nature of youth unemployment in Italy

More than three million young people between the ages of 15 and 24 were unemployed in the 28 member states of the European Union (EU) in 2018. It represents over 15% of the entire unemployed population. The data also show that even before the economic crisis the rates of youth unemployment were substantially higher than those of adult unemployment. This intensified further in the years following the economic crisis. Indeed, the European Commission has raised concerns about the evolution of the youth unemployment rate (persons under 24 years) since the beginning of the Great Recession in 2008. Various studies by Borjas (2007), Dietrich (2013), and Gontkovičová et al (2015), confirm a strong relationship between youth unemployment and the economic cycle compared to adult unemployment. One of the most pressing problems of European societies, youth unemployment involves a reduction in the efficiency of investments in education and training, high assistance costs, social unrest and a now growing phenomenon, the 'brain drain', whereby highly qualified people leave the country, reducing the growth potential of the country of origin (Tomic, 2018).

A heated debate exists about definitions of the youth unemployment rate. According to OECD (2016), the youth unemployment rate is the number of unemployed 15–24 year-olds expressed as a percentage of the youth labor force that includes individuals who are available to take a job and have taken active steps to find one in the previous four weeks. In defining youth unemployment, OECD (2010) also points to the 'poorly integrated new entrants' who, despite being qualified, face persistent difficulties in accessing stable employment, but are instead involved in a series of precarious jobs interspersed with periods of unemployment. These experiences are particularly widespread in Southern Europe and are becoming increasingly so. Another category of young people is 'young people left behind', a description that pertains to disadvantaged individuals, probably unskilled, minorities, immigrants or individuals from disadvantaged rural or remote areas (O'Reilly et al, 2015).

As a consequence of the 2008 crisis, youth unemployment increased rapidly. From the second quarter of 2008 the youth unemployment rate in the EU-28 followed an upward trend peaking at 23.9% in early 2013, before receding to 14.8% at the end of 2018, the lowest rate since 2002. This is of particular concern in all Mediterranean countries where even before the economic crisis unemployment was higher than the EU average. In 2018, the youth unemployment rate was very high in Greece (39.9%), in Spain (34.3%) and in Italy (32.2%).

In August 2019, a little over three million young persons (under 25) were unemployed in the EU-28, of whom 2.2 million were in the euro area. Table 2.1 shows that in 2019 the highest rates of unemployed youth are still found in Spain (32.7%), Greece (32.5%) and Italy (28.8%), far higher than those found in the EU-28 (14.4%) or in the euro area (15.7%). Lowest rates were recorded in the Czech Republic (4.9%), Germany (5.9%) and the Netherlands (7.2%). It is also noteworthy that the rates in Italy varied widely by region, where youth unemployment rates were comparable to that of the euro area in the Italian north-east and north-west, much higher in central Italy and the highest in the south, at 46%. Even more specifically, in 2018 (not shown in the table) the youth unemployment rate was 9.2% in the Autonomous Province of Bolzano and 11.9% in Trentino Alto Adige, against much higher rates in the southern regions such as Campania (53.6%), Calabria (52.7%) and Sicily (53.6%).

An alternative measure to the traditional youth unemployment rate is often used to emphasize the sluggish youth labor market. Called the NEET rate, this broader measure quantifies the share of the youth population that is Not in Employment, Education or Training. During the last decade, the recession has exacerbated economic disparities in European countries, with increases in youth unemployment rates and NEET rates especially in the Mediterranean countries. Table 2.2 shows the NEET rate from 2009 to 2018 across the EU and highlights, especially in Italy, Spain, and Greece that the size of the NEET rate is much higher than in the EU in 2018. The NEET rate in Italy when the recession hit was already at a higher level of about 17%; it continued to grow during and after the crisis to a value of 22.1% in 2014 and then decreased to 19.2% in 2018. Regional variations in the NEET rates in Italy follow a pattern that is similar to that of youth unemployment rate.

The Italian labor market generally is highly segmented, and this is especially true in Southern Italy, where a large part of the workforce is employed in the shadow economy. This makes the higher unemployment rate typical of the southern regions even more difficult to tackle. While the actual extent of this form of irregular or informal employment is not easily detectable, the effects on the functioning of local labor markets are certainly significant (Dell'Aringa and Lucifora, 2000).

Table 2.1: Youth unemployment rate in EU countries (August 2019) (seasonally adjusted %)

Countries	2019
European Union - 28 countries	14.4
Euro area - 19 countries	15.7
Belgium	12.9
Bulgaria	7.1
Czech Republic	4.9
Denmark	9.9
Germany	5.9
Estonia	10.1
Ireland	12.1
Greece	32.5
Spain	32.7
France	19.1
Croatia	17.0
Italy	28.8
Cyprus	17.2
Latvia	9.8
Lithuania	12.3
Luxembourg	14.9
Hungary	12.4
Malta	9.4
Netherlands	7.2
Austria	8.8
Poland	10.2
Portugal	18.9
Romania	17.5
Slovenia	8.1
Slovakia	17.0
Finland	17.1
Sweden	19.9
United Kingdom	11.4
Iceland	9.4
Norway	10.2
Turkey	26.1

Table 2.1: Youth unemployment rate in EU countries, August 2019 (seasonally adjusted %) (continued)

Countries	2019
United States	8.0
Japan	4.8
Italy (T2–2019 - source: ISTAT)	
North-West	18.3
North-East	16.3
Central	27.3
South and Islands	46.0

Source: Eurostat

Causes of high youth unemployment in Southern Italy

According to Brada et al (2014), there are five main causes of youth unemployment that can be categorized as cyclical, demographic, individual, social, structural, and causes related to policies and institutions. Youth unemployment tends to be more cyclical than adult unemployment (Ryan, 2001). The factor contributing to this higher cyclical volatility is the important role of aggregate demand in determining the results of the youth labor market in general and youth unemployment in particular. More recently, the focus has shifted to the role of labor market institutions, with particular emphasis on the role of minimum wages (O'Higgins, 2015).

Due to the particular characteristics of the recent economic and financial crisis, the impact that the recession has had on unemployment in general and youth unemployment in particular cannot be overlooked (ILO, 2012; O'Higgins, 2012; Marelli et al, 2012), with many studies offering empirical evidence (Choudhry et al, 2012; Bernal-Verdugo et al, 2012). Bernal-Verdugo et al (2012) also find that protected labor markets tend to exacerbate the negative long-term effects of financial crises, especially in youth labor markets.

O'Higgins (2012) reports that the countries most affected by the financial crisis have particularly high youth unemployment rates. In the years of the great crisis, fixed-term contracts became the type of dominant contract for young people, creating a segmented labor market, particularly in the Mediterranean countries (Görlich et al,

Table 2.2: Young people not in employment, education and training (NEET) rates (%)

Countries/Year	2009	2010	2011	2012	2013	2014	2015	2016	2017	2018
European Union - 28 countries	12.5	12.8	12.9	13.2	13.0	12.5	12.0	11.6	10.9	10.5
Euro area - 19 countries	12.6	12.8	12.7	13.1	12.9	12.6	12.2	11.7	11.2	10.6
Belgium	11.1	10.9	11.8	12.3	12.7	12.0	12.2	9.9	9.3	9.2
Bulgaria	19.5	21.0	21.8	21.5	21.6	20.2	19.3	18.2	15.3	15.0
Czech Republic	8.5	8.8	8.3	8.9	9.1	8.1	7.5	7.0	6.3	5.6
Denmark	5.4	6.0	6.3	6.6	6.0	5.8	6.2	5.8	7.0	6.8
Germany	8.8	8.3	7.5	7.1	6.3	6.4	6.2	6.7	6.3	5.9
Estonia	14.5	14.0	11.6	12.2	11.3	11.7	10.8	9.1	9.4	9.8
Ireland	18.3	19.4	19.1	19.2	16.4	15.3	14.3	12.6	10.9	10.1
Greece	12.4	14.8	17.4	20.2	20.4	19.1	17.2	15.8	15.3	14.1
Spain	18.1	17.8	18.2	18.6	18.6	17.1	15.6	14.6	13.3	12.4
France	12.7	12.7	12.3	12.5	11.2	11.2	12.0	11.9	11.5	11.1
Croatia	13.4	15.7	16.2	16.6	19.6	19.3	18.1	16.9	15.4	13.6
Italy	17.6	19.0	19.7	21.0	22.2	22.1	21.4	19.9	20.1	19.2
Cyprus	9.9	11.7	14.6	16.0	18.7	17.0	15.3	16.0	16.1	13.2
Latvia	17.5	17.8	16.0	14.9	13.0	12.0	10.5	11.2	10.3	7.8
Lithuania	12.1	13.2	11.8	11.2	11.1	9.9	9.2	9.4	9.1	8.0
Luxembourg	5.8	5.1	4.7	5.9	5.0	6.3	6.2	5.4	5.9	5.3
Hungary	13.6	12.6	13.2	14.8	15.5	13.6	11.6	11.0	11.0	10.7
Malta	9.9	9.5	10.2	10.8	9.9	10.3	10.5	8.8	8.6	7.3
Netherlands	5.0	4.8	4.3	4.9	5.6	5.5	4.7	4.6	4.0	4.2
Austria	8.2	7.4	7.3	6.8	7.3	7.7	7.5	7.7	6.5	6.8
Poland	10.1	10.8	11.5	11.8	12.2	12.0	11.0	10.5	9.5	8.7
Portugal	11.2	11.4	12.6	13.9	14.1	12.3	11.3	10.6	9.3	8.4
Romania	13.9	16.6	17.5	16.8	17.0	17.0	18.1	17.4	15.2	14.5
Slovenia	7.5	7.1	7.1	9.3	9.2	9.4	9.5	8.0	6.5	6.6
Slovakia	12.5	14.1	13.8	13.8	13.7	12.8	13.7	12.3	12.1	10.2
Finland	9.9	9.0	8.4	8.6	9.3	10.2	10.6	9.9	9.4	8.5
Sweden	9.6	7.7	7.5	7.8	7.5	7.2	6.7	6.5	6.2	6.0
United Kingdom	13.2	13.6	14.2	13.9	13.2	11.9	11.1	10.9	10.3	10.4
Iceland	7.7	7.4	6.7	5.9	5.5	5.7	4.6	4.1	3.9	4.9

Table 2.2: Young people not in employment, education and training (NEET) rates (continued)

Countries/Year	2009	2010	2011	2012	2013	2014	2015	2016	2017	2018
Norway	5.0	4.9	5.0	5.2	5.6	5.5	5.0	5.4	4.6	4.9
Switzerland	8.1	6.8	6.8	6.8	7.3	7.4	7.4	7.0	6.5	6.0
Montenegro	n.a.	n.a.	18.3	17.8	18.5	17.7	19.1	18.4	16.7	16.2
North Macedonia	27.7	25.5	25.2	24.8	24.2	25.2	24.7	24.3	24.9	24.1
Serbia	n.a.	20.4	21.3	21.6	19.5	20.6	20.1	17.7	17.2	16.5
Turkey	34.9	32.3	29.6	28.7	25.5	24.8	24.1	23.9	24.2	24.4
Italy										
North-West	13.6	14.5	14.0	15.2	17.4	16.7	17.0	15.6	15.4	14.3
North-East	10.6	12.8	13.5	14.8	15.1	15.5	13.8	12.0	13.0	13.1
Central	12.6	14.5	16.0	17.3	19.0	19.0	17.8	16.7	16.0	15.4
South	23.9	25.5	26.0	27.9	28.5	28.7	28.2	26.4	27.8	26.3
Islands	25.9	26.7	28.9	29.9	31.5	32.0	31.2	30.3	29.5	29.4

Source: Eurostat

2013). Avenues of entrepreneurship are also blocked for youth, with substantial reduction in credit and the lack of access to capital. During periods of recession, workers who have a job are laid off and few job seekers are hired. This slowdown in recruitment affects mainly young workers who are disproportionately represented in the group of job seekers (O' Higgins, 2001).

The Great Recession has also increased the disparities within countries. Peripheral areas, like Southern Italy, experienced the largest drops in employment (Ianoş et al, 2013). In 2014, the youth unemployment rate reached its maximum value of about 56% in *Mezzogiorno* Italian regions, which was almost twice that of the North-East regions (29%). D'Isanto et al (2014) show how the economic crisis led the most skilled youth of Southern Italy to choose between migrating or remaining unemployed, thus generating a vicious poverty cycle.

It goes without saying that youth unemployment cannot be entirely explained by means of the mismatch between supply and demand. This would be the case if jobs were available and firms were unable to fill them. There are cases, however, where jobs are not available at all and the economic cycle is largely responsible for that condition. To appreciate the extent to which youth unemployment is explained by the downturn cycle one may turn to the estimated output gap. A large output gap would point to a large role for the economic cycle; a small output gap would point to a larger role for the supply-and-demand mismatch. Recent estimates of the output gap in Italy show that in the last few years this gap has been negligible (European Commission, 2019). This means that the economy is near potential; therefore, one of the system components requiring a great deal of work is this potential, that is, working on ways of enlarging the economic pie.

Does unemployment beget more unemployment?

No agreement exists on whether early unemployment leads to more or less future unemployment. Gathering early experience in job searching may help in the future but unemployment may delay the accumulation of crucial skills hard to regain in the future. Freeman and Wise (1982) and Topel and Ward (1992) point to the former, arguing that job shopping provides young people with the necessary hints for effectively finding their way in the job market. Mroz and Savage (2006) use a general dynamic model of investment and human capital accumulation, and find that there is strong evidence of a human capital recovery response to unemployment: a period of unemployment experienced today increases the probability that a young person will train in the near future. Heckman and Borjas (1980) and other researchers (Cockx and Picchio, 2013; Gregg, 2001; Gregg and Tominey, 2005), on the other hand, argue that early unemployment jeopardizes future employment and wage prospects. Schmillen and Umkehrer (2013) use German administrative matched employer-employee data on more than 800,000 individuals over 24 years and show that unemployment is highly persistent among a group of individuals with a certain profile. The negative effects of unemployment mainly hit young people who lack basic education; for them after a failure in their first experience it is often difficult to recover, producing 'scarring' effects. The longer the spell of unemployment lasts and the lower the initial qualification level, the longer the duration of the scarring effects. However, Aldieri (2009) found that scarring effects derive more from the incidence of unemployment rather than from the duration of the unemployment spell. According to the author's estimates, the scarring effect in the northern Italian regions is 6% compared to 4.7% in the southern regions. This counterintuitive estimate is explained by the different levels of adversity tolerance between the north and the south, where in the south, a job loss may be considered almost as a normal occurrence.

Making human capital productive

An important component of youth unemployment is that young people, even with high levels of education, often do not have work experience that makes their human capital productive (Carmeci and Mauro, 2003). The existence of a 'youth experience gap' damages the employability of young people, a situation that has become common among both the low-educated, low-skilled, and those with a college degree. This is due to the marginal role of vocational training, which is mainly school-based in most Southern European countries (Eichhorst and Neder, 2014; Eichhorst et al, 2015), as opposed to the more elaborate and productive German-type dual vocational training systems that combine theoretical education and on-the-job training, with specific attention paid to firm needs and employer input in the design of dual VET.

Italy does not provide many training opportunities for school leavers. Most of the training is school-based. The appropriate training is usually provided once the job is obtained. Young people therefore end up being engaged in precarious jobs or in the informal economy. The transition system does not provide many choices, with economic security depending primarily on the extent of family support (Lenzi et al, 2004; Wolbers, 2007). The Italian vocational systems are still very incomplete and weak, a direct consequence of which is the high youth unemployment rate.

The German apprenticeship model, on the other hand, combines theoretical knowledge in specialized schools with practical work experience, a model that appears to be a very effective way to smooth school-to-work transitions and to avoid high rates of youth unemployment (Cahuc et al, 2013). The German/Austrian/Swiss dual apprenticeship system has also been shown to prevent labor market segmentation. The dual system has been discussed in more detail elsewhere in the book, but suffice it to say here that youth who are exposed to this model experience faster entry into the labor market (Parey, 2009) and fewer job losses (Wolbers, 2007).

Italy fares even worse than France in transitioning youth to labor market success. In Italy, one can notice that the education system does not accompany students from education to professional maturity. At the end of their studies, young Italians typically have no experience in the labor market due to the insufficient contact between secondary education and the labor market.

Education and its (tenuous) connection to the labor market in Italy

Given the poor state of the youth labor market in Southern Italy, it is necessary to understand its connection with the education and training system. The labor market fails for various reasons and the mismatch between supply and demand is undoubtedly one of the most important reasons in the case of youth unemployment. This happens because the education system pays little attention to what skills the productive system requires and, similarly, because the productive system pays little attention to the skills currently available among prospective young workers or makes little effort to find ways of developing these skills. If business leaders could talk to teachers and school managers to find out what they do and to let them know what they need, the mismatches can be undoubtedly minimized. This is true for higher education and vocational education alike. A tighter connection between the productive system and the educational system would definitely help reduce the information and the search cost, and possibly increase the number of jobs available, on top of those currently available, but vacant because of the mismatch.

The European Center for the Development of Vocational Training (Cedefop) serves as an interface between systems of human capital investment and labor force attachment, and provides EU member states with information on how this connection is working in their own country, along with a scorecard of their performance relative to other member states. Cedefop's European Skill Index (ESI) is the yardstick against which each country's systems are evaluated. The ESI is made of three dimensions or pillars: skills development (for example, basic education, computer skills, VET), skills activation (for example, labor force participation), and skills matching (for example, underemployment).

It would not come as a surprise to anyone to learn that Cedefop's ESI ranking for Italy puts it near the very bottom, only ahead of Spain and Greece, and is grouped with a set of 'low-achieving' countries, all of which scored below 36 out of 100 on the ESI (Cedefop, 2019). Italy's rank on the overall index is near the very bottom, 26/28, only behind Spain and Greece; it ranks particularly poorly on the skills activation component of the index, coming at the very bottom at 28/28, the score driven by the country's inability to successfully transition its youth to the labor market and to maintain strong participation (Cedefop,

2019). Italy fares a bit better on the skills matching component, with a rank of 20/28.

Various approaches can be used to tackle skills activation and to address the possible mismatch between supply and demand. Curricula could be fixed at the central level by the State. This is the case when the State is supposed to know better than anybody else what the market requires. Alternatively, schools and universities could be left free to follow their own route, fixing curricula according to their own evaluation of the skills in demand. It is taken for granted in this case that they perceive the needs of the market better than the State. Alternatively one could have a system where the State facilitates communication between education institutions and professional/business institutions, both at the Higher Education (HE) level and the Vocational Education and Training (VET) level. Quite clearly the feasibility of this coordinated alternative hinges upon information and its ability to flow smoothly within the market. In a perfect or near-perfect competitive economy the price system does the job. Whatever the market requires is effectively signalled to individual agents who in turn signal to the education institutions what they expect from them. Eventually the education system, both at the higher and at the vocational level, will provide exactly what the market really needs. If a sector of the economy is set to grow faster than the rest of the economy, it will signal its need for a larger workforce through offering higher wages to those possessing the relevant skills. Families and youngsters will perceive the signal and turn to education institutions demanding a larger provision of that kind of education. They will do that by offering to pay higher fees for that special kind of education. Finally education institutions will offer higher salaries to experts in that field to set up a new education program. If the system works, firms will have in due course the skills they need to expand production.

In actual fact, price signals are never that clear, and in Southern Italy this is very often the case. Families and youth may fail to realize that there is a growing sector of the economy where jobs will soon become available, making choices that will later prove to be wrong. It is in such circumstances that policies need to be designed to make up for the price system failings. If the private sector is not trusted as capable of capturing the relevant information, or of sharing it, then this information will need to be collected centrally and distributed by the State. This is an interventionist or statist model based fundamentally on the distrust of the private sector and the education institutions. Alternatively, education and academic institutions may be assumed to have a deeper knowledge of what the economic system requires; hence, they will be left free to organize the available supply of teaching and training. This is a kind of non-interventionist model based on trust of the education institutions, as they are assumed to select the signals emerging from the productive system successfully and effectively. Of course the most sensible and straightforward solution would be to make the business and professional actors talk directly to the education leaders, thus dispensing with the impersonal and intermediate role of prices and resorting to more personal and immediate contact.

The Italian educational system

In the following we provide a brief description of what the Italian education system looks like. We then point to the initiatives taken to make the Italian vocational education system look more like the German dual education model, where prospective employers have a say in what skills students need to garner. We also discuss a report on the VET system in Italy prepared by the national research institute INAPP (2016) for Cedefop.

Compulsory education in Italy implies ten years of schooling, until the age of 16. At the age of 14 young people complete their lower secondary education; also at that age they can decide whether to carry on with general education or turn to vocational education. One possibility is offered by the upper secondary level of education that requires students to complete five years of education, although only the first two years are compulsory. They can choose from high school, technical school or vocational school. After completing the program and passing a state exam students can have access to both university and non-university higher education programs. Students leaving lower secondary education can also take three other paths: viz., education for a shorter time, three or four years in regionally-run programs called IeFP (Sistema di Istruzione e Formazione Professionale); they can also turn to an apprenticeship system, with education taking place at the business site; and there is also a post-secondary education option available for those who have not attended a five-year higher secondary education program, that is, programs of higher technical training (IFTS and ITS).

Vocational education and training (VET) can take place both at secondary level and at post-secondary level. It can be school-based learning, company-based learning, or a combination of the two. The Italian vocational education system has always been prominently school-based. A number of attempts have been made however, to make it function more like the German dual system. One noticeable attempt has been the recent introduction of the so-called 'Alternanza

Scuola-Lavoro', which is a system of work-based learning designed to complement the existing mainly school-based system (Piras, 2017).

Given the exceptionally high youth unemployment rate in Italy it is not surprising that whatever measure concerns the labor market attracts a lot of attention and in Italy often turns rapidly into a contentious issue. The so-called 'Jobs Act' made a serious attempt to reform the labor market, paying attention to the need to make it more flexible and the need to involve employers in young people's education. However it does not look as if the transition to a dual system is anywhere near being completed. A number of obstacles get in the way of this transition; we address these a little later in the chapter.

Segmented economy and the geographical distribution of jobs

As shown earlier, there is a sharp distinction in the rates of youth unemployment across the regions in Italy – rather low in the north of the country, abnormally high in the south. Young southerners may have to wait a long time before finding a job, so that many of them choose to leave for the north of the country, lured by the supposedly higher wages and better opportunities in the northern regions (Mocetti and Porello, 2010; Napolitano and Bonasia, 2010; Di Cintio and Grassi, 2013). Hence, it looks as if the price system is working.

More jobs are available in the north of the country; this relative abundance is signalled through the price system, and young people plan to move north. This is consistent with the fact that southern universities are reporting lower and lower student enrolment in the last 20 years (Viesti, 2019). What typically happens is that young people perceive that job opportunities are in greater number in the northern regions and, based on that perception decide to move even before completing their higher education; in many cases they move right after high school. In that case the connection between the education system and the labor market seems to be working. Young people perceive that it is enough to get a degree from a northern university to find a job. Thus, combining data on youth unemployment in the northern regions with the outflow of young students from the south, the picture emerging is one of an effective redistribution system and an efficient labor market, where excess supply is driven to the regions where there is excess demand.

However, there is an inconsistency in this picture. One would expect that, precisely because of this outflow of young people, youth unemployment should decrease; unfortunately, this has not happened.

Youth unemployment in the south of the country does not seem to be getting any lower. The main reason for this is that the outflow of young people is concentrated among the skilled ones; that is, those who have followed the track leading to higher education. Those who have followed the technical or vocational track do not seem to be that much attracted by job opportunities in the northern regions. Hence, the price system appears to be working for the skilled young people, but not for the unskilled ones. It must be said in passing that even if the price system worked for all, we would still have a problem, that is, the fate of a region that is deprived entirely of its young labor force. Surely, no one could stop people from relocating within or across countries, but no one could ignore that there is a strong preference to stay close to where one was born. It follows from this that any free-market approach to the labor market, especially with respect to the education-work link, is bound to lead, in the best possible world, to the desertification of one part of the country.

Precisely because of the segmentation of the Italian economy, no free-market approach is feasible. Even if low-skilled young southerners thought they needed to attend a northern high school or vocational school to get a job, a large section of the economy would be deprived of its most productive labor force. The south of the country would end up with an economy with depreciating capital and a predominantly old population. It might take ages before a new influx of young people and capital rehabilitated the economy. In the meantime the social and economic fabric would deteriorate immensely. There is no alternative, therefore, to designing and implementing active labor market policies to support the local labor force, and there is no alternative to local development policies designed to make the southern regions grow much quicker than the rest of the country, or at least to keep pace.

Approaching a dual vocational education and training system

In 2015 La Buona Scuola was introduced in the Italian education system, legislation that was designed to strengthen the education-work link. Its purpose was to support training stages to be run both at school and at the work site, involving high schools and technical and vocational schools. Starting at the beginning of the third year, the program allocates 200 hours a year for high schools and 400 hours for technical and vocation schools. At the local Trade Board firms may join a list of firms ready to participate in the program and accept students at their productive sites. Thus, the program based on alternating training at school with training at the work site becomes a compulsory component of the whole education program. Alongside this alternating program, the Act also reformed the apprenticeship program. The firm hires an apprentice on a permanent basis with a clear understanding of its obligation to provide further education and training.

The training and apprenticeship programs were both intended to integrate the education system with the labor market, in an attempt to reduce the mismatch between supply and demand of labor, particularly noticeable in the youth sector of the market. Although it is difficult to evaluate the impact of such recent reforms on the performance of the labor market, a number of critical comments can be made. Available evidence clearly suggests that the intended integration of the two systems, education and production, has not been achieved.[2] The apprenticeship program has remained too much work-based, while the Alternanza Scuola-Lavoro program has remained too much school-based. Firms have adopted the apprenticeship program mainly to take advantage of the associated subsidies; schools have maintained full control of the Alternanza Scuola-Lavoro program, with the result that even the time spent at the business site is not working time, but a continuation of the time spent at school.

It is worth investigating why La Buona Scuola has so far failed to deliver the expected results. No doubt, the system is under-financed and needs some organizational adjustments, but the main reason for its failure lies in some distinctively Italian (especially southern Italian) cultural traits.[3] When it comes to judging education, the popular opinion puts high school on a standard superior to technical and vocational school. It is not long ago that humanities were considered disciplines of a higher standard than hard or social sciences. Work and business values are not usually taught at school. Business culture has been considered for a long time a culture of a lower standing. All this has kept the world of education apart from the world of production and business.

Can cultural traits be targeted by policy measures? There is no obvious answer to this question. It depends on what the assumed nature of cultural traits is, whether just inherited, rationally selected, rules of thumb, or habits subject to evolution. We typically view cultural traits as immutable elements. Such an approach would not justify any policy measure. We choose a more optimistic view and consider that policy measures are conceivable regardless of whether cultural traits are rationally selected or result from evolution.

Before we turn to a discussion of appropriate policy measures to curb youth unemployment it is interesting to examine the results of an empirical analysis on the work values entertained by Italian families.

Italian young adults and their work values

We use a unique and extensive set of data drawn from a survey conducted by the Cultural Pathways to Economic Self-sufficiency and Entrepreneurship (CUPESSE) European project (Tosun et al, 2019) to examine work attitudes across different countries. The survey provides refined measures of the determinants of economic self-sufficiency of about 20,000 young adults, aged 18–35, in 11 European countries (Austria, Czech Republic, Denmark, Germany, Greece, Hungary, Italy, Spain, Switzerland, Turkey, United Kingdom). The sample was randomly selected using age, gender, region of residence and occupational status.

In Tables 2.3 and 2.4 we show the mean value of the responses to a set of questions about work attitudes in the study countries, with responses from Italian youth bolded. Table 2.3 presents mean responses for the entire sample of youth, and Table 2.4 focuses only on unemployed youth. A four point Likert-scale was used to assess how much participants perceive some statements about work (1=strongly disagree/not important at all, 2=disagree/not important, 3=agree/important; 4=strongly agree/very important).

The first two questions (Q1 and Q2) ask respectively 'how important is a job that is secure' and 'how important is a high income'. The values in Italy are slightly below the mean, especially among the unemployed, meaning that Italian youngsters are not that 'choosy' when it comes to looking for a permanent and well-paid job.

Questions 3–9 provide a measure of work values in the study countries through a specific set of statements (Q3: 'To fully develop your talents you need to have a job'; Q4: 'It's humiliating to receive money without having to work'; Q5: 'If welfare benefits are too high there is no incentive to find work'; Q6: 'Work is a duty towards society'; Q7: 'Work should always come first even if it means less spare time'; Q8: 'Everyone should have the right to a minimum income even if they are not working'; Q9: 'A man's job is to earn money; a woman's job is to look after the home and family'). The scale is constructed in such a way that higher scores on the scale indicate higher work values.[4] Unlike what one would expect, work values in Italy are in line with other countries, like Germany, and even higher when we focus on the

Table 2.3: CUPESSE survey results: all youth

Country	Observations	Q1	Q2	Q3	Q4	Q5	Q6	Q7	Q8	Q9	Q3–Q9	Q10	Q11	Q12	Q13	Q14	Q10–Q14
TOTAL	19,402	3.61	3.24	3.14	2.71	2.86	3.08	2.57	2.29	3.12	2.82	3.47	3.53	3.37	3.43	3.47	3.45
Austria	1,684	3.57	3.17	3.14	2.49	2.85	2.92	2.27	2.58	3.39	2.80	3.52	3.66	3.45	3.46	3.52	3.52
Czech Republic	1,214	3.51	3.11	2.73	2.73	3.46	2.69	2.14	2.83	2.93	2.79	2.89	3.36	3.38	3.27	3.32	3.25
Denmark	1,142	3.25	2.73	2.90	2.64	2.59	3.18	2.43	2.41	3.71	2.84	3.34	3.36	3.40	3.38	3.25	3.35
Germany	3,279	3.61	3.20	3.12	2.71	3.00	3.11	2.40	2.51	3.15	2.86	3.56	3.58	3.32	3.44	3.41	3.46
Greece	1,538	3.70	3.54	3.16	2.52	2.24	2.99	2.54	2.03	3.36	2.69	3.42	3.57	3.42	3.30	3.46	3.43
Hungary	1,077	3.71	3.51	3.33	2.40	2.81	3.27	2.63	2.08	2.66	2.74	3.36	3.51	3.35	3.46	3.62	3.46
Italy	1,008	**3.50**	**3.17**	**3.27**	**2.81**	**2.79**	**3.08**	**2.80**	**2.14**	**3.11**	**2.86**	**3.34**	**3.39**	**3.21**	**3.10**	**3.31**	**3.27**
Spain	1,826	3.61	3.14	3.05	2.39	2.62	3.05	2.32	2.06	3.66	2.73	3.48	3.48	3.14	3.36	3.55	3.40
Switzerland	719	3.52	2.85	3.10	2.60	2.84	3.03	2.17	3.01	3.56	2.90	3.51	3.56	3.35	3.41	3.29	3.43
Turkey	2,911	3.79	3.66	3.54	3.20	2.90	3.40	3.38	1.70	2.25	2.91	3.68	3.68	3.63	3.67	3.77	3.68
United Kingdom	3,004	3.59	3.08	2.95	2.80	3.06	2.98	2.56	2.41	3.24	2.86	3.51	3.42	3.31	3.48	3.34	3.41

Table 2.4: CUPESSE survey results: unemployed youth

Country	Observations	Q1	Q2	Q3	Q4	Q5	Q6	Q7	Q8	Q9	Q3–Q9	Q10	Q11	Q12	Q13	Q14	Q10–Q14
TOTAL	6,994	3.60	3.22	3.12	2.66	2.72	3.06	2.62	2.11	3.08	2.76	3.48	3.53	3.37	3.41	3.49	3.46
Austria	473	3.54	3.11	3.08	2.44	2.75	2.88	2.24	2.43	3.39	2.74	3.49	3.61	3.42	3.42	3.50	3.49
Czech Republic	436	3.50	3.05	2.64	2.65	3.38	2.63	2.07	2.77	2.88	2.72	2.92	3.34	3.43	3.23	3.32	3.25
Denmark	385	3.24	2.64	2.84	2.53	2.38	3.13	2.38	2.22	3.64	2.73	3.34	3.35	3.38	3.34	3.28	3.34
Germany	932	3.51	3.05	3.02	2.57	2.76	2.96	2.29	2.42	3.19	2.75	3.56	3.55	3.30	3.41	3.40	3.44
Greece	664	3.73	3.50	3.14	2.47	2.18	2.94	2.53	1.92	3.42	2.66	3.41	3.55	3.38	3.31	3.43	3.42
Hungary	351	3.76	3.59	3.32	2.30	2.72	3.21	2.63	1.89	2.57	2.66	3.46	3.54	3.40	3.49	3.68	3.51
Italy	462	3.46	3.06	3.26	2.79	2.71	3.06	2.88	2.11	3.15	2.85	3.31	3.36	3.16	3.02	3.26	3.23
Spain	889	3.61	3.07	2.99	2.33	2.57	3.02	2.35	2.00	3.70	2.71	3.44	3.45	3.08	3.30	3.51	3.36
Switzerland	193	3.50	2.86	2.96	2.47	2.64	3.01	2.19	2.92	3.60	2.83	3.51	3.53	3.32	3.38	3.33	3.42
Turkey	1,505	3.79	3.65	3.53	3.16	2.88	3.40	3.37	1.66	2.23	2.89	3.72	3.71	3.64	3.69	3.78	3.71
United Kingdom	704	3.53	2.94	2.80	2.68	2.77	2.88	2.51	2.20	3.30	2.73	3.50	3.43	3.34	3.44	3.35	3.41

subsample composed of unemployed people. Therefore, there is no evidence that unemployment in Italy is associated with low work values.

Finally, we investigate what young people think about the skills needed to find a good job. Questions Q10–Q14 ask how important they consider: Q10: 'a good general education'; Q11: 'occupation-specific or job-specific skills'; Q12: 'having the right experience for the job'; Q13: 'getting on well with people and good teamwork skills'; Q14: 'being self-confident'. Italy reports the worst results among the surveyed countries after the Czech Republic, and it is the last when we take into account the responses of the unemployed (the average value among Q10–Q14 for Italy is equal to 3.23 – the lowest value – and Italy ranks among the last three countries in the overall five questions). All this appears to be especially worrisome since the first three questions in the set, Q10–Q12, refer to hard skills people can acquire through education and technical education. Italian youngsters therefore seem to believe that education is not an effective route to finding a job. This is especially true with the unemployed youth.

When we look at region-specific responses from the survey for Italy, we can also see that they follow a clear-cut North-South division (see Figure 2.1). The regions of *Mezzogiorno* exhibit, on average, lower values for Q10–Q14, revealing that southern youngsters deem education even less important to finding a job than their northern counterparts.

Policy prescriptions and concluding thoughts

We conclude with a discussion of potential solutions to curb high rates of youth unemployment in Southern Italy. A recurrent theme in this book has been the consideration of one of two models as a path forward: the free-wheeling American entrepreneurship model or the deeply entrenched dual education model of Germany. An ethos of risk-taking is essential for the success of an entrepreneurial model, whereas trust and cooperation are important in implementing a solution based on revamping the education-training-labor market systems. We consider each solution in turn.

Taking risks to create wealth is a basic tenet of capitalism and it is the pathway to self-employment, entrepreneurship, innovation and to the renewal of economic growth (Schumpeter, 1962, 1966; Casson, 2003; Baumol, 2010). As one might suspect, the preference for risk-taking and self-employment vary widely across countries and some of the variation has been traced to differences in cultural value orientations. The Global Entrepreneurship Monitor (GEM) ranks the US at the very top of 54 countries with respect to cultural norms and

Figure 2.1: Regional variation in survey responses

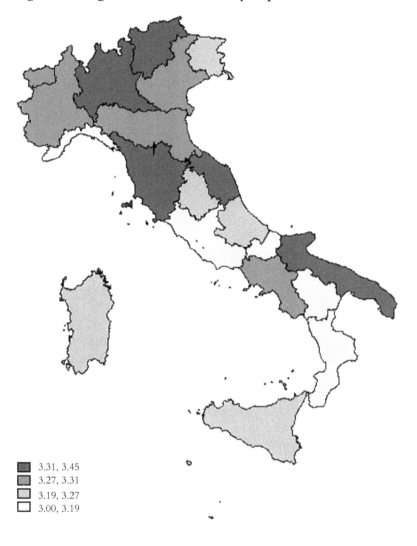

values that help foster self-employment, and Italy at 37 (Bosma et al, 2020). Moreover, nearly 56% of Italian youth reported 'fear of failure' as the reason for not starting their own business (Bosma et al, 2020). According to the GEM data, Italy's entrepreneurial ecosystem also ranks closer to the bottom, at 33 of 54 countries ranked, the ranking driven primarily by physical and commercial infrastructure, lack of supportive government policies and entrepreneurship programs, and burdensome taxes and bureaucracy. Since cultural traits such as risk-taking are slower to change, one near term strategy to make youth entrepreneurship attractive is for the government to remedy the deficits in the entrepreneurial ecosystem.

Trust and cooperation are traits that are often considered as the sine qua non for social and economic success in societies (Putnam, 1993). Many scholars have used data from the European Values Study and the World Values Survey to document the decline in indicators of trust, civic cooperation, and confidence in institutions and public services (see, for example, Sarracino and Mikucka, 2017). Particularly noteworthy is the declining trend in these indicators in Mediterranean countries such as Italy, which scores considerably below the European mean. In just about every economic or social indicator of wellbeing, Southern Italy fares much worse compared to the rest of the country, and levels of trust and cooperation, and confidence in public institutions, are no exception. While deep cultural descriptions of the Italians document an eternal struggle with deception, treachery and the fatalistic philosophy that both these beliefs help propagate, the debate within Italy seems to be 'are these beliefs and philosophy endemic to the entire country or are they limited to the south: viz., Abruzzi, Puglia, Basilicata, Calabria, Campania and the islands of Sicily and Sardinia'? Banfield and Fasano's (1958) famous ethnography, *The Moral Basis of a Backward Society*, was based on fieldwork undertaken in one village in Basilicata but the imagery conveyed by the authors soon became the symbol of Italy. The authors stated that the villagers lived their lives by following one rule: maximize the material; short-run advantage of the nuclear family; assume that all others will do likewise. Banfield went on to label people whose behavior was consistent with the rule 'amoral familist' (Banfield and Fasano, 1958: 85), and to question their commitment to community and governmental institutions.

Italian suspicions of extra-family economic and social groupings have a long history, perhaps going back as far as the 11th century. One can readily conclude from a reading of Machiavelli (1513, 1975) or more recent Italian scholars like the economist Vilfredo Pareto (1935, 1963) or political scientist Gaetano Mosca (1939, 1959), that government is largely a circulation of elites where citizens are confronted with the Hobson's choice of 'rule by force' or 'rule by fraud' (see Pareto, especially Volume 3 of *Mind and Society*).

Beginning with the work of Putnam et al (1993), the general trend in deep cultural descriptions of Italy is to embrace the tale of two Italys, the economically prosperous North and the benighted and economically struggling South. Putman traces the origins of these differences in economic performance to the Middle Ages when the northern sections of the country were governed as independent city states, while the south was subject to a series of authoritarian rulers like the Normans. In what is apparently a remarkable testament to the persistence of cultural value orientations, a number of recent research studies conducted by economists (Bigoni et al, 2016; Tabellini, 2008; Guiso et al, 2006; 2008) find that economic preferences in northern Italian regions remain strong for conditional cooperation, optimism regarding contacts with external groups (what Putnam has termed 'bridging capital') and the favorable benefits-to-cost ratios of commerce, all which were values essential to the economic prosperity of the city states. In the south, on the other hand, the choices for economic action remain rooted in the preference of betrayal aversion (Bigoni et al, 2018), 'warm glow' transactions (Andreoni, 1990; Tabellini, 2008)[5] and pessimism toward trade and investment. These result in a 'no trust – no trade' equilibrium (Guiso et al, 2008) that continues to depress the economy.

Is it possible to alter this equilibrium with well thought-out policies? The survey data we presented earlier show a clear disconnect in youth perception between education and work – there's a deeply ingrained idea that education will not get you a job; education may be valuable per se but not for finding a job. This is worrisome, since it leads to the conclusion that education is still considered an unprofitable investment. Data on the very low percentage of young people with a degree, especially in the south of the country, show that this is, indeed, still a popular belief.[6] It follows that fighting this belief is crucial to making the connection between education and work generally appreciated and effectively pursued. Only through strengthening such connections can legislators effectively turn the Italian VET system into something more in line with the German system.

As mentioned earlier, cultural traits may be the result of a rational choice or may be emerging from an enduring habit. In both cases they can possibly be modified, either by changing the incentive structure or by making a different belief spread more effectively. One could think of the following virtuous circle: if young people and their families take to the belief that education pays off in the longer term, they will make sure that their money and time make the most of the market opportunities, thus putting pressure on legislators to regulate the education-work nexus more effectively. Such a pressure would induce legislators and regulators to devote more money to creating bridging institutions between the world of education and the world of production. Such bridging institutions would enforce people's expectations that education, if properly targeted, is likely to be conducive to finding the most appropriate job.

Quite clearly then, the hardest task is changing popular beliefs or deep-seated traits. If that is accomplished, the rest follows quite smoothly. Let us assume, as a possible way ahead, that cultural traits are deep-seated habits, and assume in an evolutionary fashion that change occurs through mutations. If such mutations could be engineered, policy makers could both make sure that reproduction of those mutated beliefs occurs effectively and that they are finally selected as the most appropriate, given the existing environment. Who is responsible for engineering the mutation? This is precisely what educators are for.

Notes

[1] A few selected studies from the relevant literature can be offered: Capello (2016) offers an interesting survey of the various explanations as to why the *Mezzogiorno* has been a straggler. The lack of social capital has always figured prominently in the various explanations. Carlo Trigilia has written a good deal on this topic. See for example: Trigilia (2001) and Trigilia (2012). The ineffectiveness of policies in the southern part of the country is discussed in Paniccia et al (2011) and in Cannari and Franco (2011). Finally an interesting look at the sensitivity of southern regions to R&D expenditure is provided by Aiello and Cardamone (2012).

[2] The ineffectiveness of the Italian vocational education system has been discussed in various studies: see, for example, an IZA discussion paper on 'A road map to vocational education and training system around the world' (IZA, 2012), and a Bertelsmann Stiftung paper (Euler and Wieland, 2015) on 'The German VET system: Exportable blueprint or food for thought'. The feasibility of a German dual system in Italy has been extensively discussed in the press and on the web. See, as an example, Piras (2017).

[3] A lively debate in the press and on the web has followed the introduction of this new piece of legislation in Italian labor market law. Most commentators have noticed that the education-employment link still suffers from what has been called an excessive 'liceizzazione' of the education system. The term implies a tendency to transform the vocational and technical education into something more similar to the 'licei' (high school) where not too much attention is paid to work attitudes and values, much in favor of humanistic culture. This seems to replicate an old tendency of the Italian education world to place more value on humanistic culture than on scientific and technical culture.

[4] The Likert scale is appropriately reversed on Q8 and Q9 to make the directionality of the scale consistent with the other items.

[5] The authors refer to this phenomenon as a seemingly altruist act that provides the donor with personal gain. In this sense it is an example of a norm of 'limited morality' which in the extreme can morph into Banfield's 'amoral familism'.

[6] The European Commission in their regular Report on Economic, Social and Territorial Cohesion regularly reports data on tertiary education attainments. In their seventh report (European Commission, 2017) the map 1.11 show the population aged 25/64 with a tertiary education. It is quite clear here that the south of Italy fares rather badly, worse than most European regions, with only 15% with tertiary education.

References

Aiello, F. and Cardamone, P. (2012) Regional economic divide and the role of technological spillovers in Italy: evidence from microdata, *Structural Change and Economic Dynamics*, 23(3): 205–20.

Aldieri, L. (2009) The effects of unemployment experiences on subsequent wages in Italy, *Brussels Economic Review*, 52(2): 109–19.

Andreoni, J. (1990) Impure altruism and donations to public goods: a theory of warm glow giving, *Economic Journal*, 100(401): 464–77.

Banfield, E.C. and Fasano, L.F. (1958) *The Moral Basis of a Backward Society*, New York: Free Press.

Baumol, W.J. (2010) *The Microtheory of Innovative Entrepreneurship*, Princeton, NJ: Princeton University Press.

Bernal-Verdugo, L.E., Furceri, D. and Guillaume, D. (2012) Labor market flexibility and unemployment: new empirical evidence of static and dynamic effects, *Comparative Economic Studies*, 54(2): 251–73.

Bigoni, M., Bortolotti, S., Casari, M. and Gambetta, D. (2018) At the root of the north-south cooperation gap in Italy: preferences or beliefs? *Economic Journal*, 129: 1139–52.

Bigoni, M., Bortolotti, S., Casari, M., Gambetta, D. and Pancotto, F. (2016) Amoral familism, social capital, or trust? The behavioural foundations of the Italian north-south divide, *Economic Journal*, 126: 1318–41.

Borjas, G. (2007) *Labor Economics*, New York: McGraw Hill.

Bosma, N., Hill, S., Ionescu-Somers, A., Kelley, D., Levie, J. and Tarnawa, A. (2020) *Global Entrepreneurship Monitor: 2019/2020 Global Report*, Global Entrepreneurship Research Association, London: London Business School.

Brada, J.C., Marelli, E. and Signorelli, M. (2014) Young people and the labor market: key determinants and new evidence, *Comparative Economic Studies*, 56(4): 556–66.

Breen, R. (2005) Explaining cross-national variation in youth unemployment, *European Sociological Review*, 21: 125–34.

Cahuc, O., Carcillo, S., Rinne, U. and Zimmermann, K.F. (2013) Youth unemployment in old Europe: the polar cases of France and Germany, *IZA Journal of European Labor Studies*, 2: 1–23.

Cannari, L. and Franco, D. (2011) The *Mezzogiorno*: backwardness, quality of public services, policies, *Stato e Mercato*, 1: 103–28.

Capello, R. (2016) What makes Southern Italy still lagging behind? A diachronic perspective of theories and approaches, *European Planning Studies*, 24(4): 668–86.

Carmeci, G. and Mauro, L. (2003) Imperfect labor market and convergence: theory and evidence for some OECD countries, *Journal of Policy Modeling*, 25(8): 837–56.

Casson, M. (2003) *The Entrepreneur: An Economic Theory*, 2nd edn, Cheltenham: Edward Elgar.

Cedefop (European Centre for the Development of Vocational Training) (2019) *2018 European Skills Index*, Cedefop reference series; No 111, Luxembourg: Publications Office of the European Union, http://data.europa.eu/doi/10.2801/564143

Choudhry, M.T., Marelli, E. and Signorelli, M. (2012) Youth unemployment rate and impact of financial crises, *International Journal of Manpower*, 33(1): 76–95.

Cockx, B. and Picchio, M. (2013) Scarring effects of remaining unemployed for long-term unemployed school-leavers, *Journal of the Royal Statistical Society: Series A* (Statistics in Society), 176(4): 951–80.

Dell'Aringa, C. and Lucifora, C. (2000) Inside the black box: labor market institutions, wage formation and unemployment in Italy, *Rivista di Politica Economica*, 90: 13–55.

Dietrich, H. (2013) Youth unemployment in the period 2001–2010 and the European crisis: looking at the empirical evidence in transfer, *European Review of Labour and Research*, 19(3): 305–24.

Di Cintio, M. and Grassi, E. (2013) Internal migration and wages of Italian university graduates, *Papers in Regional Science*, 92(1): 119–40.

D'Isanto, F., Liotti, G. and Musella, M. (2014) Youth mobility and structural immobility: unemployment and economic crisis, *Rivista Economica del Mezzogiorno*, 4: 791–816.

Eichhorst, W. and Neder, F. (2014) Youth unemployment in Mediterranean countries, IZA Policy Papers 80, Institute of Labor Economics (IZA).

Eichhorst, W., Rodríguez-Planas, N., Schmidl, R. and Zimmermann, K.F. (2015) A roadmap to vocational education and training systems around the world, *ILR Review*, 68(2): 314–37.

Euler, D. and Wieland, C. (2015) *The German VET System: Exportable Blueprint or Food for Thought*, Berlin: Bertelsmann Stiftung.

European Commission (2017) *Seventh Report on Economic, Social and Territorial Cohesion*, Brussels: European Commission.

European Commission (2019) *European Economic Forecast*, Institutional paper 102, Brussels: European Commission.

Freeman, R.B. and Wise, D.A. (eds) (1982) *The Youth Labor Market Problem: Its Nature, Causes, and Consequences*, Cambridge, MA: National Bureau of Economic Research.

Gontkovičová, B., Mihalčová, B. and Pružinský, M. (2015) Youth unemployment: current trend in the labor market? *Procedia Economics and Finance*, 23: 1680–85.

Gorlich, D., Stepanok, I. and Al-Hussami, F. (2013) *Youth Unemployment in Europe and the World: Causes, Consequences and Solutions*, Kiel Policy Brief 59, Kiel: Kiel Institute of the World Economy.

Gregg, P. (2001) The impact of youth unemployment on adult unemployment in NCDS, *Economic Journal*, 111(475): 623–53.

Gregg, P. and Tominey, E. (2005) The wage scar from male youth unemployment, *Labor Economics*, 12(4): 487–509.

Guiso, L., Sapienza, P. and Zingales, L. (2006) *Does Culture Affect Economic Outcomes?* London: Centre for Economic Policy Research.

Guiso, L., Sapienza, P. and Zingales, L. (2008) *Social Capital as Good Culture,* Marshall Lecture, *Journal of European Economics Association*, 6: 295–320.

Hadjivassiliou, K., Kirchner Sala, L. and Speckesser, S. (2015) Key indicators and drivers of youth unemployment, STYLE Working Papers, 01/2015; CROME, University of Brighton, http://www.style-research.eu/publications

Heckman, J.J. and Borjas, G.J. (1980) Does unemployment cause future unemployment? Definitions, questions and answers from a continuous time model of heterogeneity and state dependence, *Economica*, 47(187): 247–83.

Ianoş, I., Văidianu, N., Stoian, D., Merciu, C. and Schvab, A. (2013) The territorial configurations of employment and lifelong learning, in R.C.L. Gonzales and V.P. Carril (eds) *European Regions in the Strategy to Emerge from the Crisis: The Territorial Dimension of the 'Europe 2020'*, Universidade de Santiago de Compostela, Serv. de Publ. e Intercambio Científico, pp 119–33.

ILO (International Labour Office) (2012) *Global Employment Trends for Youth 2012*, ILO: Geneva.

INAPP (2016) *Vocational Education and Training in Europe*, Italy: Cedefop, https://www.cedefop.europa.eu/en/tools/vet-in-europe/systems/italy

Lenzi, G., Cuconato, M., Laasch, C. and Minguzzi, L. (2004) Case study report on participation and non-formal education in the support for young people in transitions to work in Italy, Work Package 6, https://www.yumpu.com/en/document/read/6111818/italy-national-report-iris-ev

Machiavelli, N. (1513, 1975) *The Prince*, London: Penguin Books.

Marelli, E., Patuelli, R. and Signorelli, M. (2012) Regional unemployment in the EU before and after the global crisis, *Journal of Post-Communist Economies*, 24(2): 155–75.

Mocetti, S. and Porello, C. (2010) Labor mobility in Italy: new evidence on migration trends, Bank of Italy Occasional Paper 61, Bank of Italy, Economic Research and International Relations Area.

Mosca, G. (1939, 1959) *The Ruling Class*, New York: McGraw Hill.

Mroz, T.A. and Savage, T.H. (2006) The long-term effects of youth unemployment, *Journal of Human Resources*, 41(2): 259–93.

Napolitano, O. and Bonasia M. (2010) *Determinants of Different Internal Migration Trends: The Italian Experience*, MPRA Paper 21734, Munich: Munich Personal RePEc Archive.

OECD (2010) *Jobs for Youth/Des emplois pour les jeunes: Denmark*, Paris: OECD Publishing.

OECD (2016) *Society at a Glance 2016: OECD Social Indicators*, Paris: OECD Publishing.

O'Higgins, N. (2001) *Youth Unemployment and Employment Policy: A Global Perspective*, MPRA Paper 23698, Munich: University Library of Munich.

O'Higgins, N. (2012) This time it's different? Youth labor markets during 'The Great Recession', *Comparative Economic Studies*, 54(2): 395–412.

O'Higgins, N. (2015) *Youth Unemployment*, IZA Policy Paper 103, Bonn: Institute for the Study of Labor.

O'Reilly, J., Eichhorst, W., Gtbos, A., Hadjivassiliou, K., Lain, D., Leschke, J., McGuinness, S., Kurekovd, L.M., Nazio, T., Ortlieb, R., Russell, H. and Villa, P. (2015) Five characteristics of youth unemployment in Europe: flexibility, education, migration, family legacies and EU policy, *SAGE Open*, 5(1): 1–19.

Paniccia, R., Piacentini, P. and Prezioso, S. (2011) The North-Centre and the *leso* in the euro age: the same lock-in? *Rivista Italiana Degli Economisti*, 16: 2.

Pareto, V. (1935) *The Mind and Society*, New York: Harcourt.

Pareto, V. (1963) *A Treatise on General Sociology*, New York: Dover Publications.

Parey, M. (2009) Vocational schooling versus apprenticeship training: evidence from vacancy data, unpublished manuscript.

Piras, M. (2017) L'alternanza scuola lavoro in Italia e il sistema duale in Germania, www.leparoleelecose.it

Putnam, R.D., Leonardi R. and Nanetti, R. (1993) *Making Democracy Work: Civic Traditions in Modern Italy*, Princeton, NJ: Princeton University Press.

Ryan, P. (2001) The school-to-work transition: a cross-national perspective, *Journal of Economic Literature*, 39: 34–92.

Sarracino, F. and Mikucka, M. (2017) Social capital in Europe from 1990 to 2012: trends and convergence, *Social Indicators Research*, 131(1): 10.1007/s11205-016-1255-z.

Schmillen, A. and Umkehrer, M. (2013) *The Scars of Youth: Effects of Early-career Unemployment on Future Unemployment Experience*, IAB Discussion Paper, Nuremberg: Institute for Employment Research.

Schumpeter, J.A. (1962) *Capitalism, Socialism, and Democracy*, New York: Harper & Row.

Schumpeter, J.A. (1966) *History of Economic Analysis*, Oxford: Oxford University Press.

Tabellini, G. (2008) The scope of cooperation: values and incentives, *Quarterly Journal of Economics*, 123(3): 905–50.

Tomić, I. (2018) What drives youth unemployment in Europe? Economic vs non-economic determinants, *International Labour Review*, 157(3): 379–408.

Topel, R.H. and Ward, M.P. (1992) Job mobility and the careers of young men, *Quarterly Journal of Economics*, 107(2): 439–79.

Tosun, J., Arco-Tirado, J.L., Caserta, M., Cemalcilar, Z., Freitag, M., Hörisch, F. and Maloney, W.A. (2019) Perceived economic self-sufficiency: a country-and generation-comparative approach, *European Political Science*, 18(3): 510–31.

Trigilia, C. (2001) Social capital and local development, *European Journal of Social Theory*, 4(4): 427–42.

Trigilia, C. (2012) Why the Italian Mezzogiorno did not achieve a sustainable growth: social capital and political constraints, *Cambio: Rivista Delle Trasformazioni Sociali*, 2(4): 137–48.

Viesti, G. (2019) An analysis of the geographical mobility of university students in Italy, *Rivista Economica del Mezzogiorno*, 2: 439–62.

Walther, A. (2006) Regimes of youth transitions: choice, flexibility and security in young people's experiences across different European contexts, *Young*, 14(2): 119–39.

Wolbers, M.H. (2007) Patterns of labor market entry: a comparative perspective on school-to-work transitions in 11 European countries, *Acta Sociologica*, 50(3): 189–210.

3

No Jobs, No Hope: The Future of Youth Employment in Spain

José L. Arco-Tirado, Francisco D. Fernández-Martín
and Radha Jagannathan

Introduction

In order to understand youth unemployment in Spain, it is necessary to acknowledge that (a) it has been a persistent phenomenon in the last three decades; (b) the recent economic and financial crisis has hit youth harder than any other group; and (c) chronic youth unemployment is quite uneven across regions in Spain, with Andalucía reporting unemployment rates almost double that of Basque country and more than triple that of the EU–28 in 2018.

Youth unemployment problems in Spain are associated fundamentally with economic growth rates, human capital development and active labor market policies. In this chapter, we focus more on the human capital factors that either promote or depress youth unemployment and on the Spanish labor market policy efforts that have targeted youth. To be sure, Spain does not traditionally have specific policies or legislation that pertain only to youth, but any efforts aimed at the educational system as a whole, and other active labor market policies that relate to this segment of the population, can be considered under the 'catch-all' umbrella of youth-oriented policies.

In what follows, we review the nature and magnitude of youth unemployment in Spain and the regional variations. We explore the causes for these high rates, and discuss the Spanish government's efforts in boosting both the educational and labor market opportunities for youth, and whether these efforts have borne fruit. We also consider the German apprenticeship model and the American entrepreneurship model as potential ways out of high rates of youth unemployment for Spain.

The nature of youth unemployment in Spain

Youth unemployment in Spain has remained quite high in the last three decades (Scandura et al, 2018) and, as Figure 3.1 shows, the 2008 economic downturn hit youth the hardest (Carcillo et al, 2015). Young people are more vulnerable because of the transitory life periods they are going through, their lack of professional experience, sometimes inadequate education or training, often limited social protection coverage, restricted access to financial resources, and precarious working conditions. Furthermore, some young people are at a particular disadvantage or at risk of discrimination. Appropriate supportive measures are therefore required, while recognizing young people's individual responsibility in finding an entry into economic activity (Council of the European Union, 2013).

As Figure 3.1 also shows, even before the economic crisis, unemployment among people aged between 15 and 24 was twice as high as that of the adult population, the figures for Spain closely tracking that of the EU average. However, the EU and the Spanish series for youth 15–24 years diverge dramatically starting in 2007–08, with the Spanish youth exhibiting at times significantly more than twice the unemployment figures for the youth in EU.

Figure 3.2 shows the regional variation in youth unemployment in Spain. The highest unemployment rates for the NUTS 2 regions of the European Union (EU) were registered in Melilla (34.0%) and Andalucía (31.5%) in Spain (Eurostat Press Office, 2016). In particular, long-term (more than a year) youth unemployment in 2013 in Andalucía (23.8%) was almost ten points higher than in Cataluña (15.9%), almost double that of the Basque country (12.6%), and more than triple that of the EU-28 (7.2%). This pattern also held true in 2018.

As youth unemployment rates remain persistently high and transitions from education to work become increasingly difficult, a growing share of youth fall into the category of Not in Education, Employment or Training (NEET). After increasing by 5.5 percentage points between 2008 and 2013, the percentage of NEET in Spain peaked in 2013, at 22.5% (EAPN, 2017). In 2017, Spain's share of 18–24 year-old NEETs stood at 20.9% compared to an OECD average of 14.5%, and while this rate dropped slightly to 19.9% in 2019, it was still the third highest among OECD countries (OECD, 2019).

Figure 3.1: Unemployment rate by age groups in Spain and the EU-28

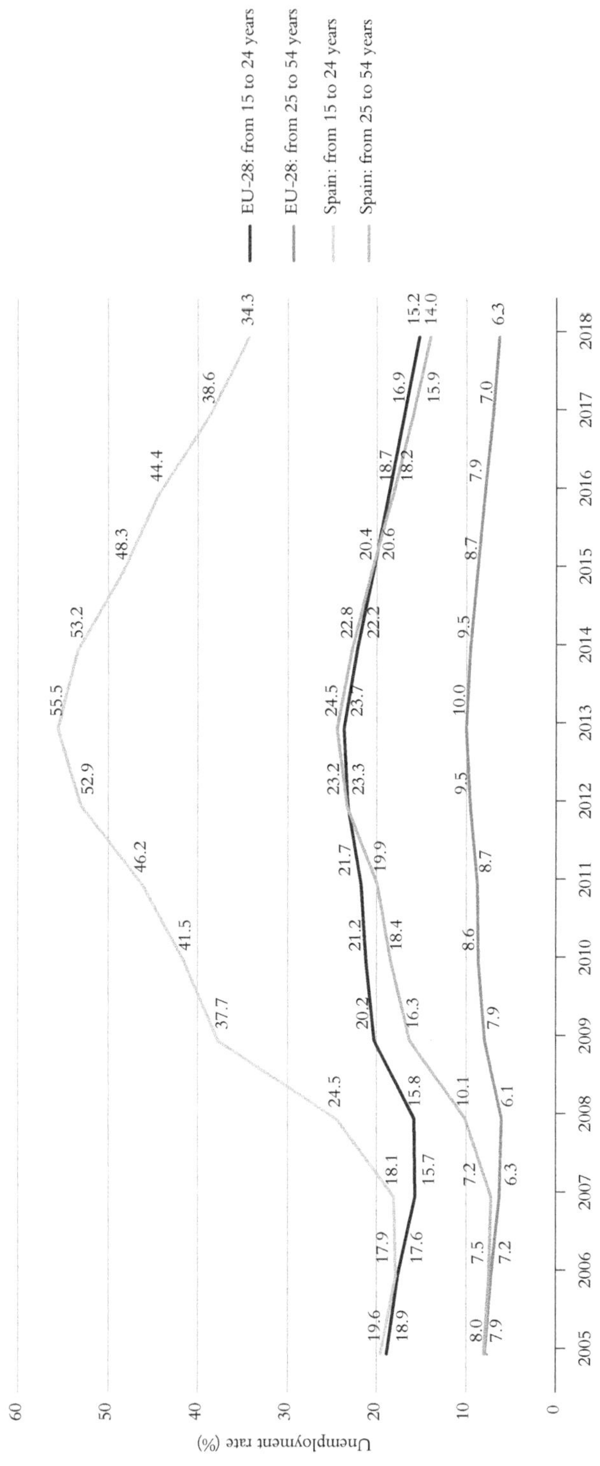

Figure 3.2: Youth unemployment (15–29) by regions in Spain

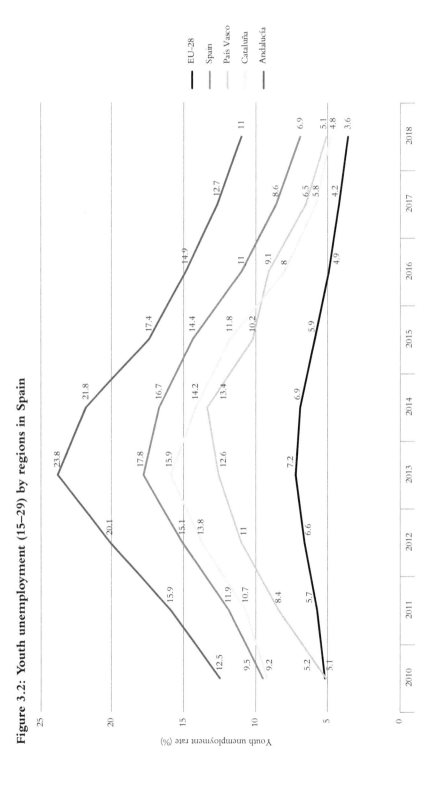

Causes of high youth unemployment in Spain

At least three groups of determinants of unemployment can be identified in the academic literature: (a) economic growth rates; (b) human capital and related factors; and (c) active labor market policies (Dvouletý et al, 2019). We briefly review how these determinants have shaped past and present Spanish youth unemployment.

Economic growth rates

Fluctuations in unemployment and growth go hand in hand, and the simplest and most widely cited indicator of this is the Okun's coefficient (Andrés et al, 2009). It has been shown that the absolute value of the estimated Okun's coefficient (initially considered to be in the vicinity of three, meaning that an increase in unemployment of one percentage point above its natural rate reduces GDP by three percentage points) not only varies considerably according to the time and spatial samples under consideration, but also tends to be well below three (Villaverde and Maza, 2007). Recent studies also suggest that the nature of the relationship has changed over time and that it is also different during expansions and recessions (Dixon et al, 2016). Although the Spanish economy has been a model for employment creation across Europe from the second half of the 1990s (Andrés et al, 2009), the Spanish unemployment rate has experienced great variability, relative to variations in GDP. Overall, economic crises have resulted in large increases in unemployment, while economic expansions have also meant higher falls in the unemployment rate than what would be expected from the Okun's law forecast (Melguizo, 2015). For example, during the 1985–1991 boom, the unemployment rate fell from 18% to 13%; however, during the ensuing recession, this rate jumped to almost 20% in 1994 (Andrés et al, 2009). Additionally, during the period 1994–2007, annual rates of growth in employment had been consistently higher compared to other countries, which had a striking effect on Spanish unemployment rates, that fell from almost 20% in 1994 to average European levels of around 8% in 2007 (Andrés et al, 2009). But following the 2007 recession the unemployment rate climbed back up to 12%. This increase was accompanied by only a 7.8% drop in GDP, which reinforces the less than perfect relationship between economic growth and unemployment in Spain. The large swings in Spanish unemployment figures and their elasticity to business cycles also do not fully capture the wide disparities among regions (Melguizo, 2015).

Dixon et al (2016) draw broad inferences on the relationship between the (equilibrium) unemployment rate and the output gap, and discuss how the performance of labor market institutions differ depending upon the age or the share of temporary workers. Their results provide significant empirical evidence that the effect of changes in the output gap on the unemployment rate decreases with age. In particular, a positive change in the output gap is likely to result in greater reduction in unemployment among younger job-seekers compared to the other age groups. Butkus and Seputiene (2019) argue that compared to the total labor force, young people are more affected by economic fluctuations and have a higher equilibrium unemployment rate, which points to the necessity of age-specific means of dealing with unemployment. From a policy perspective, it follows that an increase in economic growth (to close the output gap) will not only have the desired outcome of reducing the unemployment rate, but will also have the distributional effect of lowering youth unemployment.

Human capital and related factors

The European Center for the Development of Vocational Training (Cedefop), a research arm of the EU, ranked Spain last in the EU (28/28) on the European Skill Index, an index that captures information from both the supply (skills development, skills activation) and demand (skills matching) sides of the youth labor market. The ranking is primarily driven by deficiencies in labor demand, with skills development, activation and school-to-work transition also playing a significant role (Cedefop, 2019a).

Some of the severity in youth unemployment in Spain can be traced to its inadequate skills development in an uneven education system. Although access to education is almost universal, regional differences on registration rates for secondary post-compulsory education are substantial. For example, registration rates in Nursery (0–3 years) in some regions are double that in others, as are registration rates in higher education. Additionally, human resources in education (teachers and staff per 1,000 inhabitants) depend not only on the size of the region, but also on the range of the services offered by each educational system and the financial resources available in the various regions (for example, Basque country 36.8, Madrid 30.8, Cataluña 28.8, Andalucía 22.8 and the Canary Islands, 18).

Public spending on education in Spain fell 3% annually between 2009 and 2014 (Ivie, 2018). Much variation exists in per-pupil spending among regions, depending on their income and on the demand for post-secondary education (for example, Basque country €7,320 versus Andalucía €4,954), or the level of private investment and population concentration (for example, Community of Madrid €1,640 or Basque country €1,400 versus Andalucía €613 or Castilla-La Mancha €592). Differences also abound in the socioeconomic background of the schools, with 12% of public schools located in less favorable conditions in the Basque country and 55% in Andalucía.

Underachievement data from the PISA study shows that the share of 15-year-old students failing to reach level 2 ('basic skills level') in Spain is 22.2%, compared to Denmark (13.6%) or Germany (17.2%) (EU, 2018a). In student performance on reading, sciences and mathematics there is a 46-point difference among regions in the last PISA 2015 report, which represents a gap of 1.5 academic courses between Castilla y Leon (519 points) and Andalucía (473 points) (see Ivie, 2018 for more information). Grade repeaters at lower secondary level in general programs in Spain represent the highest number across all OECD countries at 11%, compared to 2% on average across OECD countries.

Early leavers from education who enter the labor market are more likely to occupy precarious and low-paid jobs and to depend on welfare and other social programs (ILO, 2016). In 2019, Spain stands out for its high early school-leaving rate; in fact, Spain occupies the dubious distinction of first position among EU countries on early school leaving, with 17.9% of young people between 18 and 24 showing secondary studies as the highest attainment (EC, 2019).

As is the case generally, employment opportunities increase with educational attainment in Spain. According to the OECD (2018), although the employment rate of tertiary-educated adults is below the OECD average (77% compared with 84%), it is still significantly higher than the rate of those who do not have an upper secondary qualification (61%). Of the 269 NUTS 2 regions, tertiary educational attainment rates fell in 33 regions over the period 2008–2015. Eight had declines of more than five percentage points and three of these were in Spain (Ciudad Autónoma de Ceuta, Ciudad Autónoma de Melilla, and Cantabria) (Eurostat, 2016; EU, 2018c). Between 2007 and 2017, employment rates fell for all working-age adults in Spain, but less for those with higher education: the decline was by 13% for those without an upper secondary education, 10% for those with upper secondary education and 8% for those with tertiary education. Although the tertiary-educated have much lower unemployment rates than the less-educated, unemployment rates among tertiary-educated adults are as high as 12.4%, the second highest unemployment rate across OECD countries for adults with tertiary education (OECD, 2016).

Since transitioning to a democracy in the 1970s, the Spanish young have remained the most vulnerable to economic cycles. Given flexible labor laws, the youth are the first to be hired in economic booms and are also the first to be fired during economic downturns, experiencing 'fragile employment' (Alonso, 2001; Prieto, 2014).

Temporary contracts and underemployment

Increases in part-time work and the share of fixed-term contracts have become quite common in Spain in the past few years. According to Eurostat (2016), temporary employment in the EU was most widespread among young people, with 32.5% of 15 to 29-year-olds working on a time-limited contract in 2015 – in Spain, the figure was 82.3%. Based on data from MESS (2016), this tendency continues to date; the significant over-representation of young people in temporary work reflects not only changes in labor market demand, but also structural features of education systems and cultural norms.

For many young people the choice of a fixed-term contract rather than a permanent one is not always personal or voluntary. Data on involuntary temporary employment shows an excessive use of fixed-term contracts, with 7.7% of EU employees aged 20 to 64 involuntarily working on temporary contracts in 2017; again, the share was much higher for young people aged 15 to 24, at 13.9%. With some fluctuations, the overall trend since 2006 indicates growing use of involuntary fixed-term contracts. Although fixed-term contracts could create additional opportunities and reduce youth unemployment, there is also the risk that temporary work may represent 'dead ends' rather than 'stepping stones' towards permanent jobs for young people (EU, 2018b). The picture is quite similar when we look at part-time versus full-time contracts. In 2017, 18.7% of all employed people aged 20 to 64 in the EU worked on a part-time contract. More than a quarter (27.1%) were in involuntary part-time employment, indicating severe underemployment. As with involuntary temporary employment, young people are affected the most. While part-time work can provide flexibility and better reconciliation between work and private life, and also be a valuable option for individuals who wish to be active full-time in the labor market but are unable for health or disability reasons, it is also associated with low pay and an avenue to poverty and social exclusion. Though the economic crisis was partly responsible for underemployment problems, it also continues a trend that preceded the crisis, suggesting that it is more of a structural feature of the labor market (EU, 2018b). Currently, although open-ended contracts represent an increasing share of job creation in Spain, this has not been sufficient to reduce the share of workers on temporary contracts (26.9 % in Q3–2018), which remains among the largest in the EU.

Self-employment

Although self-employment is not common among young people, some interesting trends have emerged in recent years (Hatfield, 2015). There is evidence from the Public Institute of Youth (INJUVE) that the economic recession had a positive effect on the number of business initiatives developed by young people, which probably adds to the increasing interest among public entities in promoting entrepreneurship in the Spanish economy in general and among young people in particular in recent years (EC, 2018). In fact, Spain has one of the highest self-employment rates in the context of the European Union, although it is much lower for youth (in 2014, the Spanish self-employment rate was 17.6% compared to 9.4% for workers under 30), as in the majority of other countries. Data from the Global Entrepreneurship Monitor (GEM) project shows a total early-stage entrepreneurial activity rate (TEA) for Spain of 6.15 in 2019, which is higher than Italy (2.79) or France (6.13), but much lower than neighboring Portugal (12.9) (Bosma et al, 2020). Self-employment among youth in Spain, however, may not necessarily imply a pathway to economic self-sufficiency; rather, existing data show that these youth tend to be predominantly males with poor educational qualifications, working primarily in the retail trade, food and other personal services industries, with a higher probability of being poor (González Menéndez et al, 2015).

Poor wages

Spaniards under 30 are poorer and more pessimistic than the 'mileuristas' (a neologism for people earning €1,000 a month) of a decade ago, despite being better prepared for the workplace (Doncel, 2018). Although before the crisis, €1,000 a month was considered a low salary, it is currently an unattainable goal for many workers in Spain. Four out of 10 workers in Spain earned under €1,970.50 a month in 2018, according to figures released by the National Statistics Institute (INE, 2019). And 12.62% of the workers took home the minimum wage, set at €648.60 a month, or even less if it was from part-time work (Gutierrez, 2017).

When comparing today's 20-year-olds to those in their 20s prior to the crisis, two things stand out: the precarious nature of today's working conditions, and the fact there are now far fewer youngsters. The deterioration in working conditions meant a drop in salaries for practically all employees between 2008 and 2016, but young people were the worst hit, with reductions in the range of 9% to 28% (INE, 2019). The second biggest change is the fact that the newest generation of workers is quite simply smaller. The Spanish Statistics Institute (INE) registered 4.8 million Spaniards between the ages of 20 and 29 at the start of this year – a drop of 30% compared to the 6.7 million registered in 2005 (INE, 2019). The inevitable conclusion is that the precarious conditions are no longer seen as transitory, but rather as a defining feature of today's job market (Doncel, 2018). The fact that nearly 60% of Spanish youth (18–34 years) live with their parents may be an upshot of the poor labor market outcomes these youth face (Eurostat, 2018).

A historical review of legislative and regulatory efforts to combat youth unemployment

In Spain, there is no tradition of 'youth policies' or 'youth law' or legislation that specifically concerns youth issues, or laws containing a section addressing the needs and/or rights of young people, except for policies aimed at the educational system. Rather, ad hoc targeted measures are included when legislation on structural reforms, labor market or fiscal policies is enacted. In spite of this political norm, the Spanish government and other institutions have expended significant human capital development and labor market reform efforts to combat youth unemployment. In what follows, we review these efforts along with any systematic or anecdotal data available that assess their effectiveness.

Educational reforms

Reforms in general education

After almost 40 years of dictatorship in Spain, the whole educational system needed a radical transformation to adjust its functioning to the new democratic structures. The Spanish education system has become relatively decentralized with the departments of each of the 17 autonomous regions developing and managing their educational systems based on the guidelines designed by the central Ministry of Education, Culture and Sport (Ministerio de Educación, Cultura y

Table 3.1: Policy interventions in general education in Spain

1. Organic Law 5/1980, June 19, regulating the Statute of School Centers (Ley Orgánica 5/1980, de 19 de junio, regula el Estatuto de los Centros Escolares, LOECE)

2. 1985 Organic Law 8/1985, July 3, regulates the Right to Education (Ley Orgánica 8/21985, de 3 de julio, Reguladora del Derecho a la Educación, LODE)

3. Organic Law 1/1990, October 3, regulates the General Ordering of the Education System (LOGSE) (Ley Orgánica 1/1990, de 3 de octubre, de Ordenación General del Sistema Educativo, LOGSE)

4. Organic Law 9/1995, November 20, on participation, evaluation and government of schools (Ley Orgánica 9/1995, de 20 de noviembre, de la Participación, la Evaluación y el Gobierno de los centros docentes, LOPEG)

5. Organic Law 10/2002, December 23, regulates the Quality of the Education (Ley Orgánica 10/2002, de 23 de diciembre, de Calidad de la Educación, LOCE)

6. Organic Law 2/2006, May 3, regulates Education, includes in Secondary Education Initial Vocational Qualification Programmes (PCPI) which substitutes the Social Guarantee Schemes (PGS) (Ley Orgánica 2/2002, de 3 de Mayo, de Educación, LOE)

7. Organic Law 8/2013, December 9, regulates the Improvement of the Quality of the Education (Ley Orgánica 8/2013, de 9 de diciembre, para la mejora de la Calidad Educativa, LOMCE)

Deporte or MECD). Table 3.1 shows the cascade of laws targeting key components of the educational system, ranging from an adjustment to the democratic functioning of the School Centers in 1980 to improving the quality of education taking EU input on a special focus on NEET youth.

Reforms in vocational education and training

As Table 3.2 shows, VET in Spain started during the 1980s, when the government passed the Law 51/1980 regulating professional training education. A decade later, the Royal Decree 1618/1990 made it permanent and in 1993, another Royal Decree 631/1993 established the separation of Education and VET systems. Similar to General Education, VET competencies are delegated to the Autonomous Communities, except for common content. The national system for qualifications and vocational training offers upper secondary (basic and intermediate) and higher VET qualifications (Cedefop, 2019b). The 2013 education reform introduced an alternative vocational

Table 3.2: Policy interventions in vocational education and training (VET) in Spain

1. Law 51/1980, October 8, Basic of Employment, regulates the Vocational Training Program (Ley 51/1980, de 8 de octubre, Básica de Empleo, al regular el Programa de Formación Profesional Ocupacional)

2. Royal Decree 1618/1990, December 14, National Plan for Training and Professional Inclusion (Real Decreto 1618/1990, de 14 de diciembre, Plan Nacional de Formación e Inserción Profesional) (this plan becomes permanent)

3. Royal Decree 631/1993, May 3, National Plan for Training and Professional Inclusion, separates vocational education and training from continuous education (Real Decreto 631/1993, de 3 de mayo, por el que se regula el Plan Nacional de Formación e Inserción Profesional

4. Agreement on Continuous Education and Training (signed in 1992, 1996 and 2000), develops training for employed workers (Acuerdos Nacionales sobre Formación Continua (firmados en 1992, 1996 y 2000)

5. Royal Decree 5/2000, August 4, Infractions and Sanctions in the Social realm (Real Decreto legislativo 5/2000, de 4 de agosto, de Infracciones y Sanciones en el Orden Social)

6. Organic Law 5/2002 June 19, National Catalogue on Professional Qualifications (Ley 5/2002, de 19 de junio, de las Cualificaciones y de la Formación Profesional)

7. Law 56/2003, December 16, Employment, develops the subsystem for professional training for employment (Ley 56/2003, de 16 de diciembre, de Empleo, establece las líneas generales

8. Royal Decree 1046/2003, August 1, regulates the subsystem of continuous professional education (Real Decreto 1046/2003, de 1 de agosto, por el que se regula el subsistema de formación profesional continua)

9. Royal Decree 395/2007, March 23, regulates the subsystem for professional training for employment, integrates again both subsystems (Real Decreto 395/2007, de 23 de marzo, por el que se regula el subsistema de formación profesional para el empleo)

10. Royal Decree 1631/2006, December 29, establishes the minimum curriculum for Secondary Education (Real Decreto 1631/2006, de 29 de diciembre, por el que se establecen las enseñanzas mínimas correspondientes a la Educación Secundaria Obligatoria)

11. National Agreement on Vocational Education for Employment, February 7, 2006, develops an integrated model for vocational training (Acuerdo de Formación Profesional para el Empleo, de 7 de febrero de 2006)

12. Law 14/2011, June 1, Science, Technology and Innovation (Ley 14/2011, de 1 de junio, de la Ciencia, la Tecnología y la Innovación)

Table 3.2: Policy interventions in vocational education and training (VET) in Spain (continued)

13. Royal Decree 1529/2012, November 8, develops the contract for training and learning and establish the basis for dual VET (Real Decreto 1529/2012, de 8 de noviembre, por el que se desarrolla el contrato para la formación y el aprendizaje y se establecen las bases de la formación profesional dual)

14. Organic Law 8/2013, December 9, regulates the Improvement of the Quality of Education (Ley Orgánica 8/2013, de 9 de diciembre, para la mejora de la Calidad Educativa, LOMCE)

15. Law 30/2015, September 9, regulates the VET system for employment in the labor market (Real Decreto 30/2015, de 22 de marzo, para la reforma urgente del sistema de formación profesional para el empleo en el ámbito laboral)

16. Royal Decree-law 4/2015, March 22, concerns urgent measures to reform the VET system (Real Decreto-ley 4/2015, de 22 de marzo, para la reforma urgente del sistema de formación profesional para el empleo en el ámbito laboral)

17. Royal Decree-law 694/2017, July 3, develops the Law 30/2015, which regulates the VET system for employment in the labor market (Real Decreto-ley 694/2017, de 3 de julio, por el que se desarrolla la Ley 30/2015, de 9 de septiembre por la que se regula el Sistema de Formación Profesional para el Empleo en el ámbito laboral)

path (Basic Vocational Education and Training (VET, or FP Básica in Spanish) open to Compulsory Secondary Education (ESO in Spanish) students aged 15 who meet certain academic requirements. Passing this basic vocational training with professional validity gives direct access to Intermediate VET cycles and the possibility of taking the exam to obtain the ESO diploma, opening up access to upper secondary general education programs (Sancha and Gutiérrez, 2019).

The strong relationship between the rise in youth unemployment and the promotion of alternative training models including the dual VET (López, 2017) reflects a sense of urgency by the Spanish government to promote youth employment and acquisition of a vocational qualification. For example, the Royal Decree 1529/2012, November 8, developed the contract for training and learning and established the basis for dual VET, a turning point in reform efforts. Then, the Royal Decree-law 4/2015 was passed focusing on urgent measures to reform the VET system setting, evolving into the current two types of dual VET: (a) training and apprenticeship contracts, in which the learning can be part of the education or employment systems; and (b) dual VET projects offered within the education system and implemented by the regions.

Cedefop (2018a) identified the following priorities to increase capacity and impact on VET and dual VET in Spain for 2016–2020: (a) strengthen apprenticeship and work-based learning in school-based VET; (b) improve innovation and entrepreneurship in VET schools; (c) improve information and guidance that facilitates gender-blind access to VET systems; (d) track and assess measures related to accessing quality VET recommended by the 2013 Organic Law; (e) boost continuing professional development for teaching/training staff in VET schools; (f) encourage cooperation with the chambers of commerce and other business organizations in training the trainers at companies participating in dual VET; (g) encourage organizations to offer information and communication technology (ICT)/ digital-related training to individuals enrolled in the national Youth Guarantee system; (h) ensure better skill matching and an assessment of VET's potential for creating employment; and (i) increase coordination among autonomous regions on VET criteria and quality.

The Alliance for Dual Vocational Education (Alianza para la FP Dual) was established in 2015 to support the development of dual VET and to improve young people's employability under the auspices of the Bertelsmann Foundation, the Princess Foundation of Girona, the Confederation of Employers' Organizations (CEOE), the Confederation of Small and Medium-sized Enterprises (CEPYME), and the Chamber of Commerce (Bassols and Salvans, 2016). The idea behind the Alliance is to create an attractive dual training model that would link skills development in the education sector to activation and matching in the labor sector. Ninety-five percent of Alliance members are located in three autonomous communities (that is, Andalucía, Cataluña and Madrid) and in order to be a part of the alliance, companies must: (a) pay apprentices/trainees for their in-company work/time; (b) ensure that trainers and tutors are properly trained; and (c) involve higher level managers in dual VET. The Alliance also held discussions with educational administrators and other stakeholders on future policy development, organized a forum in October 2016 to offer a prize for the most innovative dual VET practices, and produced documents that guided company mentors on dual VET (Cedefop, 2018a).

Another prominent player in the Spanish Dual VET field is the 'Dualiza Bankia', supported by Fundación Bankia. 'Dualiza Bankia' has a strategic alliance with FPEmpres, which is the association of Vocational Education School Centres in Spain. It is also a member of Alianzafpdual and the European Alliance for Apprenticeship (EAFA), and collaborates with the European Research Network on Vocational Education and Training (VETNET) and the Spanish Cámara de

Comercio (Chamber of Commerce). Similar to Alianzafpdual, Dualiza's objectives revolve around the promotion, cooperation, organization, research, and orientation among schools, companies and students interested in developing and advancing Dual VET. Currently, this organization operates throughout Spain and involves 128 schools, 297 companies, 2,662 students and 61 projects with an investment of over three million euros. The Center for Knowledge and Innovation from Dualiza Bankia, dedicated to strengthening the analysis, research and debate on VET in Spain, deserves special mention here. This resource provides key reports on the strengths and weakness of research in this field (for example, Echeverría and Martínez, 2019; Sigüenza, 2018) and on the needs and priorities of advancing a high-quality research agenda in Spain in this key strategic supply-side reform.

Effectiveness of general education and vocational education and training reforms

General education system

Quality assurance and continuous evaluation (of reforms) are baked into the Spanish education system with the involvement of a number of organizations under the purview of the Ministry of Education, Culture and Sport, such as the State Educational Inspectorate and the National Institute for Educational Evaluation. In fact, since 2000, the Evaluation Institute of the Education (INEE in Spanish), in collaboration with the autonomous regions and following EU directives, instituted various procedures and statistical indicators to enable annual assessments to serve as a basis for policy decision making. Data at the national and regional levels continue to show insufficient progress and lower than expected educational outcomes on key quality indicators like reading, mathematics, sciences, or early school leaving (EC, 2018; Eurostat, 2019; EU, 2019; Eurydice, 2019).

The poor performance of Spanish students is somewhat paradoxical when one considers the attraction of the teaching profession in Spain. Teacher salaries in Spain are among the highest in Europe, they are on average above that of workers with tertiary education; and an overwhelming 95.7% of the teachers report satisfaction with their work. However, regional differences in salaries, a high share of interim teachers, the lack of incentives for participation in continuous professional development, and the lack of candidates to school leadership are all significant challenges (EU, 2019; OECD, 2019) that counter the positive aspects of the profession.

From a policy perspective, a potential explanation for the poor performance of the Spanish educational system is the fickleness associated with changes in political leadership. Spending on education, especially on programs aimed at combating regional disparities in school leaving, professional development opportunities and upward mobility for teachers, and so on, that is much lower than the EU average, is an additional factor. Largely though, the halting fashion in which weak reforms have been formulated/implemented at the margins, coupled with a lack of stakeholder accountability in the autonomous regions, are responsible for not effectively addressing the structural problems in the education system.

Vocational education and training system

In 2006 the National Institute of Evaluation in Education (INEE) of the Ministry of Education established a quality assurance national reference point (QANRP) for the entire Spanish VET system, following the Common Quality Assurance Framework CQAF for VET (Cedefop, 2018a; Sancha and Gutierrez, 2019). More guidance on assessing VET came with the 2015 reform effort. An even more recent effort involves the creation of the State Foundation for Training and Employment (Fundación Estatal para la Formación en el Empleo, or Fundae), entrusted with a continuous assessment in concert with regional bodies, of the quality and the real impact of each new training initiative, including its potential for increasing employment probabilities, employment duration and opportunities for career mobility (Fundae, 2020).

There is limited empirical evidence available on whether the VET reforms accomplished what they set out to do. Using data on apprenticeship and training contracts development from the Public Service of State Employment (SEPE, 2019) for the period 2007–2018, Workers Commissions (CC.OO, 2019) reports that the current dual VET has not helped in increasing youth qualifications for existing jobs; nor has it succeeded in lowering early school leaving rates, and argues for new legislation that would differentiate between training contracts aimed at gaining a professional qualification (that is, dual VET) from those used to gain professional experience. Marques and Hörisch (2019) remark on the nature of implementing workplace-based training that was characterized by non-complementarity and non-coordination of labor market institutions.

According to Bassols and Salvans (2016), the pace of development and the content of Dual VET has varied across Spain (for example, remuneration of the trainee, contractual instrument used, allocation of

Table 3.3: Participation of students, schools and enterprises on dual vocational education and training in Spain

Year	Students	% of total	Schools	Enterprises
2012/2013	4,292	0.67	172	513
2013/2014	9,555	1.36	375	1,570
2014/2015	16,199	2.33	728	4,878
2015/2016	15,304	2.0	779	5,665
2016/2017	23,974	3.33	854	10,081

Source: Ministerio de Educación Cultura y Deporte

time between company and educational center, training of company tutors, dual VET start dates, and so on), resulting in many different models in practice. The authors also point out that these models are of varying quality; some even diverge quite strongly from the foundational concept of dual vocational training as a shared responsibility between educational centers and firms, and attribute this to the lack of Spanish experience among the regulating bodies, the educational centers and firms in developing a Dual VET system, and insufficient collaboration across these different stakeholders.

Others such as López (2017) are more optimistic, finding that VET reform efforts have achieved significant progress. Indeed, as Table 3.3 shows, in 2012–2013 and 2016–2017, the number of enterprises participating in the new reformed VET increased twenty-fold, and the number of students more than quintupled, although it still represents only 3.33% of the total number of students registered for VET programs.

If this system of VET guarantees 70% entry into the labor market with more than 10,000 enterprises and 900 VET schools offering 24,000 students positions in the 2016–2017 academic course in Spain (Fundación Cotec para la Innovación, 2019), then the government should scale up this model to the whole country in a consistent and financially sustainable way. It is noteworthy that approximately a third of the Bertelsmann Foundation activity in Spain is concentrated in Andalucía (Alianzafpdual, 2019), considering the much higher youth unemployment figures in this Autonomous Region.

Labor market policy reforms and their effectiveness

Table 3.4 recounts recent legislative history on various active labor market policies (ALMPs) enacted in Spain. In 2011, the government

Table 3.4: Active labor market policies (ALMPs) in Spain

1. Royal Decree 3/2011, February 18, develops urgent measures to improve employability and reform active employment policies (Real Decreto-ley 3/2011, de 18 de febrero, de medidas urgentes para la mejora de la empleabilidad y la reforma de las políticas activas de empleo)

2. Royal Decree 10/2011, August 26, urgent measures to promote youth employment, foment employment stability and to maintain the program of professional re-qualification for those people who finish their unemployment protection (Real Decreto 10/2011, de 26 de agosto, de medidas urgentes para la promoción del empleo de los jóvenes, el fomento de la estabilidad en el empleo y el mantenimiento del programa de recualificación profesional de las personas que agoten su protección por desempleo)

3. Royal Decree 1542/2011, October 31, Spanish Strategy form Employment 2012–2014 (Real Decreto 1542/2011, de 31 de Octubre, por el que se aprueba la Estrategia Española de Empleo 2012–2014)

4. Law 3/2012, July 6, urgent measures to reform the labor market (Ley 3/2012, de 6 de julio, de medidas urgentes para la reforma del mercado laboral)

5. Royal Decree-law 4/2013, February 22, measures to support entrepreneurs and to stimulate growth and employment creation (Real Decreto-ley 4/2013, de 22 de febrero, de medidas de apoyo al emprendedor y de estímulo del crecimiento y de la creación de empleo)

6. Law 14/2013, September 27, to support entrepreneurs and their internationalization (Ley 14/2013, de 27 de septiembre, de apoyo a los emprendedores y su internacionalización)

7. Royal Decree-law 16/2013, December 20, measures to favour stable contracts and to improve workers' employability (Real Decreto 16/2013, de 20 de diciembre, de medidas para favorecer la contratación estable y mejorar la empleabilidad de los trabajadores)

8. Law 3/2014, March 27, modifies the reintegrated text on the Defense of Consumers and Users (Ley 3/2014, de 27 de marzo, por la que se modifica el texto refundido de la Ley General para la Defensa de los Consumidores y Usuarios)

9. Royal Decree-law 3/2014, February 28, urgent measures to increase employment and indefinite contracts

10. Royal Decree-law 8/2014, July 4, passing urgent measures for growth, competitiveness and efficiency (Real Decreto-ley 8/2014, de 4 de julio, de aprobación de medidas urgentes para el crecimiento, la competitividad y la eficiencia)

11. Royal Decree-law 751/2014, September 5, Spanish Strategy to Activate Employment 2014–2016 (Real Decreto-ley 751, de 5 de septiembre, por el que se aprueba la Estrategia Española de Activación para el Empleo 2014–2016)

began to develop a range of initiatives to confront the alarming growth of unemployment among the young. In 2013, the Spanish Government launched the Strategy for Entrepreneurship and Youth Employment 2013–2016 (MESS, 2013) and a year later developed the Spanish National Youth Guarantee Implementation Plan. The 2017–2020 Spanish strategy for employment activation is specified each year in the employment policies annual plan (Plan Anual de Política de Empleo – PAPE), and takes into account all the recommendations made both within the framework of the National Reform Programme and by the European Network of Public Employment Services (SPE-UE Network) (Sancha and Gutierrez, 2019).

A recent study by Caliendo et al (2018) shows Spain to be the largest beneficiary of the initial YEI-specific allocation, receiving almost a billion euros. Given that the Youth Guarantee was implemented at the height of the recession, Spain, like most member states, focused on delivering short-term relief to unemployed young people through demand-side reforms such as subsidized employment and wage subsidies that were aimed at encouraging employers to offer their first employment to disadvantaged young people. However, in spite of increased outreach efforts, the employability of these youth remains low. While the share of NEETs has declined a bit (13.3% in 2017), it remains high and varies greatly across regions. Registrations in the Youth Guarantee reached 56% for NEETs aged 15–24 in 2017 (compared to 34% in 2016) and to 27.4% for those aged 25–29), and the share of youth still in employment, education or training six months after leaving the Youth Guarantee rose further to 60% in 2017 for those aged 18–24 and to 65% for those aged 25–29. However, the most vulnerable of the NEETs tended to be under-represented among beneficiaries and there is still room for greater cooperation with employers to improve engagement of those furthest away from the labor market (EC, 2019).

The Strategy for Entrepreneurship and Youth Employment includes a number of indicators to evaluate the degree of compliance of actions taken. Studies report contradictory results, with authors like Sancha and Gutiérrez (2016) pointing out that the program has not had the expected results given the high volume of youth unemployment, and others like Moldes et al (2018) describing its positive impact and outcomes on key indicators. A more recent set of evaluation studies by Fundae (2020) indicates that a total of 87 projects were funded to serve 9,202 youth under 30, and that an overwhelming majority believed that their new qualification provided them with better employment and educational potential. In addition, nearly 38% of these youth held fixed-term contracts at least a year after finishing their training, with youth who had previous work experience faring even better. About 28% of them remained in the same firm once their training period was over, and 55% remained employed (Fundae, 2020).

Another Fundae (2020) study reports on the Youth Guarantee National Registry program that funded a total of 46 projects serving 5,805 participants (60% of whom were from Madrid, Andalucía, Murcia, and Castilla y León) and involving 1,000 enterprises. These preliminary results indicate better employment outcomes for youth whose training was not linked to specific professional certificates compared to those that were so linked, possibly attributable to the versatility of the former.

Other ALMPs that were implemented in Spain provided financial incentives for self-employment, policies such as reductions of the self-employed individual's Social Security contributions and incentives for the self-employed to hire workers, and facilitating business startup capital by providing unemployment contributions in a lump sum (González Menendez and Cueto, 2015). One financial instrument the government has at its disposal in enhancing economic stability of youth is a minimum wage. Theoretically, the increase in minimum wage could have an impact not only on occupational status, but also on its composition. In particular, increased wage costs could cause a decline in salaried employment and an increase in self-employment. However, the Social Security data do not show this to be the case among workers who are potentially the most affected by minimum wage increases (BBVA, 2019).

Hiring subsidies to employers are another way for the government to promote employment and additional resources have been allocated to a new Plan for Youth Employment implemented by the regions in 2018 (EC, 2019). However, evidence from the Fundación de las Cajas de Ahorro (Reynolds, 2017) suggests that past hiring subsidies to promote youth employment have had limited success, and have failed to promote quality employment, with young workers on subsidized open-ended contracts being more likely to exit employment within two years than those employed on non-subsidized ones, casting doubts on the effectiveness of these subsidies. Jansen and Troncoso-Ponce (2018) point out that subsidized training contracts that are of too short a duration do not support skill transferability.

Finally, the newly-adopted Plan for Youth Employment 2019–2021 includes an increase in the number of counsellors for young job-seekers (+3,000), a review of the existing hiring incentives, and measures to foster entrepreneurship. The Plan envisages a review of the Youth Guarantee system and support for enhancement of skills acquisition (including digital), and job creation in rural areas that reflects demographic challenges. Although the 660 million euros budget allocated to the plan annually is still provisional and partly based on pre-existing resources, the implementation of the Plan, on a voluntary basis, falls within the competence of the regions (EC, 2019).

Feasibility of the German dual model as a solution to youth unemployment

Here we tackle one of the fundamental questions this book has sought to ask: does a full-on German dual model provide an antidote to what ails the Spanish youth labor market? Despite Spain's numerous attempts at implementing a dual VET model, doing so successfully has been elusive. In fact, despite considerable effort from the German side, most evaluations of earlier initiatives in the 1980s and 1990s indicate that only a few countries in Central Europe adopted the German system, and even there the results have been disappointing, with little evidence of long-term effects (Euler, 2013). These results have often been attributed to two sets of factors: cultural norms that are not promotive of the value of vocational training or apprenticeships, and a lack of coordination between labor market institutions and labor policies (see, for example, Valiente and Scandura, 2017 or López, 2017).

VET programs are accessible in Spain from upper secondary years all the way through tertiary education. These programs offer 2,000 hours of training over a two-year period, and some dual VET programs that last three years also offer apprenticeships. However, VET programs at the upper secondary level do not appear to bear immediate labor market benefits in countries such as Spain where general education is more dominant (Cedefop, 2018b). Even when more industry-specific curriculum and training are incorporated in full-time college-level courses in Spain, skill development and labor market effects dramatically differ from those accrued through apprenticeships. In a comparative study of the car service industry in Germany, the UK, and Spain, Grollmann et al (2017) find that while firm-based apprenticeship training in Germany and the UK leads to multiple skill development and employment, the college-based training in Spain translates to low skills acquisition, poor adjustment to market needs, and low-wage jobs. A first of its kind cost-benefit study sponsored by Bertelsmann Stiftung and the Fundación Bertelsmann shows that, if Spain were to extend its current VET model to incorporate a strong apprenticeship component, it would provide a net benefit to employers and marketable skills to trainees (Wolter and Muehlemann, 2015).

It appears that the revival of a VET system in Spain is generally welcomed, and is recognized to be critical in improving economic outcomes for youth. However, for it be more than an aesthetic solution, significant reorientation and restructuring of the system are necessary: these changes would include: (a) increasing societal acceptance of its value proposition through an information campaign; (b) making dual programs more attractive to employers through economic incentives; and (c) improving coordination across labor market institutions (education, employers, chambers of commerce, labor unions, and the government) to make training productive.

Feasibility of the American model of entrepreneurship

Most recent data from the Global Entrepreneurship Monitor (GEM) show that only 5% of 18–24-year-olds and 8.5% of 25–34-year-olds in Spain are engaged in entrepreneurial activity, compared to 15.8% and 22.1% in the US (Bosma et al, 2020). Cultural and social norms that are supportive of entrepreneurship, and citizen perception of availability of business opportunities and ease of business startups, are also comparatively much lower in Spain. In addition, a much higher proportion of GEM survey respondents reported that they would not start a business venture for fear of failure. Paradoxically, however, expert ranking of the country's overall entrepreneurship context is fairly high at 12 of 54 countries ranked by the GEM project (the US was ranked at 10). And Spain does appear to have supportive government policies that are characterized by low taxes and small bureaucratic burden, availability of entrepreneurship education programs, and a good physical, commercial and legal infrastructure. Initiatives such as Strategy for Entrepreneurship and Youth Employment and Youth Employment Plan provide evidence of the government's commitment to growing small businesses, with the topic of youth entrepreneurship continuing to take center stage in policy discussions. The presence of a strong entrepreneurial ecosystem and an equally strong government interest in promoting entrepreneurship begs the question of whether externally conducive conditions can compensate for an inherent proclivity for adventure that the Americans possess. We will have to await more conclusive assessments of Spain's policies promoting youth entrepreneurship for an answer.

References

Alianzafpdual (2019) Alianza para la FP Dual. Modelos de FP Dual en las Comunidades Autónomas, https://www.alianzafpdual.es/estudiantes/modelos-fpdual-comunidadesautonomas

Alonso, L.E. (2001) *Trabajo y Posmodernidad. El Empleo Débil*, Madrid: Fundamentos.

Andrés, J., Boscá, J.E., Doménech, R. and Ferri, J. (2009) Job creation in Spain: productivity growth, labor market reforms or both, Working Papers, BBVA Economic Research Department, https://www.bbvaresearch.com/wp-content/uploads/mult/wp_1013_tcm348-221513.pdf

Bassols, C. and Salvans, G. (2016) High-quality dual vocational learning in Spain: the Alliance for Dual Vocational Training: European case study, Fundación Bertelsmann, http://www.ippr.org/files/publications/pdf/nsaw-case-study-bassols-salvans-may2016.pdf

BBVA (2019) *Spain Economic Outlook, 2nd Quarter 2019*, https://www.bbvaresearch.com/wp-content/uploads/2019/04/spain_economic_outlook_2q19.pdf

Bosma, N., Hill, S., Ionescu-Somers, A., Kelley, D., Levie, J. and Tarnawa, A. (2020) *Global Entrepreneurship Monitor: 2019/2020 Global Report*, Global Entrepreneurship Research Association, London Business School.

Butkus, M. and Seputiene, J. (2019) The output gap and youth unemployment: an analysis based on Okun's Law, *Economies*, 7(4): 108, doi:10.3390/economies7040108

Caliendo, M., Kluve, J., Stöterau, J. and Tübbicke S. (2018) *Study on the Youth Guarantee in Light of Changes in the World of Work, Part 1, Youth Guarantee: Intervention Models, Sustainability and Relevance*, European Network of Public Employment Services, Brussels: European Commission, doi: 10.2767/371432

Carcillo, S., Fernandez, R., Königs, S. and Minea A. (2015) *NEET Youth in the Aftermath of the Crisis: Challenges and Policies, OECD Social, Employment and Migration*, Working Paper 164, Paris: OECD, http://dx.doi.org/10.1787/5js6363503f6-en

CC.OO (Comisiones Obreras) (2019) Contratos para la formación y contratos en prácticas, Secretaría de Empleo y Cualificación Profesional, https://www.ccoo.es/7dcb8c6814a7d8ae040b77d939274c50000001.pdf

Cedefop (European Centre for the Development of Vocational Training) (2018a) Developments in vocational education and training policy in 2015–17: Spain, Cedefop monitoring and analysis of VET policies, http://www.cedefop.europa.eu/en/publications-and-resources/country-reports/vet-policy-developments-spain-2017

Cedefop (2018b) *The Changing Nature and Role of Vocational Education and Training in Europe, Volume 5: Education and Labor Market Outcomes for Graduates from Different Types of VET System in Europe*, Cedefop research paper 69, Luxembourg: Publications Office of the European Union, http://data.europa.eu/doi/10.2801/730919

Cedefop (2019a) *2018 European Skills Index*, Cedefop reference series 111, Luxembourg: Publications Office of the European Union, http://data.europa.eu/doi/10.2801/564143

Cedefop (2019b) *Spotlight on VET − 2018 Compilation: Vocational Education and Training Systems in Europe*, Luxembourg: Publications Office of the European Union, http://data.europa.eu/doi/10.2801/009

Council of the European Union (CE) (2013) Council recommendation of April 2013 on establishing a Youth Guarantee, Official Journal of the European Union, https://eur-lex.europa.eu/legal-content/en/txt/?uri=uriserv:oj.c_.2013.120.01.0001.01.eng

Dixon, R., Lim, G.C. and van Ours, J.C. (2016) Revisiting Okun's relationship, IZA DP No. 9815, http://ftp.iza.org/dp9815.pdf

Doncel, L. (2018) Today's Spanish youths are worse off than a decade ago, *El País*, https://www.ine.es/prensa/ees_2016.pdf

Dvouletý, O., Lukeš, M. and Vancea, M. (2019) Individual-level and family background determinants of young adults' unemployment in Europe, *Empirica*, https://doi.org/10.1007/s10663-018-9430-x

EAPN (European Anti-Poverty Network) (2017) Poverty Watch Spain, https://www.eapn.es/archivo/documentos/documentos/1520589116_povertywatch.pdf

EC (European Commission) (2018) Employment and entrepreneurship under the Youth Guarantee, https://ec.europa.eu/social/main.jsp?catId=738&langId=en&pubId=8143&furtherPubs=yes

Echeverría, B. and Martínez, P. (2019) *Diagnóstico de la Investigación sobre la Formación Profesional Inicial en España (2005–2017)*, Dualiza Bankia Estudios, Madrid: Fundación Bankia por la Formación Dual.

EU (European Union) (2018a) Sustainable development in the European Union: monitoring report on progress towards the SDGS in an EU context, https://ec.europa.eu/eurostat/documents/3217494/9237449/ks-01-18-656-en-n.pdf/2b2a096b-3bd6-4939-8ef3-11cfc14b9329

EU (2018b) Smarter, greener, more inclusive? Indicators to support the Europe 2020 Strategy, https://ec.europa.eu/eurostat/documents/3217494/9087772/ks-02-18-728-en-n.pdf/3f01e3c4-1c01-4036-bd6a-814dec66c58c

EU (2018c) Eurostat regional yearbook, https://ec.europa.eu/eurostat/documents/3217494/9210140/ks-ha-18-001-en-n.pdf/655a00cc-6789-4b0c-9d6d-eda24d412188

EU (2019) Education and Training Monitor 2019: Spain, https://ec.europa.eu/education/sites/education/files/document-library-docs/et-monitor-report-2019-spain_en.pdf

Euler, D. (2013) Germany's dual vocational training system: a model for other countries? https://www.bertelsmann-stiftung.de/fileadmin/files/bst/Publikationen/grauepublikationen/gp_germanys_dual_vocational_training_system.pdf

Eurostat (2016) Smarter, greener, more inclusive? Indicators to support the Europe 2020 strategy, http://ec.europa.eu/eurostat/documents/3217494/7566774/ks-ez-16-001-en-n.pdf/ac04885c-cfff-4f9c-9f30-c9337ba929aa

Eurostat (2018) Share of young adults aged 18–34 living with their parents by age and sex—EU-SILC survey, http://appsso.eurostat.ec.europa.eu/nui/show.do?dataset=ilc_lvps08

Eurostat (2019) Education and training, https://ec.europa.eu/eurostat/web/education-and-training/data/database

Eurostat Press Office (2016) Unemployment in the EU regions in 2015, http://ec.europa.eu/eurostat/documents/2995521/7241268/1-28042016-bp-en.pdf/c2a7d306-73ad-4a7e-a980-5c4410d2d1e2

Eurydice (2019) Quality assurance in early childhood and school education: Spain, https://eacea.ec.europa.eu/national-policies/eurydice/content/quality-assurance-early-childhood-and-school-education-70_en#externalevaluations

Fundación Cotec para la Innovación (2019) Informe Cotec 2019, http://informecotec.es/media/informe-cotec-2019_versionweb.pdf

Fundae (Fundación Estatal para la Formación y el Empleo) (2020) Evaluación de impacto de la formación en la empleabilidad, la cualificación y la inserción profesional, https://www.fundae.es/docs/default-source/publicaciones-y-evaluaciones/evaluaciones/publicaci%c3%b3n-evaluaci%c3%b3n-j%c3%b3venes-y-garant%c3%ada-juvenil-2015.pdf

González Menéndez, M.C. and Cueto, B. (2015) *Business Start-Ups and Youth Self-Employment in Spain: A Policy Literature Review*, STYLE Working Papers, Brighton: University of Brighton, http://www.style-research.eu/publications/working-papers

Grollmann, P., Steedman, H., Jansen, A. and Gray, R. (2017) *Building Apprentices' Skills in the Workplace: Car Service in Germany, the UK and Spain*, Centre for Vocational Educational Research, London: London School of Economics and Political Science.

Gutiérrez, H. (2017) More work but less money: Spain's new salary trap, *El País*, https://elpais.com/elpais/2017/07/17/inenglish/1500277240_151930.html

Hatfield, I. (2015) Self-employment in Europe, Institute for Public Policy Research, https://www.ippr.org/files/publications/pdf/self-employment-europe_jan2015.pdf

ILO (International Labor Office) (2016) *World Employment and Social Outlook 2016: Trends for Youth*, Geneva: International Labor Office, http://www.ilo.org/wcmsp5/groups/public/---dgreports/---dcomm/---publ/documents/publication/wcms_513739.pdf

Ivie (2018) Diferencias educativas regionales 2000–2016: Condicionantes y resultados, https://www.fbbva.es/wp-content/uploads/2018/09/presentacion_cuentas_educacion_2000_2016.pdf

Jansen, M. and Troncoso-Ponce, D. (2018) El impacto de los contratos para la formación y elaprendizaje en la inserción laboral de los jóvenes, Estudios sobre la Economía Española, 27, FEDEA.

López, A. (2017) Addressing mismatch in Spain: a concern and proposal beyond the economic sphere, in M. Pilz (ed) *Vocational Education and Training in Times of Economic Crisis*, German Research Center for Comparative Vocational Education and Training (GREAT), Cham: Springer International Publishing, pp 355–68, https://link.springer.com/content/pdf/10.1007%2f978-3-319-47856-2.pdf

Marques, P. and Hörisch, F. (2019) Promoting workplace-based training to fight youth unemployment in three EU countries: different strategies, different results? *International Journal of Social Welfare*, 28(4): 380–93.

Melguizo, C. (2015) An analysis of the Okun's law for the Spanish provinces, Working Paper 1/37, Research Institute of Applied Economics (IREA), http://www.ub.edu/irea/working_papers/2015/201501.pdf

MESS (Ministerio de Empleo y Seguridad Social) (2013) Spanish national youth guarantee implementation plan, http://www.empleo.gob.es/es/estrategia-empleo-joven/destacados/plannacionalgarantiajuvenil_en.pdf

MESS (2016) Informe: Jóvenes y Mercado de Trabajo Junio 2016, Ministerio de Empleo y Seguridad Social, http://www.empleo.gob.es/es/sec_trabajo/analisis-mercado-trabajo/jovenes/numeros/2016/Junio_2016.pdf

Moldes, R., Briones, A., Gómez, F., Molina, M.J., Muñoz, J. and Sepúlveda, J. (2018) Implementation report on the 2015 and 2016 annual plan for the evaluation of the quality, impact, effectiveness and efficiency of the entire vocational training for employment system, Universidad Europea de Madrid, https://www. sistemanacionalempleo.es/pdf/abstract_of_final_report_for_the_ evaluation_program_2015-2016.pdf

OECD (2016) *Education at a Glance 2016: OECD Indicators*, Paris: OECD Publishing, http://www.oecd-ilibrary.org/docserver/ download/9616041e.pdf?expires=1474111407&id=id&accname=g uest&checksum=aad62d008d67be1286b826c68e4fa30f

OECD (2018) Education policy outlook Spain, http://www. educacionyfp.gob.es/inee/dam/jcr:a4319a40-3163-42eb-a432-74dc95dbadb3/education-policy-outlook-country-profile-spain-2018.pdf

OECD (2019) The future of work: how does Spain compare? OECD Employment Outlook 2019, http://www.oecd.org/spain/ employment-outlook-spain-en.pdf

Prieto, C. (2014) From flexicurity to social employment regimes, in M. Keune and A. Serrano Pascual (eds) *Deconstructing Flexicurity and Developing Alternative Approaches*, New York: Routledge, pp 47–68.

Reynolds, O. (2017) Is Spain doing enough to address its high youth unemployment rate? http://www.oecd.org/spain/employment-outlook-spain-en.pdf

Sancha, I. and Gutiérrez, S. (2016) Vocational education and training in Europe: Spain, Cedefop ReferNet VET in Europe reports, http:// libserver.cedefop.europa.eu/vetelib/2016/2016_cr_es.pdf

Sancha, I. and Gutiérrez, S. (2019) Vocational education and training in Europe: Spain, Cedefop ReferNet VET in Europe reports, http:// libserver.cedefop.europa.eu/vetelib/2019/vocational_education_ training_europe_spain_2018_cedefop_refernet.pdf

Scandura, R., Cefalo, R., Hermannson, K. and Kazepov, Y. (2018) Cross-national and Cross-regional Report Quantitative Analysis, Young Adult Grant Number 693167, H2020-Young-Society-2015, http://www.young-adulllt.eu/publications/working-paper/young_ adulllt_deliverable_d4_2_crossnational-and-crossregional-report-quantitative-analysis.pdf?m=1530517072

SEPE (Servicio Público de Empleo Estatal) (2019) Action Plan for Youth Employment 2019–2021, Ministerio de Trabajo, Migraciones y Seguridad Social.

Sigüenza, A.F. (2018) La Evaluación de la Competencia Profesional en programas de formación profesional Dual. Consejería de Educación, Junta de Castilla y León, ISBN: 978-84-9718-692-6.

Valiente, O. and Scandura, R. (2017) Challenges to the implementation of dual apprenticeships in OECD countries: a literature review, in M. Pilz (ed) *Vocational Education and Training in Times of Economic Crisis*, German Research Center for Comparative Vocational Education and Training (GREAT), Cham: Springer International Publishing, pp 41–58.

Villaverde, J., and Maza, A. (2007) Okun's Law in Spanish regions, *Economics Bulletin*, 18(5): 1–11.

Wolter, S.C. and Muehlemann, S. (2015) *Apprenticeship Training in Spain: A Cost-effective Model for Firms?* Gütersloh/Barcelona: Bertelsmann Stiftung and Fundación Bertelsmann, https://www.bertelsmann-stiftung.de/fileadmin/files/bst/publikationen/grauepublikationen/ll_gp_cost_benefit_study_en_final1.pdf

4

Dirigisme Pour L'Ordinaire: Vocational Training in 21st Century France

Michael J. Camasso, Guillaume Moissonnier and Radha Jagannathan

Introduction

In a 1984 report entitled Youth Unemployment in France: Recent Strategies, the Organization for Economic Cooperation and Development (OECD, 1984) provides a detailed critique of the French vocational education and job training (VET) effort and the failure of that effort to address the problem of an increasingly segmented labor market. The report's authors laid blame for the foundering at the feet of the French educational system and its organizing principle:

> Its main purpose seems to have been to select and train for the most important jobs in the country. The criteria of selection have predominantly been the talent for abstraction, the ability to simplify complex problems while leaving room for their complexities, and an overall knowledge of French history, philosophy and culture … One of the mainsprings of this system has been to let the best of each generation remain as long as possible in general education. The vocational training of this elite should therefore begin very late. It could then take place in special institutions, such as Les Grandes Écoles or on–the–job: for

example, public administration in the Foreign Service. (OECD, 1984: 57–8)

Hence, the idea of apprenticeship or technical, vocational training at an early age was viewed as an obstacle to social status and upward mobility. Moreover, as the report goes on to state, manual training has been regarded as second-class training, of less value than intellectual training (OECD, 1984: 93). Examples of poor quality vocational training sites follow, complete with poignant descriptions of inadequate tools, broken equipment, meager supplies, and the scant workplace knowledge of instructors.

Since the publication of this report the French government has implemented a variety of programs and policies to blunt the problem of youth unemployment, including a number of measures designed to make vocational education more relevant for the work setting and more attractive to young people. Over 80 of these initiatives are listed by Murphy (2017) in his book *Yearning to Labor: Youth Unemployment and Social Destiny in Urban France*. A recent endeavor, 'Les Campus des métiers et des qualifications', concentrates actors from secondary and higher education, apprenticeship training centers, employers and research institutes who comprise an industrial sector or labor specialty; for example, food and agribusiness, Information and Communication Technologies (ICT), and so on, to create smooth school-to-work transitions and workplace-based training.

Fast-forward now to a 2017 OECD report entitled Getting Skills Right: France (OECD, 2017a), and the report's assessment of the country's progress in improving vocational education and training:

> The popularity of the vocational track in secondary education is on the decline in France. The number of students in vocational education at the upper secondary level decreased by 9% in the period 1995–2015 and the upper secondary level apprenticeship declined by about 2.5% … Overall many students in vocational education specialize in sectors and occupations that are declining, and limited options are available for entering into emerging fields. (OECD, 2017a: 66)

This report continues on to point up the poor image of vocational education among employers, students and parents; the insufficient skill levels of many vocational instructors and the limited knowledge that many of these same instructors have of the workplace or the labor market. These conditions, the authors conclude, have helped France earn the dubious distinction 'as one of the few EU countries where the employment rate of vocational, non-tertiary graduates is worse than that of general non-tertiary graduates' (OECD, 2017a: 68).

Why, after over 30 years of attempted reform has the status of VET and apprenticeship remained largely unchanged? With youth unemployment rates much higher than Germany, Sweden or the US, perhaps a more pertinent question is: can the status of VET ever be improved in France? Recent efforts by the Macron government have been successful in lowering the youth (and overall) unemployment rate, raising the status of vocational education and apprenticeship for the young, and increasing the incentives for private sector work. But as a recent article in *The Economist* (2020) notes, while Macron's reforms are working, his already low popularity continues to sink. The apparent paradox can simply be credited to a problem of personality but we believe the contradiction stems from deeper cultural and institutional provenance.

The cultural *dirigisme*

We believe that in order to understand the shape of vocational education in France it is necessary to first appreciate the importance of '*dirigisme*' or the state direction of business and industry in the country. The roots of *dirigisme* can be traced to a major theme in French thinking that the idea of 'civilization' and French national character are largely synonymous, and that French culture is a direct descendant of the classical Greek and Roman civilizations (McClelland, 1964: 96–7; Lefebvre, 1962; Durant and Durant, 1963). Building upon such a legacy would require extraordinary intellectual leadership that insured that symbolic capital was not overwhelmed by the materialism of uncontrolled capitalism (Bourdieu, 1989; Murphy, 2017). As Lefebvre aptly points out, France lagged behind England in industrial and business activity because French nobles feared falling into the common mass if they followed the bourgeois ways of English lords (Lefebvre, 1962: 14).

France entered into the Industrial Revolution in halting fashion with the highly centralized government seeking to strike a balance between the preservation of legacy and the necessity of pursuing mercantilistic capitalism in a fashion that assured maximum profits. As Paul Kennedy (1987) reminds us, war in Europe had become very expensive to wage and funding increasingly difficult to obtain. Well before the French Revolution, the monarchy began to rely upon a non-hereditary nobility – what Bourdieu (1989, 1996) termed the state nobility – to consult and ultimately provide direction for both the war efforts and the economic activities needed to sustain them.

The institution that has provided continuity for the intellectuals and professionals who are responsible for *dirigisme* is the system of Grandes Écoles, that is, highly selective educational establishments, some of which were founded during the Ancien Régime. In his exhaustive research of French elites, Bourdieu (1989, 1996) identifies four Grandes Écoles that fuel France's managed capitalism, viz., École Normale Superieure (training for intelligentsia), Ecole des Hautes Études Commerciales (future captains of business and industry), École Polytechnique (engineering) and École Nationale d'Administration (heads of state). This last institution is identified by Bourdieu as the place where symbolic and material capital are blended, a kind of elites switching station allowing the extraordinary to circulate without restriction among the realms of business, academia and government. It is worthy of note that it is the École Nationale d'Administration that President Macron (a graduate) has called for to be closed as an important step toward educational equity (Colin, 2019).

It can be argued that many countries, including the US, also have cadres of elites who exert a disproportionate impact on the affairs of state and the economy. Charles Murray (2012) and C. Wright Mills (1956), a half-century earlier, have identified upper-class actors with strong connections to Ivy League (and a small handful of highly selective public) universities. These elites, however, lack the control of both symbolic and material capital that Bourdieu (1989, 1996) observes in France. Dominance over symbolic capital that stems from elite credentials requires the veneration of those qualifications by ordinary citizens, along with their belief that they do not nor cannot know what is best for themselves. These ideas have not been popular in America from its very inception as a nation state, even in matters that would appear to cry out for scientific expertise. De Tocqueville's (1840, 1945) chapter on 'Why the Americans are more addicted to practical than to theoretical science' is an early example of this skepticism.

The disparity in the control of symbolic capital between the two countries is nowhere more evident than in a study conducted by Slovic and his colleagues (Slovic et al, 2000) on nuclear power generation and public response. Samples of over 1500 citizens from each nation were asked a series of questions about trust in institutions, health risks, public policy, and so on. While 68% of French respondents believed they could trust the country's experts on the health risks of nuclear energy, only 24% of Americans voiced such trust. French respondents were also more likely to trust their government about the technological risks of nuclear power than were Americans, yet were much less likely than Americans, 80% vs. 35%, to believe they had control over their health risks.

Another important difference in the level of control French and American elites hold over symbolic capital involves the consequence given to the accoutrements (trappings) of expert status. D'Iribarne, among others (Gannon and Pillai, 2016; Murphy, 2017), talks about the significance of 'form', that is, the beauty of how things are carried out (D'Iribarne, 2009: 518), as an indication of excellence in France. In their investigation of business practices, Gannon and Pillai declare that 'how one speaks makes as much an impression as what one says' (Gannon and Pillai, 2016: 188) in French companies. While of some import, form in America is usually trumped by results.

Germany, too, has sought to create a system of elite universities, but since the inception of the endeavor in 2004 under the Schroder regime questions have been raised about its real purpose; that is, to create academically elite institutions or to create institutions for the already elite (Deutsche Welle, 2004). This initiative was renewed recently to extend it through 2026 with press coverage generally lauding the attempt to replicate the US's Ivies and Britain's Oxford and Cambridge (see, for example, German Center for Research and Innovation, 2019). Mention of Les Grandes Écoles is a very rare occurrence in these press releases, however.

French capitalism and labor market demand

Free-market capitalism has always been viewed with suspicion in France and these misgivings can be traced back at least as far as the French Revolution (Lefebvre, 1962; Gannon and Pillai, 2016). Singled out for special opprobrium is the 'dangerous strain of free-wheeling American capitalism' that is seen as a threat to France's long tradition of social welfare (Murphy, 2017: 219).

In Esping-Andersen's (2002) typology of welfare states, France and Germany are identified as conservative/corporatist nations distinguished by meritocracy, rigid labor markets and welfare linked to work-related pension credits. Hall and Soskice (2001) place France and Germany in the category of coordinated market economies (CMEs) characterized by market equilibria outcomes that rely less on demand and supply and more on interaction between firms and the government and labor unions. It would be a mistake, however, to elide the corporatism of France and Germany, especially in the context of labor demand: France conducts business from a much more firm-centric institutional platform.

In their 2020 Index of Economic Freedom, the Heritage Foundation (2020), a Washington, DC think tank, ranks 180 countries on the degree to which market capitalism is believed to thrive. The Index includes a number of economic criteria including property rights, individual and corporate tax burdens, investment, business and trade freedom. On this Index the US ranks 17, Germany 27, Sweden 22 and France 64. As we have seen in the Slovic et al (2000) study, the French public has high trust in government experts; their trust in private industry is much lower. When asked if they believed economic growth can only lead to pollution, French respondents expressed agreement at a level of 70%. In the US the level of agreement was only 45%. An attitude survey of individuals in 33 democratic countries conducted by Guillaud (2013) found that 52% of French respondents believed that the government definitely has a responsibility to reduce income disparities created by capitalism; the proportion of respondents with such belief in the US was 29%, in Germany 34%, and in social–democratic Sweden, 37%. These rankings and many others like them indicate that France is, indeed, a special case of corporate capitalism – much more centrally controlled. Hancké et al (2007) acknowledge this special case status in their essay 'Beyond varieties of capitalism' removing France from CME standing and placing the nation in a new category 'Étatisme'. The reason they cite for the move is the 'deep interpenetration of the state and the economic elites', weak business organization and state dominance (Hancké et al, 2007: 25).

Étatisme and *dirigisme* have had a great impact on the structure of labor demand in French business and industry. According to Hancké (2001), the elite-based coordination mechanism immanent in close *Étatisme* and *dirigisme* have provided the conditions for corporate autonomy from both the state and the stock market. This 'self-management by management' has, in turn, served as an impediment to the restructuring of work and labor relations in any meaningful way. Hancké (2001) maintains that *dirigisme* (he does not use the term in his argument, preferring elite coordination) has left the core contents of production jobs intact, preserving a Taylorist atmosphere where working rhythms are repetitive, dictated by machines and computers. While new workers possessed general knowledge in the form of mathematics, software and computer knowledge and social skills, they do not possess 'the deep technological kind that the German system produces' (Hancké, 2001: 324).

In a 2016 OECD report entitled *Job Creation and Local Economic Development* (OECD, 2016), readers are given a matrix which classifies European cities on the dimensions of skill supply and demand.

Major cities across France other than Paris (for example, Lyon, Lille, Marseilles) are categorized as 'skill surplus' cities. The label is a bit misleading however, since it can conflate over-education with over-skilling (Cedefop, 2018b). In Hancké's (2001) description he is clearly identifying a labor demand issue resulting from over-education in terms of mathematics, computer, social-psychological and communications knowledge but under-skilling with respect to mechanical, technological and production abilities.

Rather than creating the work place and labor relations conditions that would facilitate the younger, better-educated workers transition to a skill set of the 'deep technological type', French corporations, says Hancké, have merely added peripheral tasks to core production jobs: 'Workers now perform primary maintenance tasks, low-level personnel administration, quality control, inventory management and sometimes online contacts with suppliers. It may still be Taylorism, but it certainly takes on a different form.' (Hancké, 2001: 325). And since French companies had disproportionately more administrative, supervisory and maintenance workers than companies in other countries they were able to increase production efficiency without creating more efficient production processes.

The arguments of Hancké (2001) have been repeated and amplified by Michael Goyer (2007) in his comparison of firm-level institutions in France and Germany. Goyer notes a fundamental difference in the capacity that company CEOs and top managers in France and Germany have in their ability to unilaterally reorganize the workplace. In Germany, decision-making power is diffuse with managers seeking the consent of work councils, says Goyer, while in France workers and labor unions are typically left out of the process. This power concentration has three implications for the manner in which firms are organized: viz., skill certification and formation, segmentation of work activities and the autonomy of workers in problem-solving tasks.

We believe we can summarize Goyer's (2007) implications as follows:

1. The promotion process in German firms rests upon the acquisition of the required technical expertise and completion of relevant training for the bulk of the workforce. Most of this training is provided in vocational schools or apprenticeship programs. In France, managers and technical consultants select workers for promotion and then provide them with the appropriate training/education. Attempts to impose the recognition of vocational training as a prerequisite for

holding specific jobs has been resisted by French employers (Goyer, 2007: 208–09).

2. Because of German firms' reliance on the bulk of the company's (technically credentialed) workforce to carry out production function, segmentation of work activities is low with work rules applied to broad functions. In French firms the sharp separation between production planning and execution predominates as does a strict division of authority between management and workers (Goyer, 2007: 211). This is to be expected within a system bearing the characteristics of Taylorist production principles (Hancké, 2001).

3. Possessing only a narrow range of skills, French employees are capable of making very limited contributions to problem solving and business objectives. In Germany, workers' deeper and broader sets of knowledge, abilities and skills allow them to partner with management to achieve work efficiencies and organizational goals (Goyer, 2007: 213).

Dirigisme, *Étatisme*, and labor supply

Human capital, a term coined by Gary Becker in 1964 (Becker, 1993), is produced by changing individuals in ways that give them knowledge, skills and abilities (KSAs) which, in turn, allow them to act in new ways. Becker identifies schools and other training institutions as the principal organizations where this socialization takes place and where labor market supply is created. The educational structure in a country, and the type, quantity and quality of the KSAs it generates, reflect the demands of the market but also the historical and cultural orientations of its citizens. Nowhere is this confluence of economic and non-economic factors more evident than in France.

In Figure 4.1, we present the basic architecture of the French education system. There are two aspects of this system that will serve to focus our discussion on French labor supply: viz., high school vocational education and post-secondary degree programs. High school-level vocational education, that is, lycée professionnel, can take the form of a two-year program, Certificat d'aptitude professionnelle (CAP) or Brevet d'Études professionnelle (BEP) or a three-year program leading to a Baccalauréat professionel or Baccalauréat technologique. Many of these vocational options are provided in vocational lycées although some can be found in lycées technologique or lycées général (general university oriented education).

Figure 4.1: The French education system

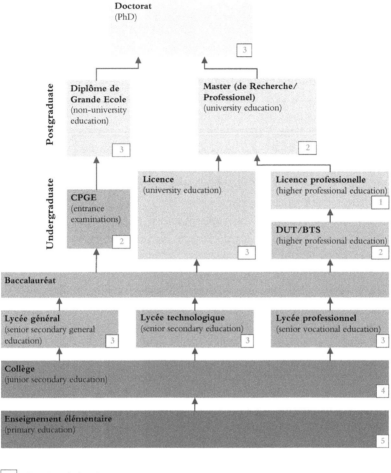

As we noted early on in this chapter, the vocational programs emanating from lycée professionnel have generally done a poor job in facilitating school-to-work transitions (OECD, 1984; 2017; Hancké, 2001; Goyer, 2007; Cahuc et al, 2013). In their cohort analyses of school-to-work transitions the Centre d'études et de recherches sur les qualifications (CEREQ) report consistently higher unemployment rates for BEP and CAP recipients than for students with the Baccalauréat général (Ilardi and Sulzer, 2015; Barret et al, 2014). Individuals with a vocational baccalauréat, especially those in a manufacturing specialization, do better but as Cahuc et al (2013) observe,

BEP/CAP students are resistant to the extra year of academic instruction that includes courses in history, literature, and so on, necessary for the Baccalauréat professionnel. In theory, CAP/BEP students and those with the Baccalauréat professionnel have a skillset that prepares them for work in some 19 economic sectors, ranging from hotel management and tourism and hairdressing and beauty treatments to automotive mechanics and construction and roofing (Baret et al, 2014). The high unemployment rates for these individuals, often in the 20–30% range, would seem to indicate otherwise.

Figure 4.1 also shows that the recipient of a Baccalauréat professionnel can pursue short two-year courses of study at University Institute(s) of Technology (IUT) or at Higher Technician's Section(s) (STS) in order to receive a Diplôme Universitaire de Technologie (DUT) or Brevet de Technicien Supérieur (BTS). Longitudinal data from CEREQ indicate lower unemployment rates for youth with BTS/DUT credentials than for youth with CAP, BEP or the vocational (professional/technical) Baccalauréat (Barret et al, 2014) but very small salary differentials of about €90 per month (Barret et al, 2014: 6). It would appear that the principal reason for pursuing these advanced degrees is job security: BTS/DUT graduates are more likely to report having permanent work contracts three years after joining the labor force than non-graduates, 74% vs. 52% in the case of DUT, 67% vs. 56% for BTS (Grelet et al, 2010).

One avenue open to individuals seeking to pursue vocational careers that is not shown on Figure 4.1 is apprenticeship or 'alternance'. In 2017 France had approximately 400,000 young people alternating their education/training between school and work settings; the number in Germany was 1.3 million individuals (Cedefop, 2018a). The European Centre for the Development of Vocational Training (Cedefop) classifies the French approach to apprenticeship as a 'Type B' effort, that is, a type of VET delivery that occurs within the VET system. The BEP/CAP programs have been identified by the government as the logical place to anchor apprenticeship, adding a work-on-site component to existing curriculum. In contrast apprenticeship in Germany is classified by Cedefop (2018a) as a 'Type A' effort, that is, it is nationally defined training in specified occupations that is recognized by all German companies and that takes place outside the VET system.

Unlike the German model where the qualifications sought, training content, curriculum, form of organization, and duration of instruction are fixed by government, businesses and union agreement at the national level, French apprenticeships are the results of highly individualized contracts between individuals and employers. And while

German apprenticeships last from three to three-and-a-half years the typical 'contrat de professionnalisation' averages around 18 months and the 'contrat d'apprentissage' can be in effect for one to three years, depending on the qualification being sought (Cedefop, 2018a). In one of the few nationwide studies of broken apprenticeship contracts, Cart et al (2010) estimate that 17% of these contracts are broken; about half of them by the apprentice primarily because of what was perceived as an unsatisfactory occupational environment.

France is unique among European educational systems in the government's designation of Grandes Écoles rather than universities as the apex of higher (tertiary) education. We have discussed their role earlier as the switching stations facilitating the circulation of elites from science, technology, business and state. If it is fair to say that VET is neglected in France it is equally fair to say that the Grandes Écoles are cherished – they epitomize the legacy of Greco-Roman civilization and the French resolve to maintain it, *mutatis mutandis*.

Entry into this Grandes Écoles system is meant to be exceedingly more rigorous than admission to university. Classe préparatoire aux grandes écoles (CPGE) is an intensive two-year program of study offered at a number of lycées général and lycées technologique upon the student's receipt of the Baccalauréat. Admission to CPGE is also highly competitive and is based on the student's Baccalauréat academic ranking and examination performance. There are three general programs of study in the CPGE: economics/commerce, literature, and science. CPGE ends with a series of rigorous examinations and application to one or more Grandes Écoles. The acceptance rate is around 5%; in public universities, on the other hand, acceptance is open to all students with a Baccalauréat – space permitting. Government spending for students in Grandes Écoles is estimated to be four times higher than it is for university students, a ratio that both signals and helps preserve Bourdieu's 'state nobility'.

We close this discussion on labor supply with an observation by Philippe d'Iribarne (2009) on the nature of work in France. D'Iribarne asserts that in France one's métier (that is, one's calling or occupation), no matter the status of the calling, signals liberty, honor and even nobility. One has to wonder out loud if this cultural capacity to find honor in the performance of Tayloristic tasks or adoption of 'la petite contrat' lasting a week or less, bodes well for any effort to reform the nation's school-to-work profile.

A note on entrepreneurship in France

Entrepreneurship, the dynamic process of creating incremental wealth, is at the very soul of capitalism, and it is a pathway for bringing disadvantaged and unemployed youth into the labor market. Following the classic discussion of Schumpeter (1939, 1964) the entrepreneur is the innovator, the risk taker, the rule challenger, irreverent to traditions, the disrupter. Sounds like a poor fit for the France of *dirigisme* and *Étatisme*. Indeed, in Bosma and Kelley's (2018) profiles of 54 countries, France ranks 34 on the criterion of cultural norms and values that are conducive to entrepreneurship; the US ranks first. These researchers also report that while 58% of survey respondents in France believed entrepreneurship to be a good career opportunity, only 35% believed it was easy to start a business there.

Two features of French business culture have been identified that can be serious obstacles to entrepreneurship and innovation: uncertainty avoidance and a penchant for abstraction/complex thinking divorced of practice (OECD, 1984; Gannon and Pillai, 2016; Hancké, 2001). For example, on the well-known dimensional analysis of cultures and organizations pioneered by Geert Hofstede (Hofstede et al, 2010), French managers garner a risk avoidance score of 85 out of 100. Countries with similar scores are Italy (75) and Spain (85). By way of comparison Sweden (30) and the US show low levels of risk avoidance. To illustrate this preference for intellectual challenge we offer Ulijn and Fayolle's (2004) study of engineering startup companies in France, Germany and the Netherlands. In their observations of the operations of these firms and through questioning of employees Ulijn and Fayolle (2004) find that French engineers appeared most comfortable with the intellectual stimulation of the problem while German engineers were keen on the connection between design and fabrication/implementation. Lastly, Dutch engineers placed their highest priority on designs that were marketable. Based on their data, these researchers construct an informal 'entrepreneurial urge' scale, ranking the Dutch very high and the French, very low.

Lest we leave the reader with the impression that there is little hope for the young entrepreneur in France, we provide the French score on the National Entrepreneurial Context Index (NECI) reported by Bosma and Kelley (2018). This index takes into consideration 12 indicators of country context, indicators like availability of startup finance, physical infrastructure, internal market dynamics, and government programs. On the NECI, France ranks 10 out of the 54 listed countries; the United States 6 and Italy 40. France gets its highest marks on available infrastructure and entrepreneurial education post-high school.

The changing French labor market

Dirigisme pour L'Ordinaire has helped create a more educated workforce in France, but it has also created the chronic problems that accompany labor market segmentation due to over-education/under-skilling. Askenazy (2019) has documented the steady rise of short-term, temporary work contracts over the past 20 years, now reaching the point where nearly half of the labor force is working under this condition of continuous uncertainty. He also notes that only about 20% of these short-term agreements last for a month or more, with the median duration only eight days. Cahuc et al (2013) view the increasing use of this instrument as a major barrier to school-to-work transitions and a contributor to a cyclical form of unemployment and underemployment.

Another consequence of the precipitous rise in short, temporary contracts is the emergence of a new group of the self-employed, that is, 'entrepreneurs out of necessity' not choice. As Askenazy (2019) points out, these new 'micro-entrepreneurs' are not the skilled artisans of the trade unions and guilds, but are, instead, independent contractors, many of whom constitute a new category of the working poor.

In Table 4.1, we present a set of time series that we think will help the reader gauge the economic dynamics produced by France's form of corporate capitalism. From the Table it is clear that the country's GDP per capita has grown by about $4,000 from 2000 to 2017, that is, from $38,461 to $42,576. During the same period in Germany the increase was from $37,998 to $46,752; in Sweden $44,694 to $56,992; and in the US, $45,056 to $53,222. Per capita exports in France rose about $3,000, from $4,987 to $7,799. In Germany the increase was from $6,685 to $17,539, in Sweden from $9,799 to $15,223; and in the US from $2,771 to $4,764. Both sets of comparisons indicate France's slow growth economy without the huge domestic market that the US possesses for its own goods.

It is also useful, we believe, to contrast the unemployment, labor force participation and early stage entrepreneurial activity (TEA) of France with those of Germany, Sweden and the US. As we see in Table 4.1, the French overall unemployment rate has, until recently, remained in the 11% to 12% range over the time series and the country's youth unemployment is double that. In Germany youth unemployment has averaged about 9%, in Sweden about 17%, and in the US about 11%. The French labor force participation rate has remained steady at 56 per 100 eligible-to-work individuals. In Germany this rate is about 59 per 100, in Sweden 72 per 100 and in the United States, 64 per

Table 4.1: Demography, economy and labor in France (2001–2017)

	2000	2001	2002	2003	2004	2005	2006	2007
GDP in US constant $ (in billions) [0,1,2]	2,342.74	2,388.52	2,415.24	2,435.03	2,502.88	2,543.12	2,603.52	2,665.00
GDP per capita (computed)	38,461	38,928	39,078	39,120	39,915	40,252	40,922	41,630
GDP annual growth rate % [1]	3.17	1.22	0.39	0.11	2.03	0.84	1.66	1.73
GNI per capita [2]	35,557	35,963	35,825	35,947	36,751	37,168	37,881	38,565
Total population (in millions) [1]	60.91	61.36	61.81	62.24	62.70	63.18	63.62	64.02
Population 15–24 years (in millions) [1]	7.70	7.71	7.74	7.79	7.82	7.83	7.82	7.79
% Population 15–24 (computed)	12.64	12.56	12.53	12.51	12.47	12.39	12.30	12.17
% Unemployment rate (yearly) [1+]	10.2	8.6	8.7	8.3	8.9	8.5	8.5	7.7
% Youth unemployment rate 15–24 [1+]	20.6	18	18.9	17.3	19.8	20.3	21.3	18.8
% NEET (youth not in employment, education, or training) [3]	15.0	14.5	14.7	14.1	14.6	14.5	15.2	14.5
% Labor force participation rate – 15+ [1*]	54.77	54.74	54.89	56.34	56.32	56.24	56.15	56.27
% Labor force participation rate – 15–24 [1*]	29.3	29.9	30.2	38.1	38.1	38.1	38.1	38.4
Employment [4]								21.83
Exports in U.S. $ (in millions) [5]	303,758	289,599	304,892	358,132	413,708	434,354	479,013	539,731
Imports in U.S. $ (in millions) [5]	295,345	293,866	303,831	362,517	434,242	475,857	529,902	611,364
Per capita exports (exports/total population) (computed)	4,987	4,720	4,933	5,754	6,598	6,875	7,529	8,431

Table 4.1: Demography, economy and labor in France (2001–2017) (continued)

2008	2009	2010	2011	2012	2013	2014	2015	2016	2017
2,670.21	2,591.67	2,642.61	2,697.56	2,702.48	2,718.06	2,743.81	2,773.10	2,806.04	2,857.09
41,479	40,052	40,638	41,283	41,159	41,183	41,375	41,642	41,969	42,576
-0.36	-3.44	1.46	1.59	-0.30	0.06	0.46	0.65	0.78	1.43
38,443	36,999	37,632	38,320	37,876	37,892	38,085	38,367	38,702	
64.38	64.71	65.03	65.34	65.66	66.00	66.32	66.59	66.86	67.11
7.75	7.71	7.67	7.61	7.57	7.53	7.51	7.51	7.56	7.62
12.04	11.91	11.79	11.65	11.52	11.41	11.33	11.28	11.31	11.35
7.1	8.7	8.9	8.8	9.4	9.9	10.3	10.4	10.1	9.4
18.3	23	22.6	21.9	23.7	24.1	24.2	24.7	24.6	22.3
14.0	15.6	16.6	16.4	16.6	16.3	16.3	17.2	17.2	16.5
56.36	56.58	56.51	56.26	56.47	56.45	56.3	56.15	56.04	55.86
38.5	39.6	38.9	37.9	37.4	37.4	37.1	37.3	37.2	37.2
21.74	21.93	21.79	21.39	21.23	21.31	21.38	21.39		
594,505	464,113	511,651	585,724	558,461	567,988	566,656	493,941	488,885	523,385
695,004	540,502	599,172	713,675	666,675	671,254	659,872	563,398	560,555	613,133
9,235	7,173	7,868	8,964	8,505	8,606	8,545	7,417	7,312	7,799

(continued)

Table 4.1: Demography, economy and labor in France (2001–2017) (continued)

	2000	2001	2002	2003	2004	2005	2006	2007
Per capita imports (imports/total population) (computed)	4,849	4,789	4,916	5,824	6,925	7,532	8,329	9,550
Total early stage entrepreneurial activity (TEA) [6]		5.72	3.13	1.63	6.03	5.35	4.39	3.17
Established business ownership rate [6]		1.62	1.27	1.64	1.45	2.27	1.33	1.74

[0] Data are in constant 2010 U.S. dollars. Dollar figures for GDP are converted from domestic currencies using 2010 official exchange rates.

[1] Source: https://stats.oecd.org/Index.aspx?DatasetCode=SNA_ (Appropriate table) and World Bank Data Online https://databank.worldbank.org/home.aspx

[2] Source: https://data.worldbank.org/indicator/NY.GNP.PCAP.KD?_Locations=GNP Gross National Income is equal to a country's GDP (Gross Domestic Product) + the country's net property income from abroad. If a country has many multinational corporations that repatriate income from local country production back to a home country, then GNI will be lower than GDP in the local country.

[1+] Unemployment Rate is the total number of unemployed individuals divided by the total number of individuals who are in the labor force, i.e., employed and unemployed seeking work. Youth unemployment rate is an age specific rate of the total number of individuals between 15 and 24 years old who are unemployed divided by the number of 15–24 year olds in the labor force i.e., employed and unemployed but seeking work.

100. Finally, on total early-stage entrepreneurial activity (TEA), that is, the average number of new jobs entrepreneurs expect to create, the French mean is about 5 over the series while the mean is also about 5 in Germany, 7 in Sweden and 12 in the US.

Viewing these particular indicators jointly we can conclude that *dirigisme* in France has not produced the level of growth or wealth found in social-democratic Sweden, conservative corporatist Germany or liberal market US. We believe it is fair to say that the cultural, labor force demand and human capital elements discussed have contributed to an economy of slow growth, low labor force participation and high youth unemployment. The problem of growing labor market segmentation suggests these issues will linger if not become exacerbated. Lacking the institutional structure to create a VET/apprenticeship mechanism like

Table 4.1: Demography, economy and labor in France (2001–2017) (continued)

2008	2009	2010	2011	2012	2013	2014	2015	2016	2017
10,796	8,353	9,214	10,922	10,153	10,171	9,950	8,460	8,384	9,137
5.64	4.35	5.83	5.73	5.17	4.57	5.34		5.32	3.92
2.8	3.21	2.44	2.38	3.23	4.09	2.94		4.3	3.58

[1*] Labor Force Participation Rate is the total number of individuals actively participating in the labor force (unemployed, employed, looking for work) divided by the number of individuals eligible to participate in the total working population group but who do not participate because of their status as full time students, retirees, homemakers, prisoners, the disabled and also includes people who simply do not want to work.

[3] The NEET (Neither in Employment, Education or Training) rate is more inclusive than the unemployment rate and is measured as the total number of youth aged 15–24 who are unemployed, economically inactive, not in education or training in the last four weeks divided by 15–24 year olds in the population. https://data.oecd.org/youthinac/youth-not-in-employment-education-or-training-neet.htm

[4] Source: https://stats.oecd.org/Index.aspx?QueryId=78408#

[5] Source: https://wits.worldbank.org/CountryProfile/en/Country/SWE/Year/2015/TradeFlow/EXPIMP

[6] Source: https://www.gemconsortium.org/data/key-aps

Germany's and lacking the value orientation of on-the-job training, residential mobility and 'free-wheeling' capitalism as practiced in the US, the French government has sought a third way out of this state of affairs through a series of active labor market policies (ALMPs).

Much as Germany's dual system and America's dynamic of residential/sectoral mobility and on-the-job training have prevented labor market segmentation, Sweden has utilized ALMPs quite successfully for the same purpose. These interventions have been far less successful in France notwithstanding *dirigisme* (Murphy, 2017; Cahuc et al, 2013).

Murphy (2017) provides an excellent example of how an ALMP designed to lower youth unemployment in France may have, in fact, helped to contribute to the problem. In 2006 the labor law was changed around youth work arrangements from a policy of 'contrat de travail à durée indéterminée' (CDI) to 'contrat première embauche' (CPE). The new law allowed employers to terminate a worker any time during a mandated two-year probationary (consolidation) period without justification. Under CDI there was no probationary period but an employee could be terminated at any time for cause. CPE liberalized employees' rights to seek training, the receipt of unemployment benefits and, as Murphy (2017) indicates, offered more protection for workers during the probationary than did CDI. Nonetheless, the new law was met with large protests because the onus to prove wrongful termination had moved from the employer to the employee. ALMPs, introduced into an environment of mistrust and adversarial relationships – conditions infrequent in Swedish labor relations but more common in France – account for their relative ineffectiveness in opening up rigid labor markets without fragmenting them.

Some views from the ninety-five percent

In his ethnographic study of Limoges, a medium-sized city in Central France, Murphy (2017) interviewed several dozen youth living in the city's poor, multiethnic banlieue, that is, the outer ring around the city. Many of these young people had completed their Baccalauréat but a significant number had not finished their high school degrees. Murphy discusses, quite eloquently, the economic insecurities, social challenges and hopes of youth facing an increasingly turbulent labor market. The author traces a good deal of youth unemployment and underemployment in this French city to the destruction of the 'social anaesthesia state' that dulls the pain of the real culprit: economic liberalism.

As we have sought to show in this discussion, the precarity or uncertainty of youth unemployment in France is not a function of unbridled free-market capitalism, per se, but a consequence of Étatisme, a centralized hybrid that preserves an elite operating core of government, business and educational interconnections and, in so doing, preserves a pillar of French history and culture. We link this Étatisme to underfunded public university and vocational education systems, to highly segmented labor markets and to 'remedies' like 'petite' and even 'miniscule' labor contracts for an increasing number of youth.

Murphy (2017) conducted his interviews at a time when French labor laws were subject to great changes – the CPI and CPE transition being one of them. President Macron's current reforms have resulted in similar upheaval. In an effort to gauge the sentiments of French youth in today's job market we conducted a dozen interviews with young people from Marseilles, Paris and Nice. We do not claim these survey responses are exhaustive or representative but we do assert that they were gathered without the respondents having any knowledge of the thesis advanced in the previous sections of this chapter. Unlike Murphy's interlocutors our youth are older and more likely to have an education beyond the Baccalauréat. Two have completed DUT programs and about half are working on a Master's (de Recherche/ Professional). The authors know one of the twelve respondents on a personal level; we have never met the others. As an incentive for completing a five-page questionnaire (available from the authors) these youth were each paid €10.

Our main purpose for conducting these interviews was to find out if French youth thought the German system of VET and/or the American approach of on-the-job training could work in France. There was complete consensus that the former would work and all but three individuals thought the American approach could or would be effective. These twelve individuals were also asked to respond to a set of closed and open-ended questions around the reasons for youth unemployment in France, who was most responsible for the situation, and what government, businesses and the universities should to improve things.

Nine of the twelve respondents thought the main problem was a system that provided too much education but not enough skills. Three individuals believed the problem resided in education limited only to high school. As to responsibility for unemployment, 10 individuals named the central government as the source of primary responsibility, followed by local government, lycée and university. The business community was ranked number one or two only twice. When asked what government should do to improve the employment situation, five individuals called for more skills training, four said taxes on employers should be reduced, and three advocated for government job creation programs. These youth believed universities needed to work more closely with the business community (8) or have more internships and job fairs (3).

We believe these interviews affirm to a large extent the arguments we have advanced in this chapter. We also believe that one of these respondents has summed up the French school-to-work transition for a great many young people in France in a simple yet elegant fashion: 'We need to stop learning everything and nothing at the same time because it is too general, uninteresting and [does not] put theory into practice'.

References

Ashkenazy, P. (2019) The changing of the French labor market, 2000–2017, *IZA World of Labor*, https://wol.iza.org/articles/the-changing-of-the-french-labor-market/long

Barret, C., Ryk, F. and Volle, N. (2014) 2013 survey of the 2010 cohort: The gap between levels of qualification widens as the crisis deepens, *Training and Employment*, No. 109–110, Marseille: Cereq.

Becker, G.S. (1993) *Human Capital: A Theoretical and Empirical Analysis*, 3rd edn, Chicago, IL: University of Chicago Press.

Bosma, N. and Kelley, D. (2018) *Global Entrepreneurship Monitor, 2018–2019 Global Report*, Wellesley, MA: Babson College.

Bourdieu, P. (1989, 1996) *The State Nobility Elite Schools in the Field of Power*, Cambridge: Polity Press.

Cahuc, P., Carcillo, S., Rinne, U. and Zimmermann, K.F. (2013) Youth unemployment in old Europe: the polar cases of France and Germany, IZA Discussion Paper 7490, Institute of Labor Economics (IZA), https://www.iza.org/en/publications/dp/7490/youth-unemployment-in-old-europe-the-polar-cases-of-france-and-germany

Cart, B. Toutin-Trelcat, M.H., and Henguelle, V. (2010) Apprenticeship contracts: why they are breached, *Training and Employment*, No. 89, Marseille: Cereq.

Cedefop (European Centre for the Development of Vocational Training) (2018a) Apprenticeship schemes in European countries: a cross-nation overview, Luxembourg: Office of the European Union, https://www.cedefop.europa.eu/files/4166_en.pdf

Cedefop (2018b) Insights into skill shortages and skill mismatch, Luxembourg: Office of the European Union, https://www.cedefop.europa.eu/files/3075_en.pdf

Colin, N. (2019) Closing the ENA government school will not change an elitist culture, *Financial Times*, April 19.

De Tocqueville, A. (1840, 1945) *Democracy in America*, vol 2, New York: Vintage Books.

Deutsche Welle. (2004) German press review: an elite university or a university for the elite? January 7, https://p.dw.com/p/4Wwf

D'Iribarne, P. (2009) National cultures and organizations in search of a theory, *Journal of Cross-Cultural Management*, 9: 309–21.

Durant, W. and Durant, A. (1963) *The Story of Civilization, Part VIII: The Age of Louis XIV*, New York: Simon & Schuster.

Esping-Andersen, G. (2002) *Towards the Good Society, Once Again? Why We Need a New Welfare State*, New York: Oxford University Press.

Gannon, M.J. and Pillai, R.K. (2016) *Understanding Global Cultures: Metaphorical Journeys Through 34 Nations, Clusters of Nations, Continents, and Diversity*, 6th edn, Los Angeles, CA: Sage.

German Centre for Research and Innovation (2019) German to strengthen eleven universities to elite status, https://www.dwih-newyork.org/en/2019/07/24/excellence-universities/

Goyer, M. (2007) Capital mobility, varieties of institutional investors, and the transforming stability of corporate governance in France and Germany, in B. Hancké, M. Rhodes, and M. Thatcher (eds) *Beyond Varieties of Capitalism: Conflict, Contradictions, and Complementarities in the European Economy*, New York: Oxford University Press, pp 195–217.

Grelet, Y., Romani, C. and Timoteo, J. (2010) What becomes of students joining a Higher Technician's Section (STS) or a University Institute of Technology (IUT)? Training and Employment 90, Marseille: Cereq.

Guillaud, E. (2013) Preferences for redistribution: an empirical analysis over 33 countries, *Journal of Economic Inequality*, 11: 57–78.

Hall, P.A. and Soskice, D. (2001) *An Introduction to Varieties of Capitalism*, New York: Oxford University Press.

Hancké, B. (2001) Revisiting the French model: coordination and restructuring in French industry, in P.A. Hall and D. Soskice (eds), *An Introduction to Varieties of Capitalism*, New York: Oxford University Press, pp 307–34.

Hancké, B., Rhodes, M. and Thatcher, M. (2007) *Beyond Varieties of Capitalism: Conflict, Contradictions, and Complementarities in the European Economy*, New York: Oxford University Press, pp 3–38.

Heritage Foundation (2020) *2020 Index of Economic Freedom*, Washington, DC: The Heritage Foundation, https://www.heritage.org/index/

Hofstede, G., Hofstede G.J. and Minkov, M. (2010) *Cultures and Organizations: Software of the Mind*, New York: McGraw Hill.

Ilardi, V. and Sulzer, E. (2015) Crisis makes school-to-work transition of CAP-BEP holders even more difficult, Training and Employment 116, Marseille: Cereq.

Kennedy, P. (1987) *The Rise and Fall of the Great Powers: Economic Change and Military Conflict from 1500 to 2000*, New York: Vintage Books.

Lefebvre, G. (1962) *The French Revolution, I: From its Origins to 1793*, New York: Columbia University Press.

McClelland, D.C. (1964) *The Roots of Consciousness*, Princeton, NJ: Van Nostrand.

Mills, C.W. (1956) *The Power Elite*, New York: Oxford University Press.

Murphy, J.P. (2017) *Yearning to Labor: Youth, Unemployment, and Social Destiny in Urban France*, Lincoln, NE: University of Nebraska Press.

Murray, C. (2012) *Coming Apart: The State of White America 1960–2010*, New York: Crown Forum.

OECD (1984) *Youth Unemployment in France: Recent Strategies*, Paris: OECD Publishing.

OECD (2016) *Job Creation and Labor Economic Development 2016*, Paris: OECD Publishing.

OECD (2017) *Getting Skills Right: France*, Paris: OECD Publishing.

Schumpeter, J. (1939, 1964) *Business Cycles*, New York: McGraw-Hill.

Slovic, P., Flynn, J., Mertz, C.K., Poumadère, M. and Mays, C. (2000) *Nuclear Power and the Public: Cross-Cultural Risk Perception*, Dordrecht: Springer, pp 55–102.

The Economist (2020) Emmanuel Macron's reforms are working, but not for him, https://www.economist.com/europe/2020/02/20/emmanuel-macrons-reforms-are-working-but-not-for-him

Ulijn, J. and Fayolle, A. (2004) Towards cooperation between European startups: the position of the French, Dutch, and German entrepreneurial and innovative engineer, in T.E. Brown and J. Ulijn, *Entrepreneurship, Innovation and Culture: The Interaction Between Technology, Progress and Economic Growth*, Cheltenham: Edward Elgar, pp 204–32.

5

Educating Youth for Future Unemployment in Greece

Radha Jagannathan and Ioanna Tsoulou

Introduction

It is difficult to imagine that a society which inspired advancements in science, mathematics, philosophy, and architecture, and which formed the bedrock of ancient western civilization, can find itself in such dire economic straits. One thing that has not changed from the ancient to modern times, however, is Greece's often difficult relationship with the rest of Europe. Starting with its independence from the Ottoman Empire in 1832, Greece has been romanticized by European elites in art and literature (Shelley, Goethe, Byron) and along the way, the seeds of historical mistrust between Greece and the rest of Europe were also sown, seeds that have since blossomed and flourished to this day (Zarkadakis, 2011).

The debt crisis that began in earnest in 2008, and the EU bailout that followed with austerity conditions attached, didn't help improve this troubled relationship. In the largest such economic bailout of a bankrupt country in history, Greece received a €320 billion loan from European authorities and private investors, and according to the European Commission, only 13% of the loan has been repaid as of last year (European Commission, 2019). The economic crisis plunged the country into a deep recession with the economy shrinking 25%, unemployment rising to 25%, and youth unemployment exceeding 50%. Greece had a labor force participation rate of 51.6% in 2019, the lowest of any EU country (Eurostat, 2019). With nearly half the working population not on the labor force, how has the country emerged from the economic crisis? Amadeo (2019) summarizes the Greek recovery as follows:

> Despite austerity measures, many aspects of Greece's economy are still problematic. Government spending makes up 48% of the GDP while EU bailouts contribute around 3%. As of 2017, Greece relies on tourism for 20% of GDP. Bureaucracy often delays commercial investments for decades. The government has shrunk, but it is still inefficient. There is too much political patronage. Government decision-making is centralized, further slowing response time. Tax evasion has gone underground as more people operate in the black economy. It now comprises 21.5% of GDP. As a result, fewer people are paying higher taxes to receive less from the government than they did before the crisis. Many of the jobs available are part-time and pay less than before the crisis. As a result, hundreds of thousands of the best and brightest have left the country. Banks haven't completely recuperated and are hesitant to make new loans to businesses. It will be a slow road to recovery. (Amadeo, 2019)

The need-hate relationship between Greece and the EU has garnered the former the moniker of 'black sheep' of the EU, characterized by a non-conformist attitude on foreign policy, passive aggressiveness on EU-set targets or implementing and upholding EU legislation, and misuse of EU funds (Featherstone and Papadimitriou, 2008). This game of opposites leads to a 'profile of contradictions' where there is a strong tendency among the Greeks to assert and maintain a national and cultural identity while simultaneously and consistently supporting EU development – as Featherstone and Papadimitriou (2008) put it:

> in crude terms, the Greek system welcomes 'Europe' for its political and resource advantages while sustaining barriers to its legal, economic and cultural adaptation. The profile contrasts self-confidence about Greece's place in Europe with a sense of vulnerability on matters of policy substance and a defensiveness about the Greek way of 'doing things'. (Featherstone and Papadimitriou, 2008: 29)

We will have a bit more to say about the 'Greek way of doing things' later in the chapter when we discuss findings from a survey the authors conducted.

In order to understand the political economy of a country and the specific role of the state in generating its economic outcomes, scholars have attempted to develop typologies of economic performance, welfare state, or a combination of the two that are based on a country's distinctive structural economic, social and political features (Esping-Andersen, 1990; Featherstone, 2008; Hall and Soskice, 2001; Hancké et al, 2007; Oscar and Rhodes, 2005). Greece has stoutly defied these attempts at neatly fitting it into any of these classifications (Featherstone, 2008). Greece does not strictly follow the mold offered by these theoretical classifications. Feathersone (2008) attempts an empirical classification based on data extracted from the European Commission and draws a picture that is characterized by: (1) an economy that is predominated by many micro and small firms and an ambiguity in the power structure of the state vis-à-vis the economic actors; (2) an employment structure with pronounced structural unemployment and low wages, especially among youth, and with scant unemployment benefits; (3) a strong public sector union; (4) business representation that is skewed toward a few large corporations, with little influence exerted by small firms; (5) high state regulation of labor, low market competition, high costs of doing business, and a substantial black economy; (6) market-distorting effects of political and economic corruption; (7) a welfare state that is largely dependent on which way the political wind blows; and (8) a relatively large but largely ineffective public administrative structure.

With the preceding as a backdrop, we focus on the country's youth and its labor market institutions and labor policies that have resulted in enormously high rates of economically inactive youth. We focus primarily on the supply side of the labor market, specifically on the Greek educational system that has produced increasingly over-educated cohorts of youth, and the labor market that has failed to absorb the generous output of the education sector. And given Greece's adversarial relationship with the major EU actors, especially the Germans who were the primary contributors to the bailout, we ask whether the Greeks would be willing to adopt a dual education system that is quintessentially German as a pathway for youth productivity. We also ask whether the Greek youth would embrace a more unstructured, free-wheeling path to economic self-sufficiency, much as the Americans do.

Current status of Greek youth

Since the beginning of the Great Recession, youth unemployment in Greece remains at worryingly high rates. Specifically, the unemployment rate of Greek youth under 25 years is 36.1% and is the highest in the EU, surpassing that of Spain (30.6%) and Italy (29.3%) (Statista, 2020). In addition, youth 15–29 years who are not in employment, education or training, the NEET rate, has reached 21.4% and is the second highest in the EU, ranking only behind Italy in 2018 (OECD, 2020). These rates, moreover, were quite high even before the recession (Bell and Blanchflower, 2015; Kretsos, 2014), in an era when labor demand in the EU was actually high.

Complicating matters, a high proportion of the country's unemployed youth – both males and females – are tertiary education graduates, which signifies a critical difference between Greece and other states of the EU (Bell and Blanchflower, 2015; Mitrakos et al, 2010). Standing (2011) warns of the rise of a 'precariat', a term he used to describe millions of youth around the world who were left 'without an anchor of stability' (Standing, 2011: 1). He referred to this class of young people as highly intellectual, whose heroes included Bourdieu, Foucault, Habermas, Hardt and Negri, and who are disillusioned with the neoliberal model where market competitiveness determines economic outcomes, and where in the name of labor market flexibility all risks and insecurities are borne by workers and families. The precariousness does not stop with job instability, such as working part-time or in temporary and poorly paid jobs, but extends to poor working conditions as well (Kesisoglou et al, 2016), earning them the additional status of 'working poor'.

Themelis (2017) points out that this 'precarianization' among young Greeks has become more acute with dramatic shifts in their sectoral preferences for employment. Whereas prior to the economic crisis there was an express preference for public sector employment because of the stability and educational orientation that used to be associated with such jobs, in 2016, an overwhelming majority of youth expressed a preference for employment in the private sector (73%), given the low esteem and the low wages and increasing instability that now accompany public sector jobs. With high rates of both education and unemployment, the school-to-work transition had now become extraordinarily sluggish. Themelis (2017) attributes this rather protracted transition to: (1) the economic crisis that weakened an already anemic connection between education and work; (2) a labor market that is highly segmented along the lines of education, residence, gender and age; and (3) the lackluster potential of higher education for employment and social integration, and its increased potential for precariousness and emigration out of Greece. He opines that, collectively, these problems 'point to a ticking bomb at the foundations of the Greek society' (Themelis, 2017: 59).

The deterioration of the youth labor market, however, cannot be solely attributed to the economic crisis; it appears that the pre-existing structural deficiencies in the education system (for example, low levels of degree completion and rather low returns to education (OECD, 2008)), and in the labor market (high rates of self-employment, especially among females, and higher than average unemployment for degree holders) (Papadopoulos, 2000; Livanos, 2010a)), also contributed to the dismantling of the Greek economy. The ever-prevailing norms of clientelism, nepotism and non-meritocracy didn't help matters any (Themelis, 2013). Existing market rigidities, along with continued dependence on the EU, created a Greek economy that nominally subscribed to the free-market philosophy without accruing the attendant benefits for its youth population. Emigration of youth, while contributing to 'brain drain', provided some relief to young graduates who were 'opportunity-starved' (Labrianidis and Pratsinakis, 2016; Christopoulou and Pantalidou, 2018; Dalla et al, 2013). While in the past such brain drain would be followed by a 'brain gain' when these youth returned home to enter the labor market with a competitive edge, this has not generally been the case following the crisis, representing additional net costs to the government in unrealized returns to human capital investment (Themelis, 2013). In fact, many scholars point out that the size of the current wave of migration is similar to that which occurred back in the late 1950s and 1960s (Ifanti et al, 2014). These same scholars highlight major differences, however, between these two migration waves; many current migrants are not low-skilled workers, rather they are young (late twenties, early thirties), well-educated university graduates with at least a bachelor's and often with a postgraduate degree (Ifanti et al, 2014; Malkoutzis, 2011). Even the adoption of several labor market reforms in recent years has not stemmed the flow of this outmigration (see, for example, Cholezas and Kanellopoulos, 2015). As Malkoutzis (2011) and Dalla et al (2013) emphasize, Greece's educated youth seek not only a better job, but they also want to escape the lack of professionalism and meritocracy, a persistent culture of corruption at all levels, and general dissatisfaction/disillusionment with elected officials.

In addition to high economic costs, unemployment in Greece has several individual, social and political costs. A substantial literature documents serious concerns for health, including increased levels of stress, anxiety and depression, limited access to medical health coverage and poor physical health (see Bambra and Eikemo, 2009; Kawachi and Wamala, 2006; Paul and Moser, 2009). It has further been suggested that unemployment of young adults may result in higher mental health impacts at a later stage (Virtanen et al, 2016). Greek youth has experienced rising levels of such adverse health effects, which have become more pronounced in recent years due to significant increases in unemployment (Drydakis, 2015). Anxiety and depression symptoms have also been shown to be stronger for young NEETs, and for those who have been unemployed for more than a year (Basta et al, 2019). These effects are likely worse, considering that Greece has the highest percentage of young people who have been without work for more than a year, compared to other EU states (Bell and Blanchflower, 2015). These researchers also evaluate the response to a Eurobarometer question on life satisfaction for the years 2000–2012, a period that straddles the economic recession. They find that while levels of wellbeing *increased* from pre- to post-recession in Northern European countries like Sweden, Netherlands, and Denmark, it declined quite substantially in Southern Europe, especially Greece, Spain and Portugal.

Labor market institutions, over-education, and skills

In a 2014 survey conducted by the publishing house Pearson, Greece ranked at the bottom of all European countries, and 33rd in the world (Siraj and Taggart, 2014) on a global education index. This index score was constructed from student performance on international tests such as OECD's Programme for International Student Assessment (PISA) tests, Trends in International Mathematics and Science Study (TIMSS) and Progress in International Reading Literacy Study (PIRLS), as well as student graduation rates from higher education. The Greek government reacted to the news with an announcement saying that 'Greece's education system has been without any strategies for years, something that actually makes up part of the structural causes of the crisis the country is experiencing today' (GB Times, 2014).

The curricula in the Greek educational system are highly centralized; they are developed and enforced by the Ministry of Education. An online blog from a Greek graduate of chemistry perfectly sums up the frustrations expressed by Greek parents and students:

> the time allotted for classes is based on more than educational needs. Mostly, it's outside factors. We have a lot of Greek literature teachers; we keep on teaching 10 hours Greek. The Archbishop demanded that we keep teaching Religion, the Education Minister is friends with the representatives of the IT teachers, he cuts Chemistry, adds computers. His

successor is on better terms with the chemists it goes the other way. No plan at all! (Triantafyllidou, 2016)

In Figure 5.1, we provide a description of the Greek education system, which is public and state-owned, under the control of the Ministry of Education and Religious Affairs. It is composed of three stages: the first includes primary education (Dimotiko), which lasts for six years and upon successful completion, students are awarded a certificate (Apolytirio Dimotikou); the second stage corresponds to secondary education, which is divided into two levels: the lower secondary education (Gymnasio) that lasts for three years resulting in a certificate (Apolytirio Gymnasiou), and the upper secondary education that corresponds to high school (Lykeio) which lasts for another three years.

Figure 5.1: Education system in Greece

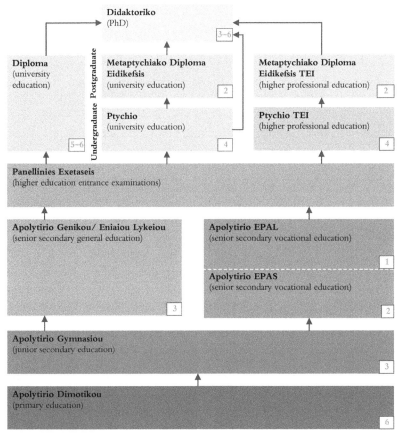

| | Duration of education |

Students in Greece have two different options for Lykeio; they can either attend the general high school (Geniko/Eniaio) or follow the vocational path (EPAL or EPAS). Upon completion of the general high school, students are granted a certificate (Apolytirio Lykeiou). If they wish to enroll in a higher education institution they need to successfully complete the Pan-Hellenic exams (Panellinies). Similar options are also available to those following the vocational path. However, the School Leaving Certificate they receive indicates specialization in a particular field. In addition, students can either take Panellinies or receive a license to practice a particular profession based on their specialization (again with relevant exams), or enroll in a vocational training institute (IEK).

The third stage of the Greek education system corresponds to higher or tertiary education. The two sectors of higher education include the university or the technological sector. The first includes research or technical (Polytechneia) universities, as well as the school of fine arts and the open university. Upon successful completion, a degree is awarded in all cases (Ptychio or Diploma for Polytechneia). The second sector includes technological education institutions (TEI) or schools of pedagogical and technological education (ASPETE), which award professional education degrees (Ptychia). In terms of postsecondary education, the university sector offers Master's programs (Metaptychiaka), while the technological sector offers more specialized Master's programs. Lastly, the university path also offers PhDs (Didaktorika), which can be attended by the university or technological sector graduates.

The race towards higher education begins in upper secondary school, training for the Panellinies. It is not uncommon to find parents making significant economic investments in private tutoring during high school in order to prepare for and score well in the Panellinies (Kyridis et al, 2017). The Greek society's penchant for over-education is well documented; obtaining a university degree is seen as a path by most towards social mobility and social standing, and a way to eventually secure a decent living (see Aravani, 2017; Livanos, 2010b; Pseiridis et al, 2018; Psacharopoulos and Tassoulas, 2004). Parental influence in both university enrollment and field choice has widely been documented in the literature (see Karamessini et al, 2019).

Unlike Germany and more like France, Greece has traditionally favored general education over Vocational Education and Training (VET). Both systems suffer from chronic underfunding; and because of the country's marginal focus on the latter, it has been affected even more, resulting in an underdeveloped VET with tenuous connection to the labor market (Cedefop, 2019). Cedefop serves as an interface between systems of human capital investment and labor force attachment, and provides EU member states with information on the performance of their own systems, in addition to a comparative perspective on how each member state performs vis-à-vis the others. The goal of Cedefop is to provide guidance for each country to design and implement targeted improvements and to identify best practices that can be emulated. Cedefop's European Skill Index (ESI) is the yardstick against which each country's systems are evaluated. The ESI is made of three dimensions or pillars: skills development (for example, basic education, computer skills, VET), skills activation (for example, labor force participation), and skills matching (for example, underemployment, qualification mismatch). Generally speaking, Cedefop finds that ESI is positively related to strong initial vocational education and training (IVET) spending and employment rates, and negatively related to the NEET rates (Cedefop, 2019).

With its underdeveloped VET accompanied by low spending, and generally high rates of youth unemployment and NEET, Greece does not score high on any of these dimensions. In fact, Greece garners the label of a 'low achiever', the nomenclature given to the group of countries (Ireland, Bulgaria, Cyprus, Romania, Italy, Greece and Spain) that scored below 36 out of 100 on the ESI (Cedefop, 2019). Greece's rank on the overall index is at the very bottom, 27/28, only behind Spain; it doesn't do much better in the component dimensions, with a rank of 23/28 in skills development, 24/28 in skills activation and 28/28 in skills matching (Cedefop, 2019). Skills mismatches abound, with the percentage of overqualified graduates occupying sub-optimal work positions exceeding the EU average of 26% by well over 18 percentage points (Cedefop, 2019).

Another Cedefop effort, this one in collaboration with Eurofound, called Skills Forecast: Trends and Challenges to 2030, examines the demand side of the labor market and provides projections on job growth expected in specific sectors of the economy in the member states (Cedefop, Eurofound, 2018). According to this publication, the next decade will: (a) see significant job growth in service-oriented industries such as accommodation and food services which will play a significant role in economies that depend on tourism; (b) see most of the job growth in Greece coming from jobs with lower earnings potential; (c) see jobs in Information and Communication Technology (ICT) growing in all member states except Greece; and (d) see higher demand for skills in business literacy and marketing.

Active labor market policies

Broad labor market reforms, the so-called ALMPs, were designed and introduced by the EU in 2011 through efforts such as the Youth Opportunities Initiative and the Youth Employment Package, where the latter gave birth to the Youth Guarantee in 2013. The specific goal of the Guarantee was to 'ensure that all young people under the age of 25 receive good quality offer of employment, continued education, apprenticeship or a traineeship within a period of four months of becoming unemployed or leaving formal education' (European Council, 2013). The European Council also created the Youth Employment Initiative that allotted €6 billion to NUTS 2 regions that had a youth unemployment rate above 25% in 2012. In principle, the Youth Guarantee was modeled after the Nordic economies and intended to be implemented with the active participation of public and private enterprises, but inasmuch as all countries are not Nordic, it was all but certain that results would be highly variable across countries, especially in countries where the ties between the public and private sectors were already frayed due to history or culture (Pastore, 2013).

The ALMPs in Southern Europe generally took the form of training courses, job search assistance and monitoring, subsidized employment or wage subsidies, and public work programs (Caliendo and Schmidl, 2016). A burgeoning literature on the effectiveness of these labor policies does not indicate promising results even when implemented under non-crisis situations. Caliendo and Schmidl (2016) conduct a meta-analysis of 37 studies that evaluated the ALMPs directed at youth while paying particular attention to issues of non-random selection through unobserved heterogeneity. These authors find that overall evidence for ALMP effectiveness is rather scant and discouraging, with job search assistance and monitoring showing positive effects at the margins, and training courses showing mixed results depending on the structure of the training (classroom based, firm based, and so on).

How did ALMPs fare in Greece? The Greek debt crisis that triggered the three bailouts (in 2010, 2012 and 2015) by the European Commission, the European Central Bank, and the International Monetary Fund (collectively known as the 'Troika'), ensured that the arrangement reflected a 'cash-for-reform' where Greece would implement severe austerity measures in return for the bailout and to stave off further economic decline. As we have mentioned earlier, even prior to the crisis, structural deficiencies existed in the market (overly restrictive employment protection legislation, low labor mobility, low unemployment benefits, high taxes, and so on). In addition, the prevailing ethos favored a system of clientelism, statism and corporatism that produced a vertical power structure, where the politically connected reaped most of the benefits, and 'the overall system was oriented to protect jobs, chiefly of insiders, but not people' (Tinios, 2015: 18).

Without a strong foundation of well-functioning political, social and economic systems any labor market reforms are doomed to fail even under normal times; that these reforms didn't perform in a stellar fashion in Greece under a crisis situation should come as no surprise to anyone. Kougias (2018) undertakes a comparative case study of two countries – Greece and Portugal – during and after the economic crisis, when both countries went through turbulent economic times and were subjected to the same cash-for-reform programs by the EU. Kougias argues that despite the similarities in the circumstances and the types of labor reforms enacted in return for cash, the two countries experienced divergent outcome trajectories, with Portugal emerging fairly successful and Greece not doing very well. Kougias (2018) attributes this divergence to three factors: (1) political instability in Greece (which saw five different governments led by four different prime ministers in an eight-year period, 2010– 2018), combined with uneven and differential implementation of labor reforms across societal strata, contributed to less buy-in and more discontent among the citizenry, resulting in significantly limited reform progress. Portugal weathered these problems with continuity of political will amidst changes in government and with more public receptivity of labor reforms; (2) while a strong coalition of stakeholders comprising the government, employers, labor unions, and a continuous social dialogue helped Portugal implement structural market reforms, Greece experienced the opposite. The country failed to have any significant social dialogue in order to influence the social mood and rally a partnership of important economic actors. Labor unions balked at proposed wage and pension cuts and took the government to national and international courts on constitutional grounds, with employers' associations and the general public no happier with the reforms; and (3) differences in reform content aimed at economic growth mattered: whereas Greece chose to increase revenues through higher corporate taxes (29%) and social contributions, a policy choice that led to 'disastrous GDP decline outrageous for any country not in wartime' (Kougias, 2018: 19), Portugal opted for lower corporate taxes (21%), cutback on public expenditures and strengthening of exports, a policy mix that resulted in a dramatic rise in its GDP, from -4% in 2012 to 2.7% in 2017.

A German-type dual education system in Greece?

In the context of internal political, social and economic turmoil which infected the administration of the Youth Guarantee program, Greece has begun to implement 'voucher schemes' targeted at youth 18–29 who have completed high school or beyond, with special focus on the NEETs. The Youth Employment Initiative (YEI) and the European Social Fund (ESF) are the main funding sources (with a total price tag of well over half a billion euros for the period 2014–2018) for these voucher schemes that aim to provide the target population with: '(i) (theoretical) training of young participants in transversal competences; (ii) work experience placements in the private sector; and (iii) guidance and counselling of participants during the placement which should not exceed six months' (European Commission, 2016: 3). The programs are implemented by a central authority (the ESF Actions Implementation Authority), under which an unemployed youth receives a voucher and gets connected to a training provider who is responsible for identifying and matching the individual's skills to a private sector host company's needs, is assigned a supervisor at the work placement site and, most importantly, is provided with additional services aimed at encouraging the host company to absorb the trainee for full-time employment.

In the words of the European Commission, these voucher schemes have 'fostered a culture of collaboration between all relevant stakeholders which, within the Greek context and in some instances, is quite novel' (European Commission, 2016: 4). The Commission goes on to say that in the interest of:

> designing a proper skills anticipation system, the Ministry of Labour started to work closely with the Ministry of Education and the Ministry of Economy. These are now also working more closely with the social partners who were asked to conduct a survey of the employers and employees about the skills needs in their respective sectors (to feed into the skills foresight exercise and the reform of the Greek vocational education and training (VET)) system. (European Commission, 2016: 4)

Even with the injection of these EU funds, Greece still struggles given the sheer numbers of youth looking to work and a concurrent reduction in labor demand. While countries like the US or Germany might spend up to 4% of their GDP towards curbing unemployment at times of recession, in Greece this amounts to about 0.1%, which includes the EU contribution. While an up-to-date assessment of how effective the YEI has been in Greece is not yet available, a preliminary evaluation of the YEI voucher schemes conducted by the Labour Institute of the Greek General Confederation of Labour (INE-GSEE) in 2015 reveals some good news on how voucher recipients fared on becoming employed, but also identified structural problems in the implementation of the schemes. Based on telephone interviews with 500 YEI participants, the evaluation report found that 51% of the jobs offered were full-time positions, and 41% were part-time positions, with a net average monthly pay that ranged between €300 and €600 depending on region, education level, and so on. About 44% of youth found that the job placement well reflected their education/training background. The report also traces the structural weaknesses to two sources: information asymmetry, and a gaming of the system by both employers and employment seekers. In the words of the evaluators:

> a basic weakness in the planning of the Voucher programmes is the lack of appropriate, adequate, relevant and reliable awareness/knowledge among participants so that they are in a position to make informed choices, especially in relation to choosing options with the best employment prospects. This lack of awareness has given rise to some 'bad' practices which, according to some interviewees, shift the focus back to the training providers. For example, there have been instances where the training providers have offered incentives in the form of, for example, a free computer/tablet, a mobile phone or even cash, to participants in order for participants to choose them. On the other hand, such practices have also led to participants using the Voucher as a bargaining chip so that they get more presents from the providers. (European Commission, 2016: 16)

Additionally, data on job placements show that nearly three-quarters of the 261 YEI participants interviewed accepted a second placement offer by the firm at the completion of their first one. This poses problems on two fronts: on the one hand, instead of regular employment, this may lead to a series of precarious placements for the trainee; on the other hand, firms may choose to replace their regular staff with these (cheaper) trainees. Suffice it to say that this experiment with a German-style dual system shows that successful adoption requires further refinements.

Self-employment/entrepreneurship in Greece

Greece has typically had the highest share of self-employed workers in all of Europe (30% in 2018, according to Eurostat (2019)). Even through the crisis, the self-employment rate declined more moderately than rates of wage/salary work (Kougias, 2018). According to Eurofound (2017), compared to the EU average (20%), a much higher proportion of the self-employed in Greece (28%) believed that they did not have other viable work options. Another 22% said that their status was at least partly due to lack of alternatives. The percentage of self-employed who preferred this status (47%) was also lower than the EU average, with 75% of the self-employed (the highest among EU member states) expressing concerns for financial security should they succumb to long-term illness. It is not hard to conclude that self-employment in Greece comes about mainly due to economic necessity, and that for many it doesn't net much more than the 'working poor' status. In fact, the in-work at-risk-of-poverty for the self-employed is the highest among all classes of workers in Greece (Ziomas et al, 2019).

The National Entrepreneurship Context Index (NECI) developed by the Global Entrepreneurship Monitor (GEM) provides an indicator of the ease with which business startups occur in 54 economies (Bosma et al, 2020). Greece is ranked number 40 on the NECI, lower than the other Mediterranean countries of Portugal (38), Italy (33) and Spain (12). This ranking closely mirrors the World Bank rating of ease of doing business, where Greece has the lowest score of these countries at 68.4 out of 100, and the World Economic Form global competitiveness rank of 59 of 141 economies, again the lowest in Southern Europe (Bosma et al, 2020). Bosma et al (2020) trace Greece's low rankings on these indices to the country's less than hospitable entrepreneurial ecosystem that features: (a) inimical social and cultural norms; (b) a shortage of financial capital; (c) business-unfriendly government policies on taxes; and (d) a lack of entrepreneurship education programs at school or post-school age. With a Total Entrepreneurial Activity (TEA) score of 8.2, Greece shows a higher activity level than Italy (2.8) or Spain (6.2), but much lower than Portugal (12.9) or the US (17.4). Nearly half the Greeks surveyed for the GEM study agree that there are good opportunities to start a business in their country, and an equal proportion also believe in their own capabilities to do so. It appears that if the government were to make structural improvements to the entrepreneurial context – make it less cumbersome to start a business, lower taxes, make more venture capital available, and make entrepreneurship part of the educational curricula – Greece has the potential to use entrepreneurship as a pathway for youth to achieve economic self-sufficiency.

An odyssey to economic security: a sampling of youth voices

In their qualitative study of 'Boomerang Kids in Contemporary Greece', Tsekeris and his colleagues (2017) carry out in-depth interviews of 15 highly-educated Greek youth who have returned to their parental homes after completing education and often having become unemployed or precariats. Among other things, these authors explore the homing instinct as a 'biographical disruption' that requires the individual to reconfigure his/her life. Some of the pain, frustration and disappointments are captured in these young people's own words:

> 'I imagined that I would have my own job that I would have a lot of money … that I could travel a lot, have my own car and a modern apartment. Finally, I haven't achieved anything of these and I still try to find a job'.
>
> 'I've been highly affected, sometimes I feel I am in a state of paralysis and this feeds me with pessimism, a huge sense of vanity … This makes me feel that nothing will occur among those things that used to be obvious some years before, namely, to have a job, a house and just to maintain myself, nothing more … Now, I regard these things as utopic and this is very disappointing, as this is not the normal progress of a human individual.'

Like Tsekeris et al (2017), we also believe that the observations, opinions and experiences of Greek youth are critical for any real understanding of the real crisis that is Greece.

We conducted a survey of 30 Greek citizens in the 18–35 age group who went through the Greek educational and labor market experiences but are all currently employed. In Table 5.1, we provide sample descriptions and responses to the closed-ended questions on the survey. We do not claim that the survey responses are exhaustive or that they are completely representative; only that they shed a good deal of light on what it is like to be employed in present-day Greece. We used a convenience sampling approach, where one of the authors knew a substantial number of the respondents through an academic network of Greeks in the US. Eight of the respondents reside in Greece, six in other European countries, and 18 in the US. The survey contained

Table 5.1: Survey responses to closed-ended questions

Question/characteristic	Responses (n=30)
Age?	• 18–23= 1 • 24–29= 10 • 30–35= 19
Gender?	• Female: 16 (5 with a bachelor's, 8 with a master's, 3 with a PhD) • Male: 14 (1 with high school, 1 with a bachelor's, 10 with a master's, 2 with a PhD)
Educational level?	• High school: 1 • Bachelor's: 6 • Master's: 18 • PhD: 5 completed
From which institution did you obtain your high school diploma?	• Athens:12 • Other: 18 • Private: 4 • Public: 26
From which institution did you get your undergraduate degree?	• Greece: 26 • Other: 3 • Engineering: 20 (17 of whom reside abroad) • Other: 9 (5 of whom reside abroad)
From which institution did you get your graduate degree?	• Master's: 12 in Greece 11 abroad • PhD: 0 in Greece (5 completed – 13 yet to complete)
What is your current employment status?	All employed (except for one who is in between jobs)
Where do you reside?	• 8 in Greece (4 of which are in Athens) • 18 in the US • 6 in Europe
Which of the following do you believe that a young Greek would find most unacceptable?	1. Having a tertiary school degree and having to work in a job that requires only a primary or secondary school education: 22 2. Having a highly developed set of technical skills and having to work in a job that does not require the use of these technical skills: 14 3. Having a tertiary school degree and having to work in a job that requires you to learn a highly developed set of technical skills: 1 4. Having a highly developed set of technical skills but needing to acquire an advanced degree (master's or doctoral) for career mobility: 7

Table 5.1: Survey responses to closed-ended questions (continued)

Question/characteristic	Responses (n=30)
The main reason for youth unemployment in Greece?	• Too much education but not enough technical skills: 16 • Too much education and too many technical skills: 5 • Too many technical skills and too much education and too many technical skills: 1 • None of the above: 6
German system can work?	• Yes: 20 • No: 8
Enough opportunities for a young person to start a business?	• Yes: 5 • No: 25
Have you ever participated in any programs?	• Yes: 5 • No: 25
Who do you think is the most responsible for youth unemployment in Greece? Rank these in order of responsibility.	First: Central government: 25. Local government: 1. Business community: 2. Primary education: 1. Second: Central government 2. Local government 4. Business community 13. Primary education: 1. Secondary education 4. Tertiary education 5.

both closed-ended and open-ended responses, and was distributed to 42 individuals, netting 30 responses. A copy of the survey instrument is available from the authors.

Table 5.1 shows that our sample is highly-educated and gender-balanced, with 60% having completed a master's degree and about 17% with a doctoral degree. Many of those who had completed a master's degree are currently pursuing doctoral studies. Most of the youth we surveyed are critical of skill mismatches in the labor market, and would find it unacceptable to be underemployed in jobs that do not require the advanced education or training they have acquired. Our respondents place the responsibility for high youth unemployment squarely on the shoulders of the Greek central government, and to a system that permits over-education and under-skilling while failing to make the education-labor force transition logical or smooth. A main reason for conducting the survey was to ascertain if Greek youth thought that the German dual education model or an entrepreneurship avenue would prove useful in curbing unemployment. As the table shows, overwhelming majorities believe that the German model can succeed in Greece (68%). Even more overwhelming are responses that indicate the potential failure of entrepreneurship as a solution to unemployment (83%).

We now turn to some of the representative responses to the open-ended questions on the youth's educational choices, the status of the current labor market, and what ought to be the Greek government's role in improving it.

While roughly two-thirds of our interviewees currently live abroad, all have expressed a strong desire to return and bring 'an air of change' to their home country. Yet most also say that they are unwilling to do so unless drastic socioeconomic and cultural changes occur in the country's landscape. Besides the fact that they cannot easily find a job with good wages that is consistent with their expertise, respondents also express concerns with the absence of work mobility, unprofessional work culture and disrespect from the employer(s). Respondents felt that a culture of openness, transparency and meritocracy are currently absent in Greece, while 'favoritism, nepotism and all the -isms that are associated with government corruption' are persistent. There is also evidence for clear distrust of Greece's political leadership and of intolerance for the inertia that characterizes the current Greek landscape. Many respondents believe that 'highly educated people cannot find their place in Greece'.

Many of the youth also expressed frustration over the mismatch between supply and demand in the job market, reflecting Mitrakos et al's (2010) statement that this is either due to the education system's failure to adjust to the needs of the labor market, or because of the Greeks' insistence on acquiring tertiary education. A closer look reveals that a strong personal interest, although important, is more of a secondary factor for pursuing higher education: pursuit of advanced education is seen as a 'social standard in Greece' and a 'natural next step'. While respondents agree that the family plays a strong role in pushing students to become 'doctors, lawyers or engineers', most of them believe that students go on to postgraduate studies (master's) because of lack of employment alternatives, with the hope of securing a better-paid job later, in addition to having international mobility.

Respondents had a lot to say about skills mismatch and the role of academia; our youth suggest that besides financial limitations, which may restrict support for students, the country's higher education institutions (HEIs) are 'more academic or scientific than technical'. They felt that academia was for the most part detached from the needs of industry, both domestically and abroad, with students having to depend on 'the advisor's connections' as their only safety net to promote mobility. Related arguments include the absence of networking and internship opportunities and the promotion of self-marketing and leadership skills. In addition, university space is characterized by high internal political activity, linking it firmly to a persistent culture that believes 'universities are sacred grounds and should stay away from evil companies', therefore, at the end of the day, 'it's all about which party you belong to'. The following suggestions from our youth on improving academia and its connection to the labor market are aligned with Aravani (2017): (a) make changes in legislation to tackle nepotism through external evaluation committees and/or peer-reviewing practices; (b) devise policies to address the issue of 'eternal students' (entering HEIs but not graduating and still remaining registered); (c) increase academic ranking by establishing programs in English; (d) link research to industry through merging departments; and (e) introduce new programs with a focus on finance, business and technology.

Interviewees did have good things to say about the Greek HEIs that make their graduates more competitive in the international market. They pointed to the fact that HEIs are publicly owned, with no tuition or fees charged for undergraduate (and for the most part postgraduate) studies. While this can (and often does) result in funding problems for the HEIs, it can also promote brainstorming and collaborative work among students, as they are often required to adapt to challenging environments with limited resources. Respondents felt that HEIs also promote independent thinking and enable knowledge 'to move away from a client-inspired culture evident in academic institutions abroad'. They also liked the fact that the HEIs place a strong emphasis on insuring solid theoretical foundations and critical thinking; and that being taught advanced topics from their early undergraduate years prepares them well for higher education.

Our respondents took a rather skeptical view of the ALMPs that Greece has attempted. They argued that: 'they are not enough as stand-alone actions, as they should belong to a wider plan for economic growth', also adding that 'they cannot fundamentally improve the situation, as they just aim at making the unemployment rates look better'.

When asked if the dual education model could potentially work in Greece, two-thirds of our interviewees answered positively; still, they appeared skeptical as to how such a model could become practical. Arguments they advanced included that: 'the Greek society is too immature to accept such a protocol'; 'education is not governed by private sector needs'; and that 'the industry in Germany is different from Greece'. Others expressed their opposition and concerns that such an approach implies unequal education opportunities and would split students into those who follow a traditional educational path (advantaged) and those who follow dual education (disadvantaged). The latter would end up serving 'short-term needs of companies as low-cost trainees'. They further argued that most high school students do not know their preferences for the future, so following the dual education path would be a risky decision.

When asked about the potential for a young person to start a business in Greece, more than two-thirds of our sample appeared pessimistic, stressing that there are not enough opportunities. Besides the lack of initial capital and the inability of the country to support a more diverse industry with connections to the international market, interviewees highlighted several macro-level obstacles. Specifically, the main points included high taxation ('every year you pay projected taxes for the next') and high insurance costs, combined with inflexible regulations, complicated bureaucratic processes, and the inability to get loans. Our youth added that there are no education or mentoring programs on entrepreneurship and how to compete in the marketplace, especially 'if [other existing firms] have proper connections and can skip certain rules'. Reflective of the GEM finding (Bosma et al, 2020) that Greece has difficulties in maintaining existing business, our youth felt that 'the challenge is not to start a business but to manage keeping it for at least three consecutive years'.

Interviewees also addressed significant cultural obstacles to the entrepreneurship avenue to employment. Once again, the refrain was on corruption and 'the absence of transparency and the persistence of nepotism from both the left and the right side, while venture spirit is seen as something evil from both sides'. They also expressed risk aversion to new enterprise because they felt that there is 'a lack of support from the local community, as there is distrust to young entrepreneurs due to their limited experience'.

It is clear from these responses that youth in Greece understand the challenges facing economic growth and employment in their country as well as any governmental official or business commission. The real question remains: can they rely on these institutions to improve their futures?

References

Amadeo, K. (2019) Greek debt crisis explained, *The Balance*, December 14.

Aravani, E. (2017) To invest or not to invest in higher education: that is the question for the crisis-shaken Greek government and households, http://www.lse.ac.uk/hellenic-observatory/assets/documents/ho-phd-symposia/the-8th-ho-phd-symposium/session-1/2.-labour-market-economics.pdf

Bambra, C. and Eikemo, T.A. (2009) Welfare state regimes, unemployment and health: a comparative study of the relationship between unemployment and self-reported health in 23 European countries, *Journal of Epidemiology & Community Health*, 63(2): 92–8.

Basta, M., Karakonstantis, S., Koutra, K., Dafermos, V., Papargiris, A., Drakaki, M., Tzagkarakis, S., Vgontzas, A., Simos, P. and Papadakis, N. (2019) NEET status among young Greeks: association with mental health and substance use, *Journal of Affective Disorders*, 253: 210–17.

Bell, D.N. and Blanchflower, D.G. (2015) Youth unemployment in Greece: measuring the challenge, *IZA Journal of European Labor Studies*, 4(1): 1.

Bosma, N., Hill, S., Ionescu-Somers, A., Kelley, D., Levie, J. and Tarnawa, A. (2020) *Global Entrepreneurship Monitor: 2019/2020 Global Report*, London: Global Entrepreneurship Research Association, London Business School.

Caliendo, M. and Schmidl, R. (2016) Youth unemployment and active labor market policies in Europe, *IZA Journal of Labor Policy*, 5(1): 1, https://doi.org/10.1186/s40173-016-0057-x

Cedefop (European Center for the Development of Vocational Training) (2019) *2018 European Skills Index*, Cedefop reference series 111, Luxembourg: Publications Office of the European Union, http://data.europa.eu/doi/10.2801/564143

Cedefop, Eurofound (2018) *Skills Forecast: Trends and Challenges to 2030*, Cedefop reference series 108, Luxembourg: Publications Office of the European Union, http://data.europa.eu/doi/10.2801/4492

Cholezas, I. and Kanellopoulos, N.C. (2015) Labour market reforms in Greece and the wage curve, *Economics Letters*, 136: 19–21.

Christopoulou, R. and Pantalidou, M. (2018) Who saved Greek youth? Parental support to young adults during the great recession, GreeSE Papers 129, London: Hellenic Observatory, European Institute.

Dalla, E., Chatzoudes, D. and Karasavvoglou, A. (2013) The 'brain-drain' phenomenon: measuring the intention of young Greek scientists to migrate abroad, *Recent Researches in Law Science and Finances*, 278–83.

Drydakis, N. (2015) The effect of unemployment on self-reported health and mental health in Greece from 2008 to 2013: a longitudinal study before and during the financial crisis, *Social Science & Medicine*, 128: 43–51.

Esping-Andersen, G. (1990) *The Three Worlds of Welfare Capitalism*, Princeton, NJ: Princeton University Press.

Eurofound (2017) *Exploring Self-Employment in the European Union*, Luxembourg: Publications Office of the European Union.

European Commission (2016) *First Results of the Implementation of the Youth Employment Initiative: Greece*, Directorate-General for Employment, Social Affairs and Inclusion Unit F1: ESF and FEAD Policy and Legislation, Brussels: The European Commission.

European Council (2013) *Council Recommendation of 22 April 2013 on Establishing a Youth Guarantee, 2013/C 120/01*, Brussels: European Council.

European Commission (2019) *Financial Assistance to Greece*, https://ec.europa.eu/info/business-economy-euro/economic-and-fiscal-policy-coordination/eu-financial-assistance/which-eu-countries-have-received-assistance/financial-assistance-greece_en

Eurostat (2019) https://appsso.eurostat.ec.europa.eu/nui/show.do?dataset=lfsa_argan&lang=en

Featherstone, K. (2008) *Varieties of Capitalism and the Greek Case: Explaining the Constraints on Domestic Reform?* London: Hellenic Observatory, European Institute.

Featherstone, K. and Papadimitriou, D. (2008) *The Limits of Europeanization: Reform Capacity and Policy Conflict in Greece*, London: Palgrave Macmillan.

GB Times (2014) https://gbtimes.com/survey-finds-greeces-education-system-be-worst-europe

Hall, P.A. and Soskice, D. (eds) (2001) *Varieties of Capitalism: The Institutional Foundations of Comparative Advantage*, Oxford: Oxford University Press.

Hancké, B., Rhodes, M. and Thatcher, M. (eds) (2007) *Beyond Varieties of Capitalism: Conflict, Contradictions, and Complementarities in the European Economy*, New York: Oxford University Press.

Ifanti, A.A., Argyriou, A.A., Kalofonou, F.H. and Kalofonos, H.P. (2014) Physicians' brain drain in Greece: a perspective on the reasons why and how to address it, *Health Policy*, 117(2): 210–15.

Karamessini, M., Symeonaki, M., Stamatopoulou, G. and Parsanoglou, D. (2019) Factors explaining youth unemployment and early job insecurity in Europe, in B. Hvinden, C. Hyggen, M.A. Schoyen and T. Sirovátka (eds) *Youth Unemployment and Job Insecurity in Europe*, Cheltenham: Edward Elgar.

Kawachi, I. and Wamala, S. (eds) (2006) *Globalization and Health*, Oxford: Oxford University Press.

Kesisoglou, G., Figgou, E. and Dikaiou, M. (2016) Constructing work and subjectivities in precarious conditions: psycho-discursive practices in young people's interviews in Greece, *Journal of Social and Political Psychology*, 4(1).

Kougias, K.G. (2018) Comparing Greece and Portugal: common employment trajectories but divergent outcomes? *Economic and Industrial Democracy*, 38(1): 51–68.

Kretsos, L. (2014) Youth policy in austerity Europe: the case of Greece, *International Journal of Adolescence and Youth*, 19(Supp1): 35–47.

Kyridis, A., Korres, M.P., Tourtouras, C.D., Fotopoulos, N. and Zagkos, C. (2017) The puzzle on unemployment factors and the welfare state role in Greece: What university students believe, in F. Yenilmez (ed) *Handbook of Research on Unemployment and Labor Market Sustainability in the Era of Globalization*, Hershey, PA: IGI Global, pp 212–34.

Labrianidis, L. and Pratsinakis, M. (2016) *Greece's New Emigration at Times of Crisis*, Hellenic Observatory Papers on Greece and Southeast Europe 99, London: Hellenic Observatory, European Institute, pp 1–48, http://eprints.lse.ac.uk/66811/1/greese-no.99.pdf

Livanos, I. (2010a) The relationship between higher education and labour market in Greece: the weakest link? *Higher Education*, 60(5): 473–89.

Livanos, I. (2010b) The wage-local unemployment relationship in a highly regulated labour market: Greece, *Regional Studies*, 44(4): 389–400.

Malkoutzis, N. (2011) Young Greeks and the crisis: the danger of losing a generation, *International Policy Analysis*, Bonn: Friedrich-Ebert-Stiftung.

Mitrakos, T., Tsakloglou, P. and Cholezas, I. (2010) Determinants of youth unemployment in Greece with an emphasis on tertiary education graduates, *Economic Bulletin*, 26: 21–62.

OECD (2008) *Education at a Glance 2008*, Paris: OECD Publishing.

OECD (2017) *OECD Employment Outlook 2017*, Paris: OECD Publishing.

OECD (2020) *Youth Not in Employment, Education or Training (NEET)* (indicator), doi: 10.1787/72d1033a-en

Oscar, M. and Rhodes, M. (2005) Varieties of capitalism and mixed market economies, APSA-EPS Newsletter.

Papadopoulos, T. (2000) *Integrated Approaches to Active Welfare and Employment Policies: Greece*, Dublin: European Foundation for the Improvement of Living and Working Conditions.

Pastore, F. (2013) The European Youth Guarantee: an Italian perspective, *Social Europe Journal*, 1–3.

Paul, K.I. and Moser, K. (2009) Unemployment impairs mental health: meta-analyses, *Journal of Vocational Behavior*, 74(3): 264–82.

Psacharopoulos, G. and Tassoulas, S. (2004) Achievement at the higher education entry examinations in Greece: a Procrustean approach, *Higher Education*, 47(2): 241–52.

Pseiridis, A., Lianos, T.P. and Agiomirgianakis, G. (2018) Overeducation of university graduates: a voluntary and rational choice of individuals: the case of three Greek universities, *Theoretical Economics Letters*, 8(11): 2135.

Siraj, I. and Taggart, B. (2014) *Exploring Effective Pedagogy in Primary Schools: Evidence from Research*, London: Pearson.

Standing, G. (2011) Labour market policies, poverty and insecurity, *International Journal of Social Welfare*, 20(3): 260–9.

Statista (2020) Youth unemployment rate in EU countries, https://www.statista.com/statistics/266228/youth-unemployment-rate-in-eu-countries/

Themelis, S. (2013) *Social Change and Education in Greece: A Study in Class Struggle Dynamics*, London: Palgrave Macmillan.

Themelis, S. (2017) Degrees of precariousness: the problematic transition into the labour market of Greek higher education graduates, *Forum Sociológico,* Série 2, 31: 53–62.

Tinios, P. (2015) *Employment and Social Developments in Greece*, Brussels: European Parliament, Directorate General for Internal Policies, Policy Department, ESP.

Triantafyllidou, D. (2016) Why does Greek education rank so poorly on PISA? https://www.quora.com/why-does-greek-education-rank-so-poorly-on-pisa

Tsekeris, C., Ntali, E., Koutrias, A. and Chatzoulis, A. (2017) *Boomerang Kids in Contemporary Greece: Young People's Experience of Coming Home Again*, GreeSE Paper 108, Hellenic Observatory Papers on Greece and Southeast Europe, London: Hellenic Observatory, European Institute.

Virtanen, P., Hammarström, A. and Janlert, U. (2016) Children of boom and recession and the scars to the mental health: a comparative study on the long-term effects of youth unemployment, *International Journal for Equity in Health*, 15(1): 14.

Zarkadakis, G. (2011) Modern Greece's real problem? Ancient Greece, *Washington Post*, November 4.

Ziomas, D., Bouzas, N., Capella, A. and Konstantinidou, D. (2019) *ESPN Thematic Report on In-Work Poverty in Greece*, Brussels: European Commission.

6

Labor Market Policies to Fight Youth Unemployment in Portugal: Between Statism and Experimentalism

Paulo Marques and Pedro Videira

Introduction

Youth unemployment rose in Portugal from the early 2000s and reached a peak of 38.1% in 2014. Due to the severity of this problem, the past two decades saw the implementation of several public programmes to tackle the rise of youth unemployment. This chapter takes stock of these initiatives and explores the Portuguese strategy to address this phenomenon. This work is part of a book that puts forward two alternatives to address youth unemployment – the German vocational and the American entrepreneurial models – and discusses whether Portugal followed a strategy similar to either of the two alternatives. The research questions that guide the chapter are therefore: what was the approach taken by Portugal to tackle the rise of youth unemployment between 2000 and 2017? Did either the German vocational or the American entrepreneurial model serve as an inspiration for the policies addressing this phenomenon in Portugal throughout this period?

Three hypotheses are developed in this chapter. The first is based on the argument that Southern European countries lack institutional complementarities to fully implement the German vocational model or the American entrepreneurial model. Thus, we hypothesize that the state played a key role to address youth unemployment by putting in place programs to fight youth unemployment, programs that did not involve other actors and did not mean implementing a new coherent model based on the German or the American model. The second consists of hypothesizing that the transition to a knowledge-based economy was a concern of Portuguese governments. Promoting entrepreneurship and developing policies focused on graduates was seen as important. Thus, we hypothesize that the American entrepreneurial model exerted some influence throughout the period in question. The third hypothesis consists of conjecturing that, after 2008, besides the policies that were already in place, new policies were adopted to address the urgency of the youth unemployment problem. In this regard, we hypothesize that policies inspired by the EU strategy to promote apprenticeships gained momentum. Thus, we expect that a mix of policies was implemented between 2008 and 2017. To test these conjectures we have analyzed all youth-oriented active labor market policies (ALMPs) implemented in Portugal between 2000 and 2017. Policies were taken from the LABREF database, which is managed by the European Commission and contains information on the content of all ALMPs for all EU countries. The results of our study confirm the first and third hypotheses, the second is rejected.

Our results show that what we call 'statism' and 'experimentalism' captures well what happened in Portugal in the period in question. By 'statism' we mean that the state implements policies without much involvement of other actors. According to our data, the overwhelming majority of policies cover internships and wage subsidies, which are wholly designed and financed by the state and do not involve other actors. The fact that statism played such an important role is in line with the comparative political economy literature on varieties of capitalism (VoC), which argues that in Southern European countries the state plays a key coordinating role in many areas, and this is the distinctive characteristic of this model of capitalism (Amable, 2003; Molina and Rohdes, 2007). Our chapter contributes to this literature by showing that the German and the American models did not serve as models for policies to address youth unemployment because Southern European countries lack institutional complementarities that are crucial for these models to work properly. Relying on the state was thus the most obvious solution. As for 'experimentalism', our point is that although policies like wage subsidies and internships were the top priority, other policies in different areas were also implemented, including promoting entrepreneurship and workplace-based training. However, they were not implemented in any ambitious or coherent way. There was not a clear strategy behind the decision to implement these policies; it was experimentalism that guided policy makers in the face of exceptional economic circumstances.

This chapter is structured as follows. It begins by contextualizing how youth unemployment has evolved in Portugal since the early 2000s up until recent times. Thereafter, it develops three different hypotheses regarding the Portuguese approach to tackling youth unemployment. The third section presents the empirical results and the fourth the discussion. In the final section we put forward our conclusions.

The nature of youth unemployment in Portugal

The development of youth unemployment in Portugal in the last two decades can be divided into three different phases. From the early 2000s up until the 2008 global economic downturn, Portugal experienced a gradual increase in youth unemployment rates (Figure 6.1). The changing economic context was crucial to understanding this process because Portugal faced low levels of economic growth throughout the entire period (Reis, 2018: 59–69). Several factors explain these economic circumstances: (1) the Economic and Monetary Union (EMU) process in the late 1990s and early 2000s; (2) China's accession to the World Trade Organization (WTO) in 2001; and (3) the Eastern enlargement of the EU in 2003. First and foremost, the EMU process posed several challenges to the Portuguese economy. Due

Figure 6.1: Youth unemployment in Portugal (2000–2018)

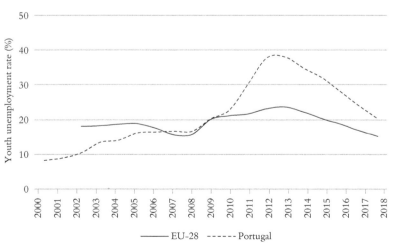

to convergence criteria, controlling inflation and reducing public debt ratios became the top priority for governments. Public policies to foster growth and social cohesion, and to tackle unemployment, became less central in the political agenda. On the other hand, the euro affected Portuguese exportations negatively because a strong currency is detrimental for a country in which many firms are still competing in low-skilled sectors (Rodrigues and Reis, 2012). Secondly, China and other Asian countries' competition hit the Portuguese manufacturing sector hard. Low-skilled industries, such as the textiles sector, were key economic sectors in Portugal in the early 2000s. Due to these countries' accession to the WTO, a massive delocalization of multinationals took place in Portugal in the early 2000s. Finally, the enlargement of the EU meant a lower capacity to attract foreign direct investment because Germany and other Continental European countries started to redirect their investment towards Eastern Europe. Furthermore, EU enlargement was also detrimental for Portugal because Eastern countries compete directly with Portugal in many sectors. As wages are lower and educational levels are higher in some of these countries, their access to the European single market was a great challenge to Portugal. Taken together, this economic context affected young labor market participants negatively, since the economy was not expanding and entering the labor market therefore became more difficult.

The second phase started with the 2008 global economic crisis and was further deepened with the EU sovereign debt crisis. From 2008 to 2010, youth unemployment rose after a period of slowdown (2005–2007); this was mainly explained by the global economic crisis, which impacted all EU countries. From 2011 up until 2013, youth unemployment rocketed and reached a historical peak of 38.1% (Figure 6.1). As is widely known, Portugal was one of the EU countries most severely affected by the EU sovereign debt crisis and had to request financial assistance in 2011 (Carneiro et al, 2014; Theodoropoulou, 2015, Reis, 2018: 64–69). As a consequence, it had to implement deep cuts in public expenditure and to further liberalize the economy (Hall, 2018; Afonso, 2019). Austerity depressed the economy even more after a period of slow economic growth, and therefore young people faced even more difficulties in entering the labor market (Marques and Hörisch, 2020).[1] Thus, Portugal faced three successive crises: from 2000 to 2008, from 2008 to 2010 and again from 2011 to 2014. All of them had dire consequences for young people as youth unemployment increased during the entire period. The negative economic context is thus a crucial part of the story behind the rise of youth unemployment.

The third phase was characterized by a reduction in youth unemployment; from 2014 onwards youth unemployment declined and is currently approaching the pre-2008 crisis level. This may partially be explained by a change in the political context and by the fact that the country is no longer under an adjustment program (since May 2014). Although public debt ratios are still very high, the government was able to return to financial markets and to finance its public debt with much lower interest rates. Furthermore, there has been an economic boom, driven by sectors like tourism and by the new political cycle (2015–2019) focused on better distribution of income to foster growth (the minimum wage increased by 20% between 2015 and 2019 and some measures taken during the 'austerity years' were reversed). As accommodation and other service sectors like restaurants are job-intensive, this led to a rapid decline of youth unemployment. Moreover, redistribution policies helped to foster internal demand and thus reduce unemployment.[2] Notwithstanding, youth unemployment levels remain above the level of the early 2000s. This means that the effects of the global and sovereign debt crises have now passed, but the structural problems that existed before 2008 are still very much in place.

Besides this negative economic context, two additional factors help to explain the persistence of high levels of youth unemployment in Portugal: the implementation of two-tier labor market reforms and the problem of skill mismatches. When unemployment began to grow, governments implemented reforms to employment protection legislation (EPL) because they believed more flexibility would have a positive effect on job creation. Up until the 2011 sovereign debt crisis, Portugal had one of the most restrictive labor laws in the OECD countries, particularly regarding regulations for permanent contracts (Venn, 2009; OECD, 2013). Although right-wing parties tried passing EPL reforms that included a relaxation in the strictness of permanent contracts, reforms were unsuccessful because the Portuguese Constitutional Court blocked them several times. Furthermore, left-wing parties and trade union confederations opposed these reforms (Marques and Salavisa, 2017). To increase labor market flexibility, right-wing parties opted for the implementation of two-tier labor market reforms, that is, regulations for permanent contracts remained strict, but regulations for temporary contracts were relaxed (Centeno and Novo, 2012; Silva et al, 2018). For instance, one of the most radical reforms implemented in the early 2000s increased the maximum duration of temporary contracts to six years. Due to the characteristics of the Portuguese economy – based on low-skilled sectors – employers have been preferring to hire through temporary contracts. Not surprisingly,

Figure 6.2: Share of involuntary temporary contracts: Portugal and EU-28 (2000–2018), 15–24-year-olds

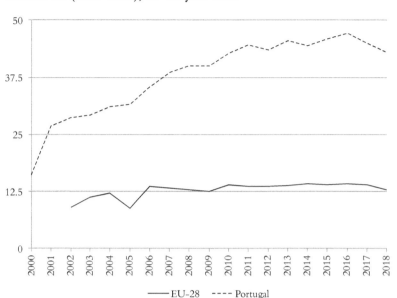

young labor market participants were penalized by this because they entered the labor market in recent years, after two-tier labor market reforms were implemented. As can be seen in Figure 6.2, the share of involuntary temporary contracts among young people rose very rapidly during the 2000s, reaching a peak of 47.1% in 2016. Because a huge proportion of young people hold temporary contracts, when an economic downturn occurs unemployment among youths rises much more rapidly than among the overall population. Taken as a whole, the liberalization agenda and its reforms on the labor legislation ultimately led to a growing segmentation of the Portuguese labor market.

Skill mismatches are an additional problem. As can be seen in Figures 6.3 and 6.4, youth unemployment among graduates is high, higher even than for those holding upper secondary and post-secondary non-tertiary education. The Portuguese government has invested massively in higher education during the past two decades. The proportion of the population with tertiary education aged 25–34 increased from 12.8% in 2000, to 33.1%, in 2015 (Eurostat, 2018). However, this growth was not matched by a transformation in the Portuguese economy, which remained largely based on low-skilled sectors. In fact, the problem was made even worse because high-tech exports dropped in Portugal from 6.2% in 2000, to 4.4% in 2014 (World Bank, 2018). This further aggravated the youth unemployment

Figure 6.3: Youth unemployment among graduates: Portugal and EU-28 (2005–2018)

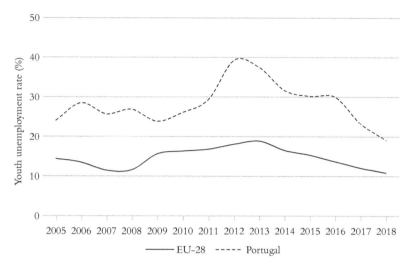

Figure 6.4: Youth unemployment among those holding upper secondary and post-secondary non-tertiary education: Portugal and EU-28 (2005–2018)

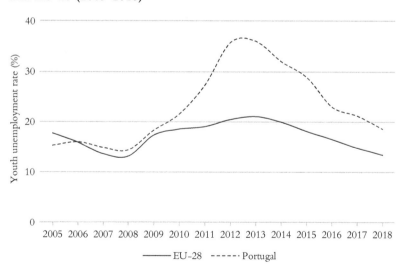

problem as graduates faced many problems on entering the labor market. Not surprisingly, Portugal ranks high on the levels of over-qualification; it is in fact the OECD country with the highest figure for this indicator (OECD, 2017a).

Taken as a whole, the rise of youth unemployment in Portugal in recent decades is thus explained by three sets of problems: sluggish economic growth between 2000 and 2014; EPL reforms that brought about a growing gap between younger and older generations; and the incapacity of the Portuguese economy to absorb a growing supply of graduates. We now turn to the discussion on how labor market policies in Portugal addressed the increasing levels of youth unemployment during this period. We begin by putting forward three hypotheses about this process, and afterwards we move on to analyse the policies implemented in Portugal.

Strategies followed by governments to address youth unemployment: three hypotheses

According to the comparative political economy (CPE) literature on VoC, Southern European countries form a specific model (Amable, 2003; Molina and Rhodes, 2007). These countries lack the institutional complementarities that characterize Liberal Market Economies (LMEs) or Coordinated Market Economies (CMEs). As argued by Hall and Soskice (2001:17): 'two institutions can be said to be complementary if the presence (or efficiency) of one increases the returns from (or efficiency of) the other'. In LMEs institutional complementarities (flexible labor regulations, access to venture capital and investment in general skills) are conducive to competitiveness in radical innovation, and the mechanism of coordination that prevails is market coordination. On the contrary, in CMEs the existing complementarities (cooperation between labor and capital in industrial relations, high job security, access to patient capital and investment in job-specific skills) contribute to competitiveness in incremental innovation, and the mechanism of coordination that prevails is strategic coordination.[3]

Instead of market or strategic coordination, it is the state that solves coordination problems in Southern European countries because these countries lack CME- and LME-type institutional complementarities. The importance of the state is clear in many areas. As the focus of this chapter is on labor market policies to fight youth unemployment, we explain the importance of the state in three areas – industrial relations, labor regulations and skill formation systems. As mentioned in what follows, we argue that the way these three areas combine is important because different strategies to fight youth unemployment (the American versus the German model) require different institutional complementarities in these areas.

In Portugal, coordination between labor and capital is weak and union density is lower than in Continental Europe and Scandinavian countries (Lima and Naumann, 2011; Marques and Salavisa, 2017). Thus, at first sight, it seems difficult to reach a high degree of collective bargaining coverage. To overcome this problem, the state uses extension ordinances, administrative regulations that expand collective agreements to non-unionised workers and non-affiliated firms (Afonso, 2019). Without this mechanism, employers would not accept signing collective agreements since they would face unfair competition from firms where collective bargaining rules would not apply. Given that sectors where firms mainly compete by price represent a high share of jobs in the Portuguese economy, this is particularly problematic. The system of industrial relations therefore depends on the state, and it can only work properly if the state is committed to extending agreements. As recently explained by Afonso (2019), if governments intend to reduce collective bargaining coverage, as happened during the EU sovereign debt crisis, the system is not sufficiently autonomous to safeguard collective bargaining (Lima, 2019). As for labor law, as explained in the first section, protection for permanent workers is very high, while regulations for temporary contracts are not. As a consequence, state intervention safeguards employment protection for the core labor force, but allows a certain degree of flexibility through the existence of precarious employment on the fringes. The state then intervenes in the economy by influencing the workings of the labor market. Finally, regarding the skill formation system, in line with other Southern European countries, Vocational Education and Training (VET) takes place predominantly in public vocational schools which possess few linkages with employers (Marques and Hörisch, 2019; Biavaschi et al, 2012; Homs, 2009; Icart and Rodríguez-Soler, 2017; Souto-Otero and Ure, 2012). Instruction typically takes place in schools and not in the workplace. Some employers have their own vocational schools, but they represent a low share of students in the Portuguese VET system.[4] Furthermore, higher education is managed by the state as the private sector represents a relatively low share of the higher education system. The skill formation system is thus coordinated by the state, which defines its priorities and scope. To sum up, the centrality of the state manifests itself in the Portuguese political economy in the three areas.

As explained in the previous section, youth unemployment grew in Portugal in the recent past. In the face of this, one can conjecture about the strategies that were followed by the Portuguese government to address this phenomenon since the year 2000. The book for which this chapter is a contribution puts forward two alternatives to address youth unemployment: the German vocational and the American entrepreneurial models. In our view, Southern European countries such as Portugal face problems with both strategies because, as explained earlier, they lack LME- and CME-type institutional complementarities.

As widely discussed in the CPE literature, the German vocational model requires the existence of a number of complementary institutions that support dual training (Busemeyer and Trampusch, 2012). According to this literature, a high level of coordination in the industrial relations system is important to allow firms to invest in their employees' specific skills as it reduces the risk of poaching (Marques and Hörisch, 2019; Thelen, 2004). This happens because if wages are set within the scope of sectoral collective bargaining, the risk is much lower. Furthermore, coordination between labor and capital is important to manage VET schools, because if training is also provided in the workplace, this requires the involvement of social partners in its provision. On the other hand, regarding employment protection legislation, the literature reveals that high job protection promotes investment in specific skills. This is because when protection is higher, individuals will be more prone to invest in specific skills. On the contrary, when job protection is low, they end up investing more in general skills to address more volatile labor markets (Busemeyer and Thelen, 2015; Estevez-Abe et al, 2001). It is difficult to implement the German model in Portugal for several reasons. As regards coordination in the industrial relations system, there is poor coordination and thus it is difficult to involve employers in the provision of workplace training. Furthermore, due to lack of autonomy in the system it is difficult to guarantee that collective bargaining coverage will remain high. In terms of labor law, although employees with permanent contracts have high job security, the opposite happens for workers with temporary contracts. As temporary workers cover mainly young labor market participants (Figure 6.2), it therefore also becomes problematic to encourage students to enrol in dual-VET programmes. Reforms recently implemented during the sovereign debt crisis further aggravated this problem because these further deregulated labor legislation, reducing even more the incentives to invest in specific skills (Theodoropoulou, 2015; Hall, 2018; ILO, 2018; OECD; 2017b). Finally, the dual-VET system in Germany is connected with a large manufacturing sector, which hires a large number of workers with this kind of training. The Portuguese manufacturing sector is shrinking and is much less competitive. Thus, existing institutions do not favour the development of this type of training.

As for the American entrepreneurial model, there are also some difficulties when trying to import it to address youth unemployment in Portugal. A number of conditions are necessary to implement this model. Access to risk capital, the existence of top-level universities and labor market flexibility are all necessary conditions for boosting entrepreneurship. As many entrepreneurs require access to capital because they did not previously accumulate capital, access to risk capital is crucial and it has been an important characteristic of the American entrepreneurial model. Top-level universities are likewise important, as new competitive products are very often the outcome of spinoffs from fundamental research conducted in top-level universities. Flexible labor markets are a key characteristic of this model because the transfer of technology in LMEs occurs when workers move from company to company (Hall and Soskice, 2001). If labor markets are highly regulated, this circulation is more difficult to achieve and thus it is harder to establish new firms that can provide new products and services. Portugal faces difficulties in meeting these conditions for several reasons. First, compared with LMEs where entrepreneurship is more successful, Portugal lacks access to risk capital, which is crucial to support entrepreneurship. Access to this kind of capital was not abundant before the crisis and the situation was further aggravated during the sovereign debt crisis, when Portugal lost access to international financial markets. Equally, although there has been a massive investment in higher education over recent years, Portugal does not have top-level universities as LMEs. As for the degree of flexibility, although reforms have been made to labor legislation since 2011, the degree of protection is still higher than in LMEs (OECD, 2017b; ILO, 2018).

Thus, a number of difficulties arise when trying to import the German vocational and the American entrepreneurial models. Our first hypothesis is based on this. We conjecture that due to the lack of LME- and CME-type institutions, it has been the state that has solved coordination problems by launching programs without much involvement of other actors and not requiring the implementation of a new coherent model based either on the German or the American models.

Notwithstanding, our hypothesis is not that governments ignored other international experiences during the period in question (2000–2017). Indeed, because youth unemployment rates in Germany, the US and UK were lower than in Portugal, this may have influenced policy makers. To address this, we have developed two additional hypotheses. We conjecture that during these years some public policies were inspired by an LME-type strategy as the focus was on dealing with the transition to a knowledge-based economy. The final hypothesis is focused on the period of the global economic and sovereign debt crises, and is that over these years a mix of policies was implemented because dual-training systems gained momentum in the EU agenda and because the severity of the youth unemployment problem required the use of all available strategies. We discuss each one in greater detail in what follows.

In the academic and policy debate of the early 2000s, the idea gained ground that a 'new economy' was already underway, one that throughout the 1990s had gradually replaced the Fordist era. Fordism was based on a capital labor accord where mass production and mass consumption were two interlinked characteristics. Mass production was crucial to create large economies of scale and therefore increasing productivity and mass consumption was necessary to create enough demand for a high level of production. Furthermore, a set of institutions supported this arrangement, namely, a coordinated system of industrial relations (labor accepted that real wages increased in line with productivity), a Beveridgean welfare state, and Keynesian macroeconomic policies to tackle economic downturns (Beveridge, 1942; Keynes, 1936). This arrangement came to an end during the 1980s due to the stagflation of the late 1970s, the technological transformations brought about by information and communication technologies (ICT) and the challenges posed by the globalization process (Boyer, 1986). While manufacturing was declining in the 1980s, services became the driving force of economic growth in the 1990s. Inspired by a Schumpeterian understanding of economic change (Schumpeter, 1912, 1983), neo-Schumpeterian scholars argued that due to information technologies and telecommunications innovations, knowledge replaced mass production as a key driver of economic growth and consequently radical innovation replaced incremental innovation (Rodrigues, 2002: 4–6; Boyer, 2002: 158–59; Salavisa, 2006: 191–94). As knowledge accumulation was increasingly important, argued neo-Schumpeterians, countries failing in the transition to a knowledge-based economy would certainly face difficulties in a highly competitive global economy.

Alongside this narrative, a number of scholars argued that a new welfare state was needed in order to address the new challenges posed by globalization and the knowledge-based economy (Esping-Andersen et al, 2002; Salavisa, 2006; Hemerijck, 2013: 35–38). As in the

Fordist production regime – where several institutions were in place to support mass production and mass consumption – the knowledge-based economy also required a set of institutions to support radical innovation and knowledge accumulation. Among them, a reshaped welfare state was a crucial building block of this new era. Instead of a Keynesian welfare state, scholars were speaking of a Schumpeterian one, in which investment in human capital and creative destruction management were the crucial features (Burlamaqui, 2000). The underlying idea was that in the knowledge-based economy the welfare state has to support individuals in dealing with technological change instead of being focused on preventing the fall in aggregate demand during economic downturns. This must be done, they argued, by increasing training throughout life (childcare policies, regular education and lifelong learning) and by investing in active labor market policies (ALMPs). This transformation of the welfare state led a number of social policy scholars to coin the term 'social investment welfare state' to characterize this change, which was presented as an alternative to the Beveridgean and neoliberal welfare state (Esping-Andersen et al, 2002; Morel et al, 2012; Bonoli, 2013: 17–19; Midgley et al, 2017; Hemerijck, 2018).

The second hypothesis is that this narrative inspired labor market policies in Portugal for several reasons. First of all, the third-way perspective, which in many respects drew on this narrative, exerted a great influence on social-democratic parties across Europe, and the Portuguese socialists were no exception. Between 2000 and 2017 the Socialist Party (PS) was in office for ten years, so it is not surprising that their political strategy influenced Portuguese employment policies. Second, as some scholars have pointed out, the third-way perspective was very influential in Mediterranean countries because the idea of deregulating employment protection legislation and simultaneously investing in ALMPs was particularly appealing (Amable, 2003: 242–44). This was because these countries had one of the most restrictive labor laws in the OECD countries (for permanent contracts) but, in contrast to other continental European countries that also had higher levels of regulation, this was not important for safeguarding investment in specific skills. Indeed, these countries were still competing in low-tech sectors, where price and flexibility were very important. Furthermore, the need to invest in education was seen as a top priority by policy makers as these countries were lagging behind in educational indicators, including early school leaving and share of graduates. Thus, rechannelling public expenditure from passive to active labor market policies and simultaneously reducing job protection seemed an attractive strategy for addressing unemployment. To test this hypothesis we will analyse the importance of policies promoting entrepreneurship and policies targeting graduates. Policies focused on graduates are important as the objective of increasing the supply of graduates was a top priority for the knowledge-based economy agenda.

Our third hypothesis is focused on the period after the onset of the global economic crisis. Youth unemployment rates escalated in Portugal in the late 2000s and early 2010s: thus, we expect that labor market policies were influenced by the need to address this problem. Regarding the two approaches mentioned earlier – the American entrepreneurial and German vocational models – we expect that both were influential in Portugal. As for the LME-type strategy, we expect the same reasons mentioned in the second hypothesis continued to apply because Portugal still needed to invest in education and training, and thus investment in ALMPs remained a top priority. Furthermore, EU institutions pressured highly-indebted countries such as Portugal to conduct structural reforms that consisted of policies to further deregulate the labor market (Marques and Hörisch, 2019a; Hall, 2018). Thus, the idea of investing in ALMPs and simultaneously deregulating EPL seemed a viable strategy.

As for the German vocational model, contrary to what we hypothesize regarding the first period, we expect that some attempts were also made to expand this type of training. This is so for several reasons. As Marques and Hörisch (2019: 1) have pointed out, during the crisis 'youth unemployment rates were lower in countries with a collective skill formation regime, that is, those with a high level of firm involvement in the provision of initial vocational training and a strong public commitment to vocational training'.

Indeed, compared with LMEs, CMEs were much more successful in preventing the rise in youth unemployment. Thus, many scholars and organizations spoke of the need to implement policies focused on promoting dual training and apprenticeships. This was the case with the most important EU policy to address youth unemployment – the Youth Guarantee. As explained by the same authors: 'the EU's Youth Guarantee encouraged countries to: strengthen partnerships between employers and relevant labor market players (employment services, various levels of government, trade unions and youth services) in order to boost employment, apprenticeship and traineeship opportunities for young people' (Marques and Hörisch, 2019: 2).

As highly-indebted countries were being pressured by EU institutions to cut public expenditure, EU programmes such as the Youth Guarantee played a key role throughout these years because they financed youth-oriented ALMPs in Southern European countries. For instance, Portugal received 160 million euros under this program (Tosun, 2017: 41). Without these EU programmes, Portugal would not have been able to implement youth-oriented ALMPs during this period.

In line with this explanation, we expect that since 2008 new areas of intervention were included. Given the importance of the EU Youth Guarantee in financing youth-oriented ALMPs, we expect policies promoting apprenticeships to have gained momentum in these years. To test this hypothesis, we will analyse whether the mix of policies increased since 2008 and if indeed apprenticeships became more important after this year.

To sum up, we develop three hypotheses:

1. The first hypothesis is based on the assumption that Southern European countries lack institutional complementarities to fully implement the German vocational model or the American entrepreneurial model. Thus, we hypothesize that the state played a key role to address youth unemployment by putting in place programmes to fight youth unemployment. In this process the state did not need to involve other actors and it did not implement a new coherent model based on the German or the American model.
2. The second consists of hypothesizing that the transition to a knowledge-based economy was a concern of Portuguese governments. Promoting entrepreneurship and developing policies focused on graduates was seen as a priority. Thus, we hypothesize that the American entrepreneurial model exerted some influence throughout the period in question (2000–2017).
3. Although the objective of dealing with the emergence of the knowledge-based economy continued after 2008, we hypothesize that new policies were also adopted to address the urgency of the youth unemployment problem. In this regard, we conjecture that especially since 2008 new policies inspired by the EU strategy to promote apprenticeships gained momentum. Thus, we expect that a mix of policies was implemented.

Labor market policies to fight youth unemployment in Portugal between 2000 and 2017

In this section our main aim is to present the empirical data on the implementation of ALMPs to fight youth unemployment in Portugal 2000–2017. In order to better answer the hypotheses raised in the previous section, we have divided our analysis into two steps: in the first, we analyse the different types of ALMPs targeting young people in Portugal 2000–2017 and assess their content and relative importance; in the second, we further examine the composition of these different types of measures throughout three periods (2001–2007; 2008–2014; and 2015–2017) in which Portugal faced, as we have seen, distinct but extremely challenging national and international situations. These severely impacted the economy and led to a dramatic rise in unemployment rates, particularly among the younger or more vulnerable cohorts of the active population.

The empirical data that supports our analysis of ALMPs in Portugal 2000–2017 was drawn from the LABREF database (European Commission, 2019) which collects and shows all related policies in each member state from different national and European sources. This data was then coded into different categories which were based on a typology developed by Tosun et al (2017), who also used the LABREF database to study youth-oriented ALMPs. This typology was adapted to better suit the aims of this study, resulting in the following categories: investment in vocational education and training (except 'dual training schemes'); workplace-based training; labor market training and internships; job search assistance and monitoring; wage subsidies; public sector employment programs; promotion of self-employment and entrepreneurship; and other. To compare with their typology, we have divided their first category of 'human capital investment' into our first two categories of 'investment in vocational education and training' and 'workplace-based training', with the latter focusing on the promotion of dual training schemes and the promotion of apprenticeships. We believe this will allow a more fine-grained analysis of the different types of vocational education measures which are important in assessing the implementation of programs more commonly associated with the German vocational model. By the same reasoning, we have added a new category of 'promotion of self-employment and entrepreneurship', a type of measures typical of LMEs as epitomized by the American model. Lastly, we have excluded the category 'packages' since we counted each program separately. It should nevertheless be pointed out that this compartmentalization is often debatable since some measures encompass different dimensions of ALMPs at the same time and in others the boundaries are often blurred (such as in the distinction between apprenticeships and internships which in the Portuguese system is often unclear in the design of the measures). When this happens, we have opted either for coding these policies simultaneously in the several categories to which they pertain (and thus the same measure may have several different codes at the same time), or in choosing the category that better captures the spirit and scope of the measure.

Table 6.1 summarizes the results of coding the different ALMP measures addressing the youth in Portugal for the period under analysis. This has allowed us to assess the relative importance of each policy area. A second column shows the number of measures specifically addressing higher education graduates, a topic which will likewise be important in our analysis. Prior to the description and reflection on the ALMPs in Portugal between 2000–2017, a word of caution is still perhaps needed regarding the limits to the conclusions we may draw from that analysis. We focus exclusively on: (1) new measures or ones which were changed throughout this period (therefore excluding measures and programs which continued active without significant changes); (2) policies which specifically target the youth (and there was for instance a large body of measures on vocational training and upskilling of the adult population); and (3) by analysing the number and content of policies we are still leaving out important aspects such as the volume of investment or the number of participants in each measure. However, it is our contention that within these analytical confines it is still possible to help reflect on the content and orientation of ALMPs aimed at youth in Portugal and thus to successfully address our hypotheses.

Table 6.1: Youth-oriented ALMPs (2000–2017)

	Overall	Directed at HE graduates
Investment in vocational education and training (except dual training)	1	0
Workplace-based training	5	0
Labour market training and internships	15	5
Job search assistance and monitoring	1	0
Wage subsidies	15	4
Public sector employment programmes	1	0
Promotion of self-employment and entrepreneurship	4	1
Other	1	0
Total	43	10

Source: Own table based on the LABREF database (European Commission, 2019)

The first three categories in our analysis concern the measures taken in relation to training, with 'investment in vocational education and training' focusing exclusively on school-oriented training; 'workplace-based training' addressing the promotion of dual training schemes and apprenticeships (training schemes which combine school and workplace-based vocational education programs); and 'labor market training and internships' focusing on the type of temporary programs which generally mark the transition periods between formal training and the workplace. Training programs are generally found in the literature to be one of the most effective types of ALMPs, even though their effects may take some time to materialize (Vooren et al, 2018; Card et al, 2018), and to be particularly suited for periods of economic recession when the opportunity costs for the participants are comparably lower (ILO, 2018).

As we can see from Table 6.1, throughout this period of extended recession there was indeed a strong focus on ALMPs on training in Portugal. However, the bulk of these interventions can be found in the more temporary programs, such as the promotion of internships, followed at distance by workplace-based training and with training taken in a school-based environment accounting for only one new measure addressed at young people. The latter was a measure adopted in 2004 which stipulated that minors who were admitted to jobs without having completed compulsory school or without a professional qualification should attend either an education module, or a training cycle or combined education and training cycles, providing together the missing educational attainments.

The literature also points out that dual training programmes that combine school and work training, are even more effective than the ones addressing only one of these components (Card et al, 2018). A number of such workplace-based training policies were implemented in Portugal throughout the period in question. In 2002, the government designed a set of new rules for the employment of early school leavers. This provided flexibility in recruitment for firms but subjected the signing of the new contract to the condition of attendance by the young person in question on a training course conferring compulsory schooling credentials and vocational qualifications, and establishing a minimum period of working time to be used for training. Other measures concern the revision of the curricula and organization of apprenticeships in 2008, training courses which function under the National System of Qualifications and provide both professional training and an upper secondary qualification, and the establishment of a broader definition of working student in 2009 to include people that work and attend any level of education, including vocational education courses or temporary youth occupation programs. In 2010, when the effects of the economic crisis were deepening, the government launched an overarching program, the Employment Initiative, which covered several dimensions of ALMPs: (1) the creation of a professional traineeship program for young people who attend professional and technological courses or who have a secondary school education or equivalent qualification level; (2) a program to support the recruitment of young people who have already completed a traineeship program, particularly in technological areas; and (3) offered re-qualification opportunities for up to 5,000 young people with a university degree in sectors of low employability to help integrate them into the labor market. Some of these measures were later merged and further expanded as part of the Youth Guarantee program, which invested in several areas relating to training and the transition to the labor market. Finally, in 2013 a measure was designed to activate the unemployed registered in the Public Employment Service (PES), including younger workers but also adults, regardless of their educational attainment, through a qualification process based either on training (modular but often complemented with practical training in the workplace) or on the recognition, validation and certification of competences (RVCC) of dual nature (professional and educational) and of the skills acquired throughout life, in different contexts.

As we have pointed out before, most of the measures on training in Portugal throughout the period in question (15 out of 21) involved temporary programs and, especially, subsidized internships. These internships had initially been designed as an instrument to facilitate and promote the transition between education and training and the labor market for young people, but were significantly expanded in both their aims and recipients with the onset of the economic crisis. In fact, it can be argued that the bulk of the response by the Portuguese government to the dramatic rise in unemployment levels throughout this period, particularly youth unemployment, revolved around the two main axes of internships and wage subsidies. Even though the specific measures on internships are too numerous to address individually, a few of the more significant and overarching programs and measures should nevertheless be detailed.

The first of these is the group of measures on professional internships which at its origin were directed at people aged under 30, looking for their first job or, in exceptional conditions, looking for a new job with higher level (level IV and V) or intermediate qualifications (levels II and III). However, the aims and scope of these professional internships were the object of numerous changes and revisions during the economic crisis, in order to better answer the effects of rising youth unemployment at all levels of qualifications. Chronologically, in 2009 a specific measure was designed aimed at creating more than 12,000 professional training placements for young people, especially young higher education graduates in areas of low employability, and at increasing the number of young people supported through professional placements to 37,000. This measure included financial compensation for employers, as well as exemption from social security payments for up to two years for recruitment of young people on an unlimited work contract. At the same time, the Professional Internship Program, specifically aimed at promoting youth employability, was widened throughout this period to include 35-year-olds, to target other levels of qualifications and even, in specific circumstances, people above the 35-year-old threshold. At the same time its duration was reduced from 12 months to 9 months and the financial support for its recipients greatly reduced in order to cover more beneficiaries in a time of stringent budgetary restraints. A number of measures on subsidized internships were also introduced in 2010, as we have seen, under the Employment Initiative and Employment Passport, which were later merged and rebranded under the name Employment Internships, as one of the four pillars of the Youth Guarantee in 2013. Again, the changes operated during the reform period were generally aimed at increasing the number of recipients of these programs (namely NEETs and other vulnerable groups at the margins of the labor market) and broadening their coverage, a purpose which was successfully achieved throughout this period (OECD, 2017b). In spite of the positive outcomes observed of these programs in fighting youth unemployment, with for example 67% of participants in Employment Internships in work nine months after the conclusion of the program, several challenges remain. Among these is the need to reach out to the unregistered NEETs and improve the monitoring of the program and its participants (ILO, 2018), as well as possibly redirecting it to those who need them most as the recovery takes hold (OECD, 2017b). The latter concerns were already partially addressed with two measures taken in 2017, namely the creation of the Contract-Employment in 2017, which not only focused on providing financial support for employers hiring under more permanent basis, such as fixed-term and especially through permanent contracts, but also prioritizes vulnerable groups, namely young people, older workers, refugees, former convicts and others.

Another significant group of measures relates to the INOV program which concentrates a number of different subsidized professional internships targeting higher education graduates in different areas relating to international commerce (INOV-Export); sustainable development and renewable energies (INOV-Energi@); culture and arts (INOV-Art); social economy (INOV-Social); multinational entities (INOV-Contacto); cooperation for development (INOV-Mundus); and innovation and company development in small to medium-sized firms (INOV-Jovem). This was a program launched in 2005 but further developed in 2008 which combined the objectives of encouraging the transition of young people to the labor market with the promotion of the political agenda of the Lisbon Strategy, namely in its three pillars of the economy, social cohesion and the environment (Costa Dias and Varejão, 2012). The changes promoted in 2008 were again a response to the onset of the crisis and placed the program even more firmly under the domain of ALMPs by increasing the coverage to target more recipients, now exclusively unemployed, and facilitating the professional integration of young graduates in areas of low employability.

Another typical area of intervention in ALMPs, which in our typology comes under 'job search assistance and monitoring', relates to those activities such as intensive counseling interviews, CV reviews, advice on job-search strategies or interview techniques, referrals to specific policies and other elements relating to PES delivery which have been found to significantly increase the employability of job-seekers in a cost-effective manner (OECD, 2017b). In line with this, the Portuguese government launched an initiative in 2015 to improve the institutional response of its employment service. This included merging existing Job Centres with Professional Training Centres to achieve a closer alignment between employment and training services offered to job-seekers, and introducing stronger performance management and evaluation mechanisms of placement efforts and job search activities, as well as a modernization of PES information systems. This was, however, an area which, in spite of known deficiencies in the Portuguese system, was not a priority throughout these years, and even these few measures were not fully implemented (OECD, 2017b).

In contrast, measures on 'wage subsidies' were indeed an absolute priority in the government's response to rising youth unemployment caused by the economic crisis. These types of measure have been found in the literature to be very effective in increasing the probability of individuals finding and retaining a job, especially in the short and medium term (Card et al, 2018; Vooren et al, 2018). Therefore, this type of ALMPs constituted one of the two main axes that governed the response to the economic and employment crisis (alongside the more temporary programs of labor market training and internships).

In fact, these two dimensions were very often combined in the form of several subsidized internship programs which showed very positive results in the chances of individuals finding and retaining a job, even after the completion of the subsidized internships (ILO, 2018; OECD, 2017b). The wage subsidies measures which were implemented throughout the period in question revolved around: (1) increasing the participation of certain groups in the labor market (namely young people, the long-term unemployed, individuals with only basic levels of education and training, and other more vulnerable groups); and (2) encouraging the substitution of temporary contracts for more permanent contracts (such as can be found under the Employment Stimulus and Employment Contract programs). Financial support for employers usually combined subsidizing the wages of the people hired under these programs, but often also other forms of support such as a temporary reduction or exemption from taxes and social security contributions in the new contracts. The nature of these types of measure, as well as the high number of participants, especially during the peak of the recession, made them a significant financial burden on the public coffers throughout this period, yet they were an important emergency measure in response to exceptional circumstances. It can be argued, though, that with the improvements in the economy and the labor market in the last few years the resources which were devoted to wage subsidies should now be directed at other more structural and cost-efficient ALMPs (ILO, 2018).

A good example of these more efficient ALMPs is the 'promotion of self-employment and entrepreneurship'. This is, as we have previously seen, a type of measure usually more associated with the American model, which we hypothesized may have exerted some influence throughout this period. Our data show, nevertheless, that the measures for promoting entrepreneurship throughout this period were scarce and not developed in a coherent way. These measures include the creation in 2012 of Passport Entrepreneurship, aimed at developing entrepreneurship and innovative projects, or with high growth potential, by highly qualified youth; and a cooperative entrepreneurship initiative, COOPJOVEM, supporting the creation of cooperative businesses or investment in projects for existing agricultural cooperatives involving the net creation of employment. Both initiatives included a series of specific support measures, linked together and complemented with technical assistance throughout the project. The scope of the latter program in cooperative businesses was broadened in 2015 to specifically address young NEETs. Finally, in 2014 the Youth Invest program also supported the creation of start-ups by the young unemployed, in the form of an interest-free loan for investment and a subsidy for job creation. However, both in terms of the number of initiatives and the level of investment and number of participants, these measures were marginal in relation to the most common and influential types of measure, namely subsidized internships and other forms of wage subsidies. Other, even more marginal types of measures aimed at youth implemented throughout this period are those relating to 'public sector employment programmes', with only one measure taken in 2010 to support professional traineeships for young people in central and local public administration, and one additional measure coded as 'other', which harmonized the criteria for proving disability and support in educating disabled people aged under 24.

Finally, while there were a significant number of policies (10 out of 43) targeting graduates, the nature and scope of these measures were significantly changed throughout the period in question. Up until 2008, we find a couple of measures relating mostly to the INOV programs, in which the political concern is both to provide a framework for a smoother transition of graduates to the labor market in selected areas, and to promote innovation processes in the firms receiving those graduates. These concerns, as well as the selected areas were, as we have seen, very much in line with the implementation of the Lisbon Strategy. In the second stage, when the full effects of the crisis were taking hold, both in youth unemployment in general but also in relation to graduates, priorities were clearly altered. The measures in this period were mostly directed at promoting the re-qualification of graduates in areas of low employability and at supporting employment creation through wage subsidies to firms and, to a lesser degree, in supporting entrepreneurship and self-employment creation by graduates. Finally, in the latter stages of the crisis, and especially in 2017 with the Employment Contract program, the focus was now on supporting more permanent forms of employment, and encouraging firms to sign those types of contracts through wage subsidies and temporary exemptions from taxes and social security payments.

The analysis conducted on the types of ALMPs implemented in Portugal 2000–2017 has already produced some insights that may help us to answer our hypotheses. Given that Southern European countries lack a coherent set of institutional complementarities to fully implement either the German vocational model or the American entrepreneurial model, we had postulated that the state had played a key role in addressing youth unemployment without significantly involving other actors in that response. The data collected in this chapter show that the state did play a key role, since the bulk of the ALMPs implemented during this period refer to internships and wage subsidies, which are designed and financed by the state. Furthermore, one cannot view the implementation of coherent reforms as resembling either the German vocational model or the American model, in spite of some measures aimed at promoting entrepreneurship and a non-negligible number integrating higher education graduates in the labor market. However, even these types of measure seem to be much more related to a certain experimentalism in public policy, under exceptional circumstances in the labor market caused by the effects of the economic crisis on youth unemployment, than to a decisive and coherent strategy aimed at implementing either of the two models. This analysis will be further debated in the discussion section where we will likewise reflect on the differences in the policies implemented throughout the three different periods under analysis (Table 6.2).

As we have seen, the first of these periods (2001–2007) corresponds to a largely stagnant economy, coupled with a gradual rise in unemployment brought about by the effects of the EMU process and increasing competition from Eastern European and Asian countries in low-skilled industries which were key economic sectors in Portugal. The second period (2008–2014), corresponds to the onset of the global economic crisis of 2008 and the EU sovereign debt crisis which followed it. This eventually led to the financial assistance program of 2011 in Portugal, which fostered austerity and the liberalization of the economy, and to a stark economic depression with dire effects on the

Table 6.2: Youth-oriented ALMPs during three distinct periods

	2001–2007	2008–2014	2015–2017
Investment in vocational education and training (except dual training)	1		
Workplace-based training	1	4	
Labour market training and internships		13	2
Job search assistance and monitoring			1
Wage subsidies	3	9	3
Public sector employment programmes		1	
Promotion of self-employment and entrepreneurship		3	1
Other			1
Total	5	30	8

Source: Own table based on the LABREF database (European Commission, 2019)

labor market. In the third period (2014–2017), the economy already shows some signs of recovery, there is a sharp decrease in unemployment rates, namely in youth unemployment, and the implementation of a different political agenda based on the reversion of some of the measures of the previous period, and a set of redistribution measures which helped to boost internal demand and the economy.

In the first period of analysis we find five different measures which fall under the categories of training and wage subsidies. The measures relating to training were taken in 2002 and 2004, and were aimed at promoting training cycles of a more structural nature by providing schooling credentials or vocational qualifications with a very substantial number of hours of training. The wage subsidies for hiring young people in this period (as well as other more vulnerable groups) usually lasted for up to 12 months and were relatively generous in the financial support for both the participants and the firms hiring them, while the use of more permanent contracts was also clearly encouraged. The political agenda of this period was thus directed at the providing young people with better qualifications and at facilitating their transition to the labor market in the context of economic stagnation, but clearly without the sense of urgency which we see in the profusion of measures taken at the peak of the crisis.

During our second period of analysis (2008–2014), the great majority of ALMPs targeting youth (22 out of 30) revolved, as we had seen, around more temporary training and internship programs and wage subsidies (often coupled as subsidized internships). These subsidized internship programs (such as the INOV and Employment Passport programs) were successively reformed during this period to cover a greater variety of recipients, and the duration and generosity of the subsidies was reduced in order to further increase the number of its beneficiaries in the context of limited financial resources. Other less significant groups of measures implemented throughout this period relate to workplace-based training programs, namely the revision of the curricula and organization of apprenticeships in 2008; a number of measures under the Employment Initiative from 2010 onwards; the Youth Guarantee from 2013, which contained dual training elements; and some measures promoting entrepreneurship and self-employment by graduates. However, both these types of measure seemed to be implemented more as additional barriers in the attempt to contain and alleviate the effects of the rising youth unemployment of the period than as part of a coherent political strategy aimed at the implementation of either the German vocational model or the American entrepreneurial one. Even measures which were originally focused on the implementation of the Lisbon Strategy, such as the INOV program, were reformed from 2008 onwards to respond to the exceptional circumstances of this period. The hypothesis we put forward that during the economic crisis the government had resorted to a great profusion of policies in the attempt to contain the rapidly rising youth unemployment, seems to be fully corroborated by the data. In fact, one pervasive critique in the literature on ALMPs in Portugal is the lack of coherence and stability in its design and implementation (Hespanha and Caleiras, 2017). This is evident in the high number of measures and programs addressing youth unemployment, the constant changes in nomenclature, beneficiaries and conditions for access, and even its equivocal classification given the variety of targets in the same measure and its diverse justification. These features not only add confusion to the system by making it more difficult for job-seekers and firms to know what help is available, and by raising costs in the adaptation of PES to the new programs or variations in existing programs, but also make a more longitudinal and in-depth assessment of specific measures and their impact particularly challenging. An illustrative example of this problem is the Youth Guarantee. As shown in Table 6.3, in the scope of this program the Portuguese government implemented 16 different measures in three different policy areas. The first refers to training, the second to internships and wage subsidies, and the final one to entrepreneurship. As expected, the bulk of investment went to internships and wage subsidies.

From 2015 onwards, the economic recovery, and especially the sharp decline in youth unemployment, have led to a significant decrease in the number of policies, even if they are still skewed towards labor market training, internships and wage subsidies (5 out of 8 measures). However, even within these categories the nature of the measures already shows some important differences when compared to the previous period, with wage subsidies being now much more directed at promoting more permanent contracts (while during the crisis this objective was clearly more relaxed). The absence of new measures specifically focusing on dual training programmes, and the single measure aimed at the promotion of entrepreneurship, further reinforce the idea that the previous initiatives in these areas were much more of an emergency response than a strategic move towards the implementation either of the German or American models. Lastly, it should be noted that in spite of recent improvements in youth unemployment, it remains high when compared with other OECD countries (OECD, 2017b). Going forward, the success in implementing ALMPs on this issue

Table 6.3: Measures implemented in the scope of the Youth Guarantee

Operational areas/ typologies	Indicative financial allocation		Indicative participants	
	€	%	N°	%
Qualification/education				
RETOMAR program	9,795,000	2.9	6,530	3
Young Active Life	20,616,000	6	128,550	59.9
Traineeships for professional retraining program: AGIR/ PERPro	902,000	0.3	266	0.1
Subtotal	**31,313,000**	**9.1**	**135,346**	**63.1**
internships/employment				
Internships	156,500,000	45.6	34,780	16.2
Young Active Employment	13,000,000	3.8	5,200	2.4
Hiring support	54,300,000	15.8	27,150	12.7
Professional Internships in Local Administration (PEPAL)	17,500,000	5.1	1,500	0.7
Internships in External Peripheral Services of the Foreign Affairs Ministry (PEPAC-MNE)	2,295,000	0.7	85	0.0003
INOV Contact: International Internships for Young Graduates	12,000,000	3.5	600	0.3
Estagiar T	17,170,000	5	2,450	1.1
PIIE	3,350,000	1	882	0.4
Young INTEGRA	1,156,000	0.3	247	0.1
Madeira Internships	12,000,000	3.5	2,685	1.3
Subtotal	**289,271,000**	**84.2**	**75,579**	**35.2**
entrepreneurship				
COOPJOVEM	16,800,000	4.9	2,700	1.3
EMPREENDE JÁ: business management and perception network	4,800,000	1.4	630	0.3
Young idea INVEST	1,286,000	0.4	200	0.1
Subtotal	**22,886,000**	**6.7**	**3,530**	**1.6**
Total	**343,470,000**	**100**	**214,455**	**100**

Source: CESOP (2018)

may depend on a higher stability of measures, on focusing resources on the more vulnerable groups (such as NEETs), on implementing more cost-efficient measures, and on further reforming PES delivery (OECD, 2017b).

Box 6.1: Effectiveness of ALMPs in Portugal

A number of empirical studies have assessed the effectiveness of ALMPs in Portugal (Nunes, 2007; Centeno et al, 2009; Costa Dias and Varejão, 2012; OECD, 2017b: 49–52; and ILO, 2018: 102–5). Most studies assess ALMPs in three areas: training, wage incentives and internships. Two studies include two additional areas: promotion of entrepreneurship and self-employment (Costa Dias and Varejão, 2012); and programmes integrating unemployed individuals into socially useful work (OECD, 2017b: 49–52). Regarding training, the majority of studies found no positive results in terms of job creation (Centeno et al, 2009; Costa Dias and Varejão, 2012; OECD, 2017b). This is especially the case in shorter training interventions, which are seen as less successful than apprenticeships, which are longer and show better results (ILO, 2018: 104). As for other policy areas, wage incentives are seen as more effective in terms of job creation than internships. For instance, according to the ILO (2018: 104), '64.1% of individuals who benefited from an employment incentive were still employed 12 months after the termination of the support', while the same figure for internships was 38.3%. The OECD (2017b: 51) report corroborates these conclusions by showing that wage incentives are more effective than internships. Notwithstanding, internships have a positive effect on job creation (on this see also Nunes (2007)). Within the scope of a report commissioned by the Portuguese Public Employment Services (IEFP), Costa Dias and Varejão (2012), found that wage incentives and promoting entrepreneurship and self-employment are the most effective policies to address unemployment. Finally, the OECD report also studied a program integrating unemployed individuals into socially useful work, and it found that the impact is small and seems to disappear in the long run. Taken as a whole, existing empirical studies point out to the following conclusions:

• Training interventions are less effective than other types of ALMPs, especially shorter training interventions;
• Internships have a positive impact in terms of job creation;
• Wage incentives and promotion of entrepreneurship and self-employment are the most effective interventions.

Discussion

This section further discusses the hypotheses put forward and summarizes the main features of the Portuguese labor market policies. In our view, statism and experimentalism were the two key characteristics of the Portuguese strategy for fighting youth unemployment.

The data collected in this chapter show that the state did indeed play a key role. The majority of policies relate to internships and wage subsidies, which are totally designed and financed by the state. Furthermore, one cannot observe the implementation of coherent reforms towards the German or the American model. Some policies were implemented but they did not mean a departure from statism. Furthermore, our results are very much in line with a recent contribution that studied the Spanish case and concluded that policies implemented after the onset of the global economic crisis were totally managed by the state and mainly consisted of traineeships and other related programs (Marques and Hörisch, 2019b: 9–11). To conclude, hypothesis one is corroborated by the empirical data.

Our results do not validate hypothesis two. Although during the period in question a number of policies targeting graduates (11 out of 43) were implemented, policies promoting entrepreneurship and self-employment were scarce and not developed in a coherent way. Some conditions need to be in place in order to boost entrepreneurship. Access to risk capital and top-level universities play a crucial role. From the policies we analysed, we cannot conclude that substantial reforms were made to address these problems. The total financing was relatively small and thus insufficient to address the lack of venture capital. On the other hand, there are no signs that the higher education system was reformed in order to boost this transition. In our view, what was done in this regard was the implementation of several programs to address the rise of youth unemployment among graduates, namely internships and wage subsidies programs. This happened because youth unemployment among graduates remained very high in Portugal during the entire period (Figure 6.3). Taken as a whole, the problems preventing entrepreneurship in Portugal remained the same and investment in graduates through internships and wage incentives was a response to the growing levels of unemployment among graduates and not part of an ambitious strategy to address the emergence of a knowledge economy.

The rejection of hypothesis two illustrates how difficult it is to implement a 'third-way type' strategy in Southern European countries. This strategy was based on the assumption that it was necessary to simultaneously liberalize labor legislation, increase investment in

ALMPs, and reduce the generosity of passive labor market policies. Portugal relaxed labor legislation in the 2000s by reducing the regulations on the use of temporary contracts and, in the light of the sovereign debt crisis, reduced the strictness of permanent contracts. But expenditure on ALMPs did not increase. In our view, this occurred for two reasons. First, investment in ALMPs requires funding; yet these countries did not have the financial capacity to do so during this period. They were in fact pressured to reduce public expenditure, not to increase it. Thus, when the socialist party was in office, the room for manoeuvre to make this investment was short. Second, during the sovereign debt crisis, the EU strategy to reduce deficits and boost employment was aligned with the neoliberal agenda of labor market deregulation (Marques and Hörisch, 2020). It was not social investment but more workfare that was the top priority, that is, a reduction in the generosity of unemployment benefits to reduce welfare dependency. The right-wing coalition government that was in office between 2012 and 2015 was fully committed to this strategy (OECD, 2017b).

The empirical evidence of this chapter corroborates hypothesis number three. The period of the economic crisis was indeed characterized by the implementation of a mix of policies, including entrepreneurship, workplace-based training, internships and wage subsidies. Besides corroborating this hypothesis, the empirical evidence shows the lack of coherence in labor market policies in Portugal. The American and the German models require different institutions to support them, and thus implementing both models is not a feasible strategy. What seems to be happening is a sort of experimentalism; policies are disconnected and many times contradictory.

Taking these three conclusions together, we argue that the Portuguese strategy to address youth unemployment is based on statism and experimentalism. Internships, wage subsidies and public sector programs represent about 75% of the policies implemented during the period in question. To implement these programs the state did not involve other actors: it designed and financed the programs. The opposite would have happened if, for instance, the government had implemented an ambitious strategy to boost entrepreneurship, or if it had promoted dual training at a large scale. In those cases, it was necessary to involve other actors in the design and financing of programmes. Thus, statism is one of the key characteristics of the policies adopted in the period in question. On the other hand, we can speak of an experimentalist approach because the strategy was not coherent. Although no ambitious strategy to boost entrepreneurship or dual training was adopted, some minor reforms were implemented. The problem is that they were not implemented in a coherent way. It is very difficult to simultaneously boost dual training and entrepreneurship because this requires the existence of different institutions. In our perspective, the continuous rise of youth unemployment for many years contributed to this because governments used all available strategies to address youth unemployment. To a certain extent it was the severity of the youth unemployment problem that led to this outcome.

Concluding remarks

This chapter has analysed how different Portuguese governments addressed the rise of youth unemployment between 2000 and 2017. By doing so, it has shown that the strategy followed over this period is characterized by a reliance on statism and experimentalism. The state implemented the great majority of policies without much involvement of other actors, and policies were implemented in different and, many times, contradictory areas. Taken together, this chapter shows that even in the context of great turmoil, where the potential for political change was high, no path-breaking initiatives were implemented.

To conclude, we look ahead to the future in order to understand the main challenges the country still faces, and to discuss the feasibility of different strategies in the near future. Although youth unemployment has dropped in recent years, it remains above the European average. The youth unemployment rate in Portugal was 18.1% in June 2019. Given also that unemployment among graduates remains high (Figure 6.3) and that the share of temporary contracts among youth is very high (Figure 6.2), young labor market participants still face huge difficulties in the labor market. Thus, political effort is still needed to address this issue. We do not expect that the government's approach will change substantially over the next years and, therefore, wage incentives and traineeships seem the most viable solution. Many empirical studies show that these are the most effective policies to fight youth unemployment (see Box 6.1). Thus, we expect the government to continue to invest in these policies. Notwithstanding, it is possible that entrepreneurship and policies focused on graduates will deserve more attention in the future. This will happen for three reasons. First, high unemployment among graduates is a pressing problem in Portugal and thus entrepreneurship can be part of the solution. The situation may become even worse because the share of graduates is still increasing and thus the oversupply of graduates will continue in the future. Second, the Portuguese government has recently announced new policies to boost entrepreneurship, including the attraction of big international conferences like the Web Summit, which has taken place in Lisbon since 2016 and attracts tens of thousands of entrepreneurs. Besides the fact that these events may provide Portuguese start-ups with access to venture capital, the Portuguese government has, very recently, launched new programs to facilitate access to risk capital (StartUP Portugal). Although this does not solve all the problems identified here (for instance the lack of top-level universities and the poor indicators in high-tech exports), it can provide better conditions to boost entrepreneurship. Third, empirical studies evaluating public programs conclude that programs promoting entrepreneurship show good results (see Box 6.1). Taken as a whole, it seems that continuing to invest in wage subsidies and internships, but simultaneously investing in entrepreneurship and programs for graduates, seems the most viable strategy in the near future.

As for the other alternative – the German model – it does not seem viable to significantly boost dual training in Portugal in the near future. First, the VET system remains untouched; the overwhelming majority of training takes place in state schools without linkages to employers. Only a few schools provide this kind of training and very often they belong to multinationals. Furthermore, no jobs are being created to include a high number of young people in this type of training. The industrial sector continues to shrink and the service sector demands different types of skills. Finally, coordination between labor and capital has not increased in the recent past. Therefore, we do not expect that the Portuguese government will boost this type of training to fight youth unemployment in the near future.

Notes

[1] Due to the rise of youth unemployment emigration soared. Permanent emigration among those aged 15–29 grew from 11,021 individuals in 2008 to 25,963 individuals in 2012 (INE, 2018). Furthermore, also as a consequence of the rise in unemployment, young people played a key role in the demonstrations against austerity; several massive protests were called by youth movements (Fernandes, 2017). Interestingly, the same happened in Spain, where the youth was also very active on the popular mobilization against austerity (Romanos, 2017).

[2] The rapid decline of youth unemployment since 2014 shows the importance of the economic context in understanding this phenomenon in Portugal. When the economic context improved, youth unemployment dropped significantly. If unemployment was mainly explained by cultural factors, youth unemployment would not have dropped so rapidly.

[3] For further details on this see: Soskice (1999) and Hall and Soskice (2001).

[4] German companies like Volkswagen have their own vocational schools, which provide this type of training. However, they represent a low proportion of students in the Portuguese VET system.

Acknowledgments

This work was financed by Portuguese funds through FCT – Foundation for Science and Technology in the framework of the project no. 030016, BRIGHET – Bringing together Higher Education, Training, and Job Quality, Reference: PTDC/SOC-SOC/30016/2017.

References

Afonso, A. (2019) State-led wage devaluation in Southern Europe in the wake of the Eurozone crisis, *European Journal of Political Research*, 58(3): 938–59.

Amable, B. (2003) *The Diversity of Modern Capitalism*, Oxford: Oxford University Press.

Beveridge, W.H. (1942) *Social Insurance and Allied Services: The Beveridge Report,* command paper 6404, London: HMSO.

Biavaschi, C., Eichhorst, W., Giulietti, C., Kendzia, M., Muravyev, A., Pieters, J., Rodríguez-Planas, N., Schmidl, R. and Zimmermann, K. (2012) *Youth Unemployment and Vocational Training*, IZA Discussion Paper 6809, Bonn: IZA, 1–103.

Bonoli, G. (2013) *The Origins of Active Social Policy: Market and Childcare Policies*, Oxford: Oxford University Press.

Boyer, R. (1986) *Capitalismes fin de siècle*, Paris: Presses Universitaires de France.

Boyer, R. (2002) Institutional reforms for growth, employment and social cohesion: elements for a European and national agenda, in M.J. Rodrigues (ed) *The New Knowledge Economy in Europe: A Strategy for International Competitiveness and Social Cohesion*, Cheltenham: Edward Elgar, pp 146–202.

Burlamaqui, L. (2000) Evolutionary economics and the economic role of the state, in L. Burlamaqui, A.L. Castro and H.J. Chang (eds) *Institutions and the Role of the State*, Cheltenham: Edward Elgar, pp 27–52.

Busemeyer, M. and Thelen, K. (2015) Non-standard employment and systems of skill formation in European countries, in W. Eichhorst and P. Marx (eds) *Non-Standard Employment in Post-Industrial Labour Markets*, Cheltenham: Edward Elgar, pp 401–29.

Busemeyer, M. and Trampusch, C. (2012) The comparative political economy of collective skill formation, in M. Busemeyer and C. Trampusch (eds) *The Political Economy of Collective Skill Formation*, Oxford: Oxford University Press, pp 3–38.

Card, D., Kluve, J. and Weber, A. (2018) What works? A meta-analysis of recent active labour market program evaluations, *Journal of the European Economic Association*, 16(1): 894–931.

Carneiro, A., Portugal, P. and Varejão, J. (2014) Catastrophic job destruction during the Portuguese economic crisis, *Journal of Macroeconomics*, 39(B): 444–57.

Centeno, M. and Novo, A.A. (2012) Excess worker turnover and fixed-term contracts: causal evidence in a two-tier system, *Labour Economics*, 19(3): 320–8.

Centeno, L., Centeno, M. and Novo, A. (2009) Evaluating job-search programs for old and young individuals: heterogeneous impact on unemployment duration, *Labour Economics*, 16(1): 12–25.

CESOP (2018) *Avaliação da Implementação, Eficácia e Eficiência da Iniciativa Emprego Jovem: Relatório Final Revisto*, Lisbon: CESOP.

Costa Dias, M. and Varejão, J. (2012) *Estudo de Avaliação das Políticas Ativas de Emprego: Relatório Final*, Porto: FEUP.

Esping-Andersen, G., Gallie, D., Hemerijck, A. and Myles, J. (2002) *Why We Need a New Welfare State*, Oxford: Oxford University Press.

Estevez-Abe, M., Iversen, T. and Soskice, D. (2001) Social protection and the formation of skills: a reinterpretation of the welfare state, in P. Hall and D. Soskice (eds) *Varieties of Capitalism: The Institutional Foundations of Comparative Advantage*, Oxford: Oxford University Press, pp 145–83.

European Commission (2019) *Labour Market Reforms Database*, https://webgate.ec.europa.eu/labref/public/

Eurostat (2018) Eurostat Database on Education, http://ec.europa.eu/eurostat/web/education-and-training/data/database

Fernandes, T. (2017) Late neoliberalism and its discontents: the case of Portugal, in D. Della Porta, M. Andretta, F. Fernandes, F. O'Connor, E. Romanos and M. Vogiatzoglou (eds) *Late Neoliberalism and its Discontents in the Economic Crisis*, Cham: Palgrave Macmillan, pp 169–200.

Hall, P. (2018) Varieties of capitalism in light of the euro crisis, *Journal of European Public Policy*, 25(1): 7–30.

Hall, P. and Soskice, D. (2001) An introduction to varieties of capitalism, in P. Hall and D. Soskice (eds) *Varieties of Capitalism: The Institutional Foundations of Comparative Advantage*, Oxford: Oxford University Press, pp 1–68.

Hemerijck, A. (2013) *Changing Welfare States*, Oxford: Oxford University Press.

Hemerijck, A. (2018) Social investment as a policy paradigm, *Journal of European Public Policy*, 25(6): 810–27.

Hespanha, P. and Caleiras, J. (2017) O labirinto das políticas de emprego, in M. Silva, P. Hespanha and J.C. Caldas (eds) *Trabalho e Políticas de Emprego: Um retrocesso Evitável*, Coimbra: Atual, pp 121–95.

Homs, O. (2009) *Vocational Training in Spain: Towards the Knowledge Society*, Barcelona: La Caixa Foundation.

Icart, I. and Rodríguez-Soler, J. (2017) The VET system and industrial SMEs: the role of employees with VET qualifications in innovation processes, *Journal of Vocational Education & Training*, 69(4): 596–616.

ILO (International Labour Office) (2018) *Decent Work in Portugal 2008–18: From Crisis to Recovery*, Geneva: ILO.

INE (2018) INE – Estatísticas Anuais da Emigração, https://www.pordata.pt/Portugal/Emigrantes+permanentes+total+e+por+grupo+et%c3%a1rio-2522

Keynes, J.M. (1936 [1973]) *The General Theory of Employment, Interest and Money*, London: Macmillan for the Royal Economic Society.

Lima, M. (2019) Portugal: reforms and the turn to neoliberal austerity, in T. Muller, K. Vandaele and J. Waddington (eds) *Collective Bargaining in Europe: Towards an Endgame*, Vol 3, Brussels: ETUI Printshop.

Lima, M. and Naumann, R. (2011) Portugal: from broad strategic pacts to policy-specific agreements, in S. Avdagic, M. Rhodes and J. Visser (eds) *Social Pacts in Europe: Emergence, Evolution, and Institutionalisation*, Oxford: Oxford University Press, pp 148–73.

Marques, P. and Hörisch, F. (2019) Promoting workplace-based training to fight youth unemployment in three EU countries: different strategies, different results? *International Journal of Social Welfare*, 28(4): 380–93.

Marques, P. and Hörisch, F. (2020) Understanding massive youth unemployment during the EU sovereign debt crisis: a configurational study, *Comparative European Politics*, 18(2): 233–55.

Marques, P. and Salavisa, I. (2017) Young people and dualization in Europe: a fuzzy set analysis, *Socio-Economic Review*, 15(1): 135–60.

Midgley, J., Dahl, E. and Wright, A.C. (2017) *Social Investment and Social Welfare: International and Critical Perspectives*, Cheltenham: Edward Elgar.

Molina, Ó. and Rhodes, M. (2007) The political economy of adjustment in mixed market economies: a study of Spain and Italy, in B. Hancké, M. Rhodes and M. Thatcher (eds) *Beyond Varieties of Capitalism: Conflict, Contradictions, and Complementarities in the European Economy*, Oxford: Oxford University Press, pp 223–52.

Morel, N., Palier, B. and Palme, J. (eds) (2012) *Towards a Social Investment Welfare State: Ideas, Policies and Challenges*, Bristol: Policy Press.

Nunes, A. (2007) *Microeconomic Studies on Programme Causal Effects: Empirical Evidence from Portuguese Active Labour Market Policy*, PhD Thesis, University of Coimbra.

OECD (2013) Indicators of Employment Protection, http://www.oecd.org/els/emp/oecdindicatorsofemploymentprotection.htm

OECD (2017a) Skills for Jobs Database, https://stats.oecd.org/index.aspx?datasetcode=mismatch#

OECD (2017b) *Labour Market Reforms in Portugal 2011–2015: A Preliminary Assessment*, Paris: OECD.

Reis, J. (2018) *A Economia Portuguesa: Formas de Economia Política Numa Periferia Persistente (1960–2017)*, Coimbra: Almedina.

Rodrigues, J. and Reis, J. (2012) The asymmetries of European integration and the crisis of capitalism in Portugal, *Competition and Change*, 16(3): 188–205.

Rodrigues, M.J. (ed) (2002) *The New Knowledge Economy in Europe: A Strategy for International Competitiveness and Social Cohesion*, Cheltenham: Edward Elgar.

Romanos, E. (2017) Late neoliberalism and its indignados: contention in austerity Spain, in D. Della Porta, M. Andretta, F. Fernandes, F. O'Connor, E. Romanos and M. Vogiatzoglou (eds) *Late Neoliberalism and Its Discontents in the Economic Crisis*, Cham: Palgrave Macmillan, pp 131–67.

Salavisa, I. (2006) The State at the crossroads: from welfare to the knowledge-based society, in W. Dolfsma and L. Soete (eds) *Understanding the Dynamics of a Knowledge Economy*, Cheltenham: Edward Elgar, pp 182–99.

Schumpeter, J. (1912, 1983) *The Theory of Economic Development: An Inquiry into Profits, Capital, Credit, Interest, and the Business Cycle*, New Brunswick: Transaction Publishers.

Silva, M., Martins, L. and Lopes, H. (2018) Asymmetric labor market reforms: effects on wage growth and conversion probability of fixed-term contracts, *Industrial and Labor Relations Review*, 71(3): 760–88.

Soskice, D. (1999) Divergent production regimes: coordinated and uncoordinated market economies in the 1980s and 1990s, in H. Kitschelt, P. Lange, G. Marks and J. Stephens (eds) *Continuity and Change in Contemporary Capitalism*, Cambridge: Cambridge University Press, pp 101–34.

Souto-Otero, M. and Ure, O.B. (2012) The coherence of vocational education and training in Norway and Spain: national traditions and the reshaping of VET governance in hybrid VET systems, *Compare: A Journal of Comparative and International Education*, 42(1): 81–111.

Thelen, K. (2004) *How Institutions Evolve: The Political Economy of Skills in Germany, Britain, the United States, and Japan*, Cambridge: Cambridge University Press.

Theodoropoulou, S. (2015) National social and labour market policy reforms in the shadow of EU bail-out conditionality: the cases of Greece and Portugal, *Comparative European Politics*, 13(1): 29–55.

Tosun, J. (2017) Promoting youth employment through multi-organizational governance, *Public Money & Management*, 37(1): 39–46.

Tosun, J., Unt, M. and Wadensjo, E. (2017) Youth-oriented active labour market policies: explaining policy effort in the Nordic and the Baltic States, *Social Policy & Administration*, 51(4): 598–616.

Venn, D. (2009) *Legislation, Collective Bargaining and Enforcement: Updating the OECD Employment Protection Indicators*, OECD Social, Employment and Migration Working Papers 89, Paris: OECD.

Vooren, M., Haelermans, C., Groot, W. and van den Brink, H.M. (2018) The effects of active labour market policies: a meta-analysis, *Journal of Economic Surveys*, 33(1): 125–49.

World Bank (2018) World Development Indicators, https://data.worldbank.org/indicator/tx.val.tech.mf.zs?view=chart

7

Adaptability of the
German Vocational Model
to Mediterranean Countries

Jale Tosun, Julia Weiß, Alexa Meyer-Hamme and
Marcel Katzlinger

Introduction

Youth unemployment is a major source of concern in Europe. There are two reasons why the levels of youth unemployment continue to be high in certain European Union (EU) member states. First, young people have greater difficulties in finding a job than adults. In many instances, young people's skills and competences are critically assessed, and young job-seekers have to compete with adults who are already part of the labor market. Second, in recent years, European firms have reported skills mismatches among young job-seekers, making it difficult for them to hire adequately skilled staff. Therefore, youth unemployment can be regarded as a consequence of poor vocational education and training (VET) policies that result in inadequate skills, skills shortages and skills mismatches (Majumdar, 2017). If they lack the necessary skills, youths and adults alike will be confronted with difficulties in finding decent work and they are less likely to become entrepreneurs, even though entrepreneurship stimulates innovation and economic growth.

Scholars have identified such deficiencies in the VET systems of some EU member states, whereas others they regard as role models. The German VET system has been heralded as particularly successful for integrating young people into the labor market (Shore and Tosun, 2019a, 2019b). The main characteristic of this 'dual system' is its structure, as the skill formation takes place over a training period of two to three-and-a-half years through the regulated cooperation of vocational schools, on the one hand, and companies, on the other. Trainees in this system spend part of the week at the vocational school and the other part at the company, where they are involved in regular working activities. The main benefit for apprentices is that they receive work-based training that improves their chances in the labor market. Given the empirically manifest success of the German model, several countries have attempted to adopt it or at least parts of it (Marques and Hörisch, 2019).

However, the German VET system is embedded in a complex organizational structure and has matured over several decades since the adoption of the Vocational Training Act of 1969. It is based on the collaboration of the federal government, the states, private companies, and certification bodies such as the chamber of industry (Bonoli and Wilson, 2019). Employer organizations and trade unions are the drivers when it comes to updating and creating new training regulations and occupational profiles or modernizing further training regulations. In this way, the VET system has the flexibility to depart from traditional skills and adapt training practices to modern processes and technologies. In other words, skill formation corresponds to a network approach where the entirety of different bodies plays an important role (Trein and Tosun, 2019). In addition to the organizational networks involved in VET, the system is highly formalized and standardized, which ensures that all apprentices receive the same training, regardless of region and company.

While Germany has been regarded as a model country concerning its VET regime, scholars have associated the EU member states in the South of Europe with deficient regimes (Berlingieri et al, 2014). An important indicator for this assessment is the youth unemployment rate, which traditionally has been high in these countries, corresponding to double or triple the rate of general unemployment. The financial crisis of 2007–2008, and the subsequent sovereign debt crisis, have exacerbated the situation of young people across Europe (see, for example Lahusen et al, 2013; Tosun, 2017; Tosun et al, 2017). This induced the Council of the EU in June 2013 to adopt the Youth Guarantee, which marks a major milestone in the EU's political commitment to support young people in overcoming the obstacles they are confronted with on their journey from education to employment (De la Porte and Heins, 2015). The Youth Guarantee calls on the member states to adopt measures which ensure that young people receive a 'good quality' offer for a job, an apprenticeship, a traineeship, or continued education within four months of them leaving education or becoming unemployed (Chabanet, 2014; Tosun, 2017; Tosun et al, 2017).

The adoption of the Youth Guarantee represents one reason why the German model has recently received even more attention from both policy makers and firms. For example, the German government – together with other countries that have a dual VET system in place, such as Austria – launched an online 'Apprenticeship Toolbox' to provide support to decision makers throughout Europe who want to implement the key principles of dual apprenticeship schemes. Furthermore, the German government has been cooperating with the governments of Greece, Italy, Latvia, Portugal and Slovakia to develop high quality VET there.[1] German firms have launched projects or programs to transfer the German VET system to the countries in which they are operating.

In this contribution, we concentrate on German multinational companies and their subsidiaries abroad, and examine to what extent they strive to realize the German VET model or have to adjust to local factors in the host countries (see, for example, Pilz, 2019). We argue that the German VET model can be transferred to other countries if the local factors are favorable. To probe the plausibility of our argument, we present data for the subsidiaries of German multinational companies based in Spain and Italy – two countries that have experienced particularly high levels of youth unemployment (see, for example, Tosun, 2017; Marques and Hörisch, 2019; Trein and Tosun, 2019). We consider our findings important for guiding future policy action since, as we will demonstrate, even if German firms operating abroad are willing to transfer VET systems, the endeavor can be hampered by several factors.

In the remainder of this chapter we proceed as follows: (1) we provide background information on the VET systems in place in Spain and Italy; (2) we introduce the concept of Varieties of Capitalism and explain how it relates to VET systems; (3) we turn to the concepts of policy transfer and standardization models in order to identify the determinants for a successful transfer of VET systems; and (4) we illustrate the strategies of German companies that are based in Spain and Italy. In a last step, we summarize and discuss the insights offered here, before providing some concluding remarks and avenues for future research.

Background information on the Spanish and the Italian vocational education and training regimes

Youth unemployment has been a challenge to policy makers in Italy and Spain. Figure 7.1 reports the youth unemployment rates for these two countries and how they have developed between 1995 and 2019; it also presents the youth unemployment rates for Germany for the same period in order to provide a benchmark for comparison. The figure demonstrates that youth unemployment has always been higher in Italy and Spain during the observation period, although the unemployment rates approximated Germany's in 2005, as youth unemployment rose in the latter while declining in Spain and Italy. However, after 2005, the curves for Italy and Spain have increased sharply, whereas youth unemployment in Germany has gone down. In 2018, the youth unemployment levels in Italy and Spain declined sharply, at least in comparison to the levels in 2013 and 2014, though they still corresponded to three times the level of youth unemployment in Germany in the same year. One explanation for this finding is that both countries have under–institutionalized school-to-work transition regimes. The regimes in place are school-oriented, but they lack the necessary structure for guiding the transition process (see Gonon, 2017). Therefore, the performances of Spain and Italy with regard to youth unemployment can be attributed not only to the performance

Figure 7.1: Youth unemployment rates as a percentage of the active population aged 15–24 (1995–2018)

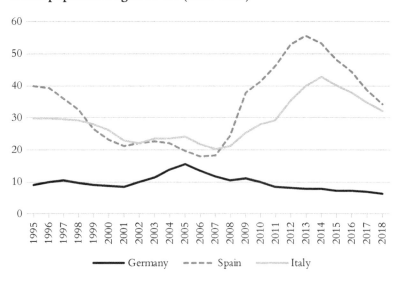

of the economy but also to the pertinent policy and institutional arrangements in place.

The sharp increase in youth unemployment induced the Spanish government to implement a set of policy measures, one of which aimed to facilitate dual vocational education and training (DVET). In fact, it was not only Spain that began to promote DVET in the last years. Between 2010 and 2018, DVET systems were introduced into a number of EU member states in which apprenticeships did not exist previously, including Spain and Italy (see Šćepanović and Martin-Artiles, 2020).

The Royal Decree 1529/2012 adopted in 2012 (BOE, 2012) represents the first policy framework for the country's implementation of DVET. Within the legal framework established by the Royal Decree, the educational authorities of the 17 regional governments are given the responsibility to develop and implement DVET measures in their respective territories.

The Royal Decree sets out the general legal framework only. However, since it does not define minimum quality standards, each region can implement the DVET system according to its respective preferences. For instance, in some regions, apprentices receive a regular employee contract, including the payment of a salary and social security contributions. In other regions, the firms training apprentices are not obliged to remunerate them at all. Another source of cross-regional variation refers to the time the apprentices spend working in the firms and studying in the vocational schools. The Royal Decree only sets out that apprentices shall spend 33% of their time in the firms, which leaves considerable leeway in the organization of the apprenticeship. Consequently, in some regions, the apprentices shift between firm and vocational school on a daily or weekly basis, whereas in others they spend up to one year in the vocational school and afterwards a whole year in the firm. As a result, there is considerable variation across the apprenticeships and in the skill sets apprentices acquire.

Apart from the lack of a quality framework, DVET in Spain currently faces three major challenges. First, DVET is not established, and many parents, students, teachers, and firms have not heard of it. Therefore, they have no or little interest in obtaining skills by means of DVET. Consequently, DVET needs to be promoted in order to attract more demand.

Second, DVET is based on sharing responsibility for the education and training of the apprentices. This requires a new training culture in companies as well as new forms of cooperation between firms, schools and the public administration. Traditionally, Spanish companies do not consider themselves as educating institutions, and schools and companies are not accustomed to working hand in hand. Hence, a paradigm shift is needed on the part of all actors involved.

Third, implementing a DVET project is especially challenging for small and medium enterprises (SMEs), since they lack the necessary resources to provide training and to release a tutor internally. SMEs, however, dominate the landscape of Spanish companies: Of the over 3.3 million companies currently registered in Spain, 99% are SMEs (with between 0 and 249 employees). Within this group, micro companies with up to 9 employees make up 93% (Dirección General de Industria y de la Pequeña y Mediana Empresa, 2018).

Regarding participation rates of students in DVET, there has been a constant increase in recent years. In the academic year 2017–2018, around 27,000 students were enrolled in dual VET programs in Spain. Compared to the overall number of students participating in the traditional school-based VET system in Spain, which was around 800,000 in 2017–2018 (Ministerio de Educación, 2019), the participation rate in DVET remains small, though it has been constantly increasing in recent years. Despite the strengths of the DVET programs and the favorable employment rate of VET graduates, Spanish youth still tend to see VET as a second-class education. At the same time, policy makers are putting a strong focus on expanding DVET.

In Italy, the Legislative Decree 81/2015 adopted in 2015 established three types of apprenticeship schemes. The first type is 'apprenticeship for vocational qualifications and diplomas, upper secondary education diplomas and high technical specialization certificates'. The duration of the contract varies between a minimum of six months and the maximum duration of the VET program it applies to. The distribution of time between training in the vocational school and the company varies between 50% and 70%. The second type is the 'occupation-oriented apprenticeship', which is a scheme outside the VET system and leads to an occupational qualification recognized by the national sectoral collective agreement. The minimum duration of the contract is six months and the maximum three years (or five years for artisanal jobs), of which out-of-company training covers a maximum 120 hours in total. The third type consists of 'apprenticeship for higher education and training', which leads to university degrees and higher technical institute diplomas, and 'apprenticeship for research activities', which leads to a contractual qualification outside the education and training systems. The latter does not require out-of-company training (Cedefop, 2017).

The challenge Italian policy makers face is that the first type of apprenticeship, which corresponds to a quality apprenticeship as defined by the EU Youth Guarantee (see Tosun, 2017), never took off – despite being around since 2003. The 2015 reform of this apprenticeship type aimed to introduce a DVET (Šćepanović and Artiles, 2020). The revised system 'foresees a relevant component of formal training at school or training centre, which systematically alternates with in-company formal training, and a work component at the workplace' (Cedefop 2017: 16). The development of the DVET is financially supported through European structural and investment funds, as well through Erasmus Plus and Youth Guarantee schemes (Šćepanović and Artiles, 2020). Despite the financial support from the EU and the supply of knowledge offered by EU member states that have had DVET in place for a long time, the Italian system suffers from flaws.

As Cedefop (2017) contends, the system is affected by a lack of coordination between the pertinent bodies at the national and regional levels, resulting in poor governance arrangements. The need to offer apprenticeships with open-ended employment contracts leads to uncertainties among employers, since apprentices have a double status as students and full-time employees. Moreover, there is a lack of clarity concerning formal training in the company. Lastly, no unified definition of quality standards exists for both in-company and out-of-company training.

Figure 7.2 provides further insights into the challenges of introducing DVET in Italy and Spain. The data originating from the CUPESSE project are depicted by means of box plots for the 11 countries covered in the corresponding dataset (see Tosun et al, 2019). Box plots are a method for visualizing groups of data through their quartiles. The lines extending from the boxes indicate variability outside the upper and lower quartiles. Individual points are used for outliers. The box plots show the levels of (dis)agreement of young people aged 18–35 with the statement: 'Young people's skills do not match with what employers are looking for'. Interestingly, the median in Germany corresponds to the value 3, which indicates that the respondents somewhat agree with this statement. In Italy, the median value is also 3, but the distribution of the responses is different for Germany as we can infer from this box plot that there is also some disagreement with the statement (value 2). Put differently, the German respondents are more aware of the link between employment and skills. Turning to Spain, the median value is 2, and the distribution of the respondents' answers indicates that there is less awareness of skills mismatch as a reason for youth unemployment. The distribution of the values for this question for the Spanish respondents corresponds to those based in Greece, which represents another EU member state with a high level of youth unemployment.

Figure 7.2: Response patterns to the question of whether skills mismatch is a driver of youth unemployment (2016)

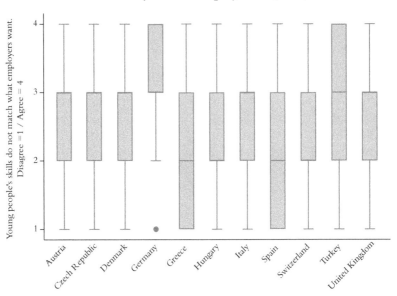

While DVET regimes have been introduced in Spain and Italy, subsidiaries of German multinational companies cannot assume that they will benefit from a situation similar to that of Germany. We therefore expect German companies operating in these two countries to attempt to establish their own DVET systems, which facilitate the recruitment of a workforce with an adequate skill set despite the costs that the endeavors entail (Mühlemann et al, 2018).

Over the last few decades, Germany has been a major source of Foreign Direct Investment (FDI) in Italy and Spain. More generally, Germany is one of the major sources of outward FDI, together with Japan and the US (OECD, 2019). As Figure 7.3 shows, the German outward FDI stock increased up until 2009.[2] As we have seen in Figure 7.1, youth unemployment increased in Italy and Spain in 2005. Therefore, subsidiaries of German multinational companies are likely to have absorbed a good share of the youth workforce available at that time in the two countries. Over this period, Italy and Spain belonged to the group of European countries that received the second-highest outward FDI from Germany (see Camarero et al, 2019). It should be noted that the EU is the single largest destination for German outward FDI (OECD, 2019). In this context, Antonakakis and Tondl (2015), for example, report that German multinational companies are

Figure 7.3: German Foreign Direct Investment stock abroad (in millions of US dollars) (2001–2011)

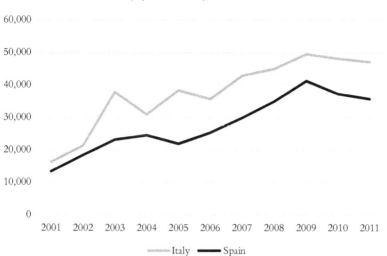

attracted by advanced markets that are characterized by high wages and productivity, which, in turn, are associated with a workforce that possesses a certain skill level. Kottaridi et al (2019: 386) find that a 'better educated workforce in vocational courses can create a more attractive investment climate', and refer to VET as a factor that enables domestic companies to 'reap the benefits of technological spillovers from foreign activities'. Therefore, a clear relationship exists between VET systems and a country's attractiveness as a destination for FDI.

To summarize, in this section we showed that Italy and Spain have experienced difficulties in integrating young people into their labor markets. The respective national governments have taken measures for improving youth employment. In this context, both countries have strengthened the dual component of their VET systems. However, initial assessments show that these are still characterized by flaws (see, for example, Berlingieri et al, 2014; Cedefop, 2014; 2017; Mühlemann et al, 2018; Marhuenda-Fluixá et al, 2019), which induces us to expect foreign firms to invest in setting up their own DVET systems.

Varieties of capitalism and the characteristics of vocational training systems

The Varieties of Capitalism (VoC) approach offers a framework, which helps to understand institutional differences as well as similarities among developed economies.[3] It is an actor-centered approach; more specifically, the VoC approach sees companies as the crucial actors in the economies (Hall and Soskice, 2001). Companies are perceived to seek 'to develop and exploit core competencies or dynamic capabilities understood as capacities for developing, producing, and distributing goods and service profitably' (Hall and Soskice, 2001: 6). As capabilities are relational, the companies encounter coordination problems. Therefore, the companies' success depends on the ability to coordinate effectively with many actors (Tosun et al, 2019; Trein and Tosun, 2019; Hörisch et al, 2020).

The VoC approach identifies five areas within which companies must develop relationships to solve the coordination problem inherent in economic activities:

- industrial relations
- VET
- corporate governance
- inter-firm relations
- employees

Based on these five areas, two ideal types of economies exist: liberal market economies (LMEs) and coordinated market economies (CMEs). In LMEs, 'firms coordinate their activities primarily via hierarchies and competitive market arrangements', whereas in CMEs 'firms depend more heavily on non-market relationships to coordinate their endeavors with other actors and to construct their core competencies' (Hall and Soskice, 2001: 8). These different forms of coordination lead to one institution supporting the functioning or efficiency of another. Put differently, coordination results in institutional interdependencies.

Whether or not it is advantageous to have a state that engages in coordination depends on the forms of innovation in which the companies specialize. They can specialize either in incremental innovations or radical innovations. The former concerns the gradual improvement of a product, while the latter centers on placing new products on the market. By specializing in certain innovation forms, the states will benefit from a comparative advantage. What is important to note is that the reasoning of VoC refers to the firm-level, but the empirical testing takes place at the macrolevel, which suggests that there are no differences across firms within countries. However, that is not correct since, according to VoC, what is important is the skill profile of a firm's workforce (Hermann and Peine, 2011). Thus, when the national VET regime is likely to have an impact on the skill profile of firms, we can still expect variation across companies or sectors within states. Furthermore, recent research in business studies has shown that both incremental and radical innovation performance are required in order to generate economic rents and to ensure a firm's survival (see, for example, Forés and Camisón, 2016). Therefore, a balance between the two forms of innovation is required, which suggests that there is even variation over time within the same company.

Going back to the original VoC approach, Hall and Soskice (2001) contend that consistently coordinated or consistently liberal forms of capitalism are successful. Conversely, they posit that mixed forms are less successful. A state can be described as a mixed-market economy (MME) within the VoC approach if it cannot be clearly assigned to either of the two categories of theory (Hall and Gingerich, 2004: 35). For example, the term 'mixed' describes the situation in which market-based coordination takes place, while the state nevertheless intervenes in various areas by means of regulation (Molina and Rhodes, 2007: 229).

Spain can be described as an MME for the following reasons: First, the country is divided into several regions with different production systems. Moreover, it was a dictatorship until 1978, within which no unions or employers' organizations were allowed. As a result, companies have never been able to practice the usual forms of cooperation for CMEs (Molina and Rhodes, 2007: 237). The result of this became apparent after the industrial crisis in the early 1980s as 'state retrenchment after the mid-1980s left a vacuum filled in many instances by liberalization and an extension of market principles' (Molina and Rhodes, 2007: 238). Thus, the influence of foreign capital increased as companies – due to the relatively well-developed infrastructure, low labor costs and Spain's entry into the EU – relocated their labor-intensive departments to Spain.

Overall, the situation in Spain continues to be marked by a policy mix that favors companies. This came about for two reasons. First, small and medium-sized companies and large companies formed a coalition against the workers' movement (Molina and Rhodes, 2007: 240). Thereby the latter lost more and more influence. In addition, large industrial and service companies entered into a coalition with the largest banks and the financial sector, accelerating the liberalization, privatization and deregulation of the labor market. As a result, hardly any elements of a CME can be found. Occasionally, there are sectoral reconcilements between unions and employers, but Spanish companies hardly have to coordinate with their workforce.

Spain's economy is therefore at best weakly coordinated and, above all, characterized by regionally different regulations. Interestingly, this finding also holds true when investigating the way in which the EU Youth Guarantee is implemented in Spain: the Ministry of Labor plays the central role in the implementation regime, but it is not embedded in a broader implementation network. This contradicts the regulations of the EU Youth Guarantee, since the formation of a network is one of the formal requirements formulated by the EU Commission concerning the implementation of this particular measure (Tosun, 2017; Trein and Tosun, 2019).

Italy, like Spain, is an MME. The country is divided by language, ethnicity and region. It is difficult to speak of one economic system as it 'is not characterized by a coherent and integrated set of national institutions' (Trigilia and Burroni, 2009: 633). Hence, the state also lacks the complementarities of the different economic systems proposed by the VoC approach. Even the great reforms that have taken place in various areas (for example, labor market, financial market and credit system, corporate governance and training, and university systems) since the 1990s have not changed this (Trigilia and Burroni, 2009). Furthermore, the Italian economy has not shifted towards one of the two ideal-types of capitalism (Rangone and Solari, 2012). For being considered a CME, the country lacks strong corporate participation and coordinated wage bargaining, as well as stronger business and banking cooperation (Schröder, 2014). It is not a liberal country, either: since capital market financing does not play a significant role, companies do not have to meet strict requirements with regard to their shareholders and the market is hardly developed for corporate management (Schröder, 2014). Instead, Italy is characterized by regional fragmentation, with the result that regional economies exist with respective governance, as well as, for example, different associations that barely cooperate. Or, as Trigilia and Burroni (2009: 634) put it: 'the Italian model as regionalized capitalism is related to the strong and persistent territorial differences in terms of the organizational architecture of firms'.

With the implementation of the EU's Youth Guarantee, the fragmentation of the Italian political economy became apparent. The program was not warmly received by young job-seekers for various reasons, including a lack of coordination between educational institutions and employers. Furthermore, the different regions in Italy did not use the EU funds for the Youth Guarantee in a uniform way. For example, some regions spent money on launching apprenticeships, whereas others have refused to do so (Manuti et al, 2015). The parallels between the political economy and the implementation of the Youth Guarantee are not surprising, since the VoC posits a close relationship between the institutional characteristics of capitalist systems and the design of their education policies.

From the perspective of the VoC approach, it is crucial that the training within the educational system fits with the demands made by the companies. Here, 'the VoC approach makes a sharp distinction between general skills systems, focusing on academic higher education on the one hand, and specific skills systems for which the provision of vocational skills is more important on the other' (Busemeyer, 2016: 69). This can be attributed to the aspect of institutional complementarities. Thus, the two types of market economies are characterized by different education systems as they make different demands for specific qualifications.

The training within CMEs tends to convey industry-specific skills that encourage employees to stay in a company for a long time. One of the countries with a typical coordinated training system is Germany. Here, the so-called 'collective skill formation system' (Busemeyer and Trampusch, 2012) exists, in which state, unions and business associations regulate the training together. For the purpose of the institutional complementarities, CMEs must then support this training system. Companies train their employees and become dependent on them, relying on their specific skills, and it would incur high costs to lose these employees. In order to maintain the system, institutionalized participation rights are important for employees. In addition, the existence of industry-negotiated wages means that there is no financial incentive to change employers. Finally, the relatively inflexible labor market makes it more appealing for the companies to train their employees themselves. The trainee does not have to finance his/her own training in these collective skill formation systems. Instead, the companies finance the practical part, while the state finances the school-based part. Workers only have to accept comparatively low wages during their training (Busemeyer and Trampusch, 2012). In general, however, such a training system is only possible if the other aspects of the economy are coordinated, so that workers and employers can learn to work together (Schröder, 2014).

By contrast, LMEs tend to produce general qualifications that are learned at school or university rather than in companies, allowing the workers to move jobs quickly on the flexible labor market (Busemeyer and Vossiek, 2016). This results from the fact that LMEs are characterized by radical and CMEs by incremental innovations, for which they demand the appropriate qualifications in the labor market. In LMEs, the problem that everybody needs skilled workers, but no one wants to pay for their education, is not solved in the companies.

Employees who would have completed vocational training when living in a CME often end up without training when living in an LME. For this reason, they often end up in the low-wage sector (Thelen, 2008). Other workers within LMEs receive training through schools and universities and thus learn skills that are more general. The costs of the educational system within LMEs is usually financed by the state, but by paying high tuition fees, the students also have to pay for a large part of the training system. This training system then complements the rest of the economy, where there is a flexible labor market that facilitates the transition between companies and where high qualifications often involve high wages (Schröder, 2014).

In Europe, two main VET designs have emerged. CMEs, like Germany and Austria, emphasize VET programs at the secondary level as they seek to prepare young people for skilled working positions in industry and services. In LMEs, such as the United Kingdom, the expansion of tertiary education has occurred largely through the privatization and marketization of education, including through VET, with a view to enabling access on a mass scale. Central and Eastern European countries, which have only developed market economies after 1990, have both designs in place – either in the form of secondary or tertiary VET, depending on whether they correspond to a CME or an LME (Kottaridi et al, 2019: 376). Turning to the South of Europe, VET systems are often considered under-developed (see, for example, Karamessini, 2008).

A glance at Spain reveals that it is more of a technologically underdeveloped country (Schröder, 2014). As a result, no radical innovations are generated, and therefore the demand for broad and higher qualifications are lower. Instead, in comparison to other EU/OECD states, Spain can be positioned in the midfield when it comes to manufacturing, machinery and equipment, and electric machinery manufacturing, and thus has a demand for specifically trained, middle-educated workers. Indeed, Spain is characterized by a high degree of skills mismatches and labor market demands, and is one of the EU/OECD countries with the highest prevalence of this problem (Dolado et al, 2013: 26). Many of the overqualified have acquired a tertiary degree and work in professions designed for graduates of higher secondary education (Dolado et al, 2013: 26).

Overall, Spain is the OECD country with the highest proportion of both overqualified and underqualified workers, who account for a total of 30% of all Spanish workers (Dolado et al, 2013: 28). A big problem, therefore, is the interplay of training and the demands made by companies, as Royo (2008: 80) describes: 'the variety of congruence between what university students learn in college versus what the laboratory market needs'.

The situation in Italy is characterized by strong fragmentation, which results in a mixed system. This is also evident for the country's VET system, which can be categorized as closer to the systems of CMEs, though it is not as coordinated, for example, as Germany's (Trigilia and Burroni, 2009). This is also due to the economic sectors, which is why 'in Italy, firm-level vocational training is not widespread since it is used only in crafts, retail, and large manufacturing companies, and is based on fixed-term employment contracts' (Eichhorst et al, 2015: 317). Here, too, a mismatch can be found between the supply of employees with suitable skills and the demand from the labor market. In Italy, this mismatch is especially 'characterized by the paradox of recurrent claims of insufficient graduates and the parallel talent drain of young professionals to foreign countries' (Cainarca and Sgobbi, 2012).

To summarize, the VoC represents a parsimonious approach that sets out how institutions governing the exchange between companies and their national labor markets, financial markets, and research and development collaborations lead to different models of capitalism. The different models translate into different types of innovations. To ensure that the economy can function as it should, national governments adapt their VET arrangements to the type of capitalism in place in the country. In CMEs, companies are more willing to invest in the skills of the workforce, whereas in LMEs companies are less willing to do so. This reasoning is plausible for the companies located in each of these types since their way of producing and inventing differs starkly from each other. CMEs give priority to long-term investment and benefits, whereas LMEs concentrate on short-term benefits. The types of capitalism and the corresponding VET systems are considered stable because of the complementarities of their underpinning institutions (Dilli et al, 2018). In Italy and Spain, the models of capitalism are not fully developed and likewise the VET institutions and systems remain underdeveloped. This situation is challenging to German companies investing in these two countries as it forces them to invest in the skill formation of their workforce themselves.

German companies as transfer agents?
Theoretical considerations

The VoC approach is useful for explaining persistent differences in the countries' VET schemes. However, it has been criticized for exactly this, that is, for providing a static and country-centered explanation (for a discussion, see, for example, Drahokoupil and Myant, 2015). We do not wish to engage with the criticism of VoC, though we would like to stress that this approach does not recognize the impact of Europeanization and globalization. More precisely, we contend that VET systems can change over time and that multinational companies represent one factor driving these changes, as they export their respective procedures and can also strive to bring about policy change at different levels of government by, for example, lobbying the national governments of their host countries. Literature strands unrelated to VoC have already discussed the patterns and causes of policy change.

The past three decades have seen a wealth of studies concentrating on how and why policies and institutions 'travel' across countries. This perspective has been predominantly examined by two strands of literature: research on policy diffusion and policy transfer (Stone, 2012). Diffusion studies investigate the spread of policies across and within political systems by stressing the importance of 'diffusion mechanisms' such as learning and emulation (Maggetti and Gilardi, 2016). This literature is characterized by large-n studies that cover long periods and test different diffusion mechanisms, together with a set of domestic-level factors such as regime type or income levels. A frequent research subject of diffusion studies has been (higher) education policies (see, for example, Christ and Dobbins, 2016), which is plausible given the important role of the OECD in defining pertinent policy benchmarks. The OECD publishes country reports that identify the strengths and weaknesses of the individual countries as well as best-practice cases. The publication of this information induces countries to reconsider their policy approach and to consider changes to it. For example, in 2015, the OECD released a publication entitled 'The Missing Entrepreneurs 2015: Policies for Self-employment and Entrepreneurship', which explicitly identified countries with effective policies in place for stimulating entrepreneurship. Comparisons like these induce governments to look abroad to find policies that could be worth adopting.

Transfer studies concentrate on the 'processes by which knowledge about policies, administrative arrangements, institutions and ideas in one political system (past or present) is used in the development of policies, administrative arrangements, institutions and ideas in another political system' (Dolowitz and Marsh, 2000: 5). The main difference vis-à-vis diffusion studies is a methodological one: transfer research tends to conduct in-depth analyses of few cases and to provide a 'thick description' of these. Much like policy diffusion, the concept of policy transfer is also interested in mechanisms that remain implicit, since the main analytical interest of this literature to identify different forms of policy transfer. According to Dolowitz and Marsh (2000), these include:

- copying (direct and complete transfer)
- emulation (transfer of the ideas behind the program)
- combinations (mixture of different policies)
- inspiration (final policy does not draw upon the original)

Both transfer and diffusion can result in an empirical phenomenon known as 'policy convergence'. Knill (2005: 768) defines policy convergence as: 'any increase in the similarity between one or more characteristics of a certain policy (for example, policy objectives, policy instruments, policy settings) across a given set of political jurisdictions (supra-national institutions, states, regions, local authorities) over a given period of time.'

The concept of policy convergence resembles that of 'institutional isomorphism', which is defined as a process of homogenization that 'forces one unit in a population to resemble other units that face the same set of environmental conditions' (DiMaggio and Powell, 1991: 66). In the EU, for example, we can observe that there has been a growing similarity of VET policies over time, which is due to direct EU effects, such as policies and funding, as well as to indirect EU effects, such as policy learning in the context of the Open Method of Coordination.[4]

Going back to policy transfer research, Stone (2004) proposed the concept of 'transfer agents' to explain why and how governments learn from abroad. Transfer agents are actors that promote the adoption of policies or institutions in a place elsewhere. They can be international organizations, such as the OECD, but also multinational companies that operate in different countries or transnational non-governmental organizations, such as foundations. Stone emphasizes the importance of these actors for transfer processing, but she does not elaborate on the rationality assumptions or the motivation of these respective transfer agents that push for a transfer of policies and institutions originating from elsewhere.

Here, VoC offers a useful complement since, in the case of VET schemes, we would expect multinational companies to engage in policy transfer in order to increase the supply of workforce that has the 'right' set of skills. More precisely, multinational companies have production processes in place that require the skill sets available in their country of origin. However, when they find subsidiaries abroad, they may not have access to workers who possess the skills needed for the specific production process. Therefore, if VET policies in the countries where multinational companies operate do not produce the necessary skill sets, the companies have to fill in this gap themselves by either transferring the VET systems directly or inducing the governments of the countries concerned to change their VET policies.

This reasoning has been discussed in the management literature on multinational companies under the term 'standardization' or 'integration'(Pudelko and Harzing, 2007). According to these literatures, standardization, or integration, means that the practices of multinational companies resemble those of the parent company. Or, put differently, this perspective posits that global management practices ('best practices') converge, despite differences in the cultural and institutional contexts (Cantwell et al, 2010; Pudelko and Harzing, 2007). Pertinent research has shown that the standardized models of reputable multinational companies have also been adopted by local companies, resulting in a convergence of standards and practices in the respective organizational field (Fortwengel and Jackson, 2016; Stockmann, 1999; Wrana and Revilla Diez, 2016; Wiemann and Fuchs, 2018).

The opposite scenario refers to 'responsiveness' or 'localization', which posits that the subsidiaries of multinational companies act and behave as local companies (Pudelko and Harzing, 2007). In other words, divergence exists across the local-level standards and practices of multinational companies that result from responses to the differing cultural and institutional contexts in which they operate. The degree of acceptable divergence depends on the specific company and can vary across the individual companies. In the specific case of DVET, a subsidiary could deem it too costly to train a new workforce, engage with local governance structures, or promote its standards, if they do not appear to be salient within the respective operation context.

Because of the high level of youth unemployment and the EU's demand to tackle this problem, both Italy and Spain have invested in developing their VET systems. German companies are an important partner in this process since their subsidiaries are of economic relevance to these countries. Do the subsidiaries of German multinational companies promote German-style DVET, or do they adapt to the local models? Existing research has shown that both the standardization and localization of VET systems can be observed (see, for example, Schippers, 2009; Stockmann and Silvestrini, 2013; Pilz and Li, 2014; Wiemann and Fuchs, 2018; Li et al, 2019; Pilz, 2019).

Businesses react to and interact with their organizational environment, which consists of other companies, government agencies, the public, and other stakeholders (Baron, 2013). Businesses often partake in specific forms of cooperation, such as joint ventures, alliance formations or 'strategic business nets' in order to engage with complex organizational environments.[5] Möller et al (2005) differentiate between three forms of strategic business – or value – nets: vertical, horizontal and multidimensional. Horizontal value nets are relevant to the present analysis; they are 'characterized by competitor alliances and cooperative arrangements involving various institutional actors (government agencies, industry associations, research institutes and universities) that aim either to provide access to existing resources or to co-develop new resources' (Möller et al, 2005: 1278). Vertical value nets include 'supplier nets, channel and customer nets and vertically integrated value systems', and multidimensional value nets include 'core or hollow organizations', complex business nets and new value-system nets (Möller et al, 2005: 1277).

Networks form around specific core issues, such as socioeconomic challenges, demands for less restrictive regulations, or demands for a more adaptive education system. All these challenges have in common that they cannot be addressed, without engaging with policy makers and stakeholders. Corporate networks achieve their goals through means of agenda-setting, communication strategies and value change on a local, regional and/or national scale (Möller and Halinen, 2017). They can compensate for information deficits, share the burden of engaging with a new market and institutional framework, and they allow for access to an extended number of capabilities. Joining such a network is therefore an efficient way for a firm to achieve its strategic goals, especially when practicing a convergence strategy.

Therefore, we contend that subsidiaries choose standardization if the networks in which they participate allow for it. This allows them to transfer their practices to other companies or even establish them as local or national policies. If the companies participate in weak networks or are confronted with other barriers, they will choose localization (Möller and Halinen, 2017).

To summarize, we contend that the subsidiaries of multinational companies have a strategic interest in transferring their practices to the differing contexts in which they operate. This reduces the companies' costs (as they do not have to establish new processes) and facilitates a smooth operation irrespective of the country in which they operate. Exporting production processes (in the narrow sense mostly referring to technology) is a comparatively straightforward task.[6] With human capital and VET, the transfer of practices and standards is more challenging since the companies cannot provide the skill formation themselves but rely on partner organizations such as vocational schools.

If they participate in networks that facilitate the transfer, the subsidiaries will choose standardization. Otherwise, they may opt for localization.

Companies' attempts to promote dual vocational education and training

Do the subsidiaries of German multinational companies promote German-style DVET in Italy and Spain? To assess this question, we first provide information on the empirical basis on which we draw, then we discuss the cases of German companies operating in Spain and Italy separately. Finally, we offer a comparative assessment.

Empirical foundation

Our empirical base comprises the Center for European Trainees (CET), which is supported by the Robert Bosch Foundation, the employer organization of Baden-Württemberg and the education academy of Baden-Württemberg's economy. The Robert Bosch Foundation comprises more than 90% of the Robert Bosch GmbH, which is an engineering and technology company with core operating areas in mobility, consumer goods, industrial technology, and energy and building technology. Thus, the company and the foundation collaborate closely. Founded in 2014, the main goal of the CET is to collect and disseminate the experience of companies, chambers of commerce and trade, business associations, and education institutions that attempt to transfer the German DVET to Italy and Spain. We conducted two interviews with the CET in order to learn about the German companies' strategies in Italy and in Spain.

The second organization we approached was the Alianza para la Formación Profesional Dual (AFP), which was founded in 2018 by the Fundación Bertelsmann in Spain. The AFP is also supported by the Princess of Girona Foundation, the Confederation of Employers' Organizations, the Spanish Confederation of Small and Medium-Sized Enterprises, and the Spanish Chamber of Commerce (Bassols and Salvans, 2016).

The AFP aims to mitigate youth unemployment in Spain by pursuing a fourfold strategy: first, communication; second, collaboration; third, training; and fourth, networking. DVET remains relatively unknown in Spain and, among those who have heard of it, its reputation is not very high. More precisely, most people in Spain associate DVET with low salaries and long working hours, making it appear unattractive to young people in the qualification phase.

The AFP strives to improve the image of DVET and to promote it across Spain. To this end, it organizes events and has initiated an information campaign that relies on 'success stories' as former apprentices share their experiences with DVET. Furthermore, the AFP network actively articulates to policy makers at the national and regional levels as well as to other relevant stakeholders, such as unions and chambers of commerce, the kind of VET policy changes that it would like to see implemented in Spain.

The members of the AFP network collaborate by means of ten working groups, each of which is led by one firm that – together with other businesses and organizations – develops specific DVET policies, such as quality standards for tutors, trainings and school curricula. The best possible scenario of this collaborative effort is that the policy output is adopted and implemented by all network members, as well as being exported to other firms by means of a group of advisors. The latter consists of ten individuals who support businesses and organizations starting their first DVET projects. For example, the AFP connects local car dealers to each other in order to establish common training standards and coordinate vacancies. Within the AFP, schools, businesses and other stakeholders learn about DVET through joint workshops. The networking aspect is covered through participation in the working groups as well as through monthly webinars and access to a digital library where businesses can find information on DVET (Interview with Guillem Salvans, AFP, October 31, 2018).

We also carried out an interview with the Spanish subsidiary of Media Markt. Media Markt is a chain of stores that sells consumer electronics and has numerous branches throughout Europe. This company offers a complement to the other branches covered in this analysis by means of the CET and the AFP.

All interviews were semi-structured, with a set of questions reflecting the main concept of interest while leaving room for additional questions and answers that might emerge from the specific conversation situation. We carried out the four interviews remotely in 2018. The transcripts of the interviews are available upon request. We are aware that the empirical basis for this study is limited and therefore we do not intend to provide a hard, empirical test of hypotheses. Instead, we seek to probe the plausibility of our main argument, namely that the question of whether subsidiaries of multinational companies practice standardization and localization depends on the respective national context in which they operate as well as the strategies that they choose. Therefore, the findings must be regarded as indicative and should be subjected to rigorous empirical testing in the future.

Spain: favorable conditions for standardization

The interviews carried out with the representatives of organizations located in Spain showed that youth unemployment, skills mismatches, and the need to change the VET system by adding dual elements, featured highly on the agenda. At the same time, it became apparent that DVET, since it is the standard in Germany, is preferred by the subsidiaries. All interviewees indicated that companies hire staff that had received DVET.

In this context, Monica Mondejar Harrando of Media Markt stated that: "at the end, you have young talents, you include your talents in your structure in your organization and these young people can be surprising talents for us" (Interview with Mónica Mondéjar, Media Markt Spain, September 25, 2018). While German companies wishing to implement DVET face a number of barriers, such as differing legal frameworks across Spain's autonomous regions, they all try to implement their specific system of training, a school-work place relationship and remuneration (Interview with Gabriela Martinez, CET, September 25, 2018). For example, the Robert Bosch GmbH and the Robert Bosch Foundation advocate the idea that "these are not cheap interns but future employees!" (Interview with Gabriela Martinez, CET, September 25, 2018).

German companies have used legal loopholes to implement a country-of-origin strategy concerning DVET to the best possible extent. Several legal requirements exist in Spain that make it difficult for companies to transfer their DVET model to the various sites on which they operate. Some Spanish regions, such as Cataluña and Madrid, mandate by law the remuneration of apprentices for the time they spend at the company, but other regions do not require apprentices to be paid at all, or stipulate that companies only have to provide them with a non-contractual form of remuneration (Interview with Guillem Salvans, AFP, October 31, 2018). Media Markt and Robert Bosch GmbH both support standardized payments across the country and implement this form of payment, even though they are not legally required to do so (Interview with Mónica Mondéjar, Media Markt Spain, September 25, 2018; Interview with Gabriela Martinez, CET, September 25, 2018). Both companies have developed strategies for dealing with the legal barriers; these include, for example, reaching informal agreements with vocational schools.

The interviewees also indicated that several German and some Spanish companies are using horizontal business networks in order to establish a DVET system. German businesses play a major role within the AFP network, since they act as initiators of DVET measures by providing examples of best practices and by acting as role models: "In my region, we have a lot of German companies from the industry, and they always used to be the ones which started the system and the ones we could present" (Interview with Guillem Salvans, AFP, October 31, 2018).

When there was a lack of interest in the training program or an insufficient number of qualified students in Germany, some companies, such as the Robert Bosch GmbH, also recruited apprentices from Spain (and other countries in which they operate), trained them at their facilities in Germany, and then employed them in their facilities abroad after they had received their diploma (Interview with Gabriela Martinez, CET, September 25, 2018; Interview with Jacopo Mancabelli, CET, November 8, 2018). This manner of proceeding reveals how important DVET is to German companies, and that they depend on this particular training method to benefit from the workforce – an observation which aligns with the reasoning of the VoC approach.

The AFP offers specific benefits to individual companies, but it also has the potential to realize the interests of the individual network members at a higher level. As Monica Mondejar Herrando puts it: "If you want to change the content of the curricula, if you want to change the law and the legal frame in general, it's going to be better if we are a kind of the group of companies like within Alianza and then talk to the government" (Interview with Mónica Mondéjar, Media Markt Spain, September 25, 2018).

This quote reveals an important finding: the network structure increases or is perceived to increase the potential of German companies to act as an advocacy group and to bring about changes in (higher) education policy. Therefore, we can infer from the empirical material that the firms prefer a policy solution to the issue of matching the job-seekers' skills with the skill demands of the employers. This is a plausible finding since, with a corresponding public policy, the companies do not have to invest in skill formation; instead, the governments must bear the costs. In other words, articulating interests and calling for the country-wide introduction of DVET is also a function of networks.

For Spanish businesses, or those who have no DVET-related experience, the AFP lowers the potential resource costs and catalyzes the expansion of DVET on a national scale by demanding policy change. The network is therefore an instrument of burden-sharing for an otherwise resource-intensive process of institutional change and for strengthening the advocacy power of companies. In addition, the network approach also prevents the German companies from losing their investment in human capital. If the German companies were the only ones to train their apprentices according to the DVET program, once completing the training the employees would be attractive to other employers and could consider accepting job offers from other (domestic) companies. Therefore, in order to ensure that the investment in human capital pays off and that the employees stay with the company for some time, it is important to involve companies with similar skill requirements in the network. In this way, not only the German companies but many or even all of the companies with similar needs concerning the skill profiles of their employees could bear the cost and enjoy the benefits of DVET, which reduces uncertainty and facilitates business operation and further investment.

However, the interviewees also indicated that the coordination of efforts required for introducing DVET is important (see Trein and Tosun, 2019). If all companies engage in similar but coordinated activities, they will all have to bear higher costs. The subsequent impact on the Spanish VET system might be marginal, since confronting local companies with too many different models can lower their willingness to consider DVET as they would not know which model to adopt.

Italy: the case for localization

When assessing the German companies' strategies concerning the adoption of German-style DVET or the implementation of an adapted approach to vocational training, the governance structure of the Italian VET system is important. Two central-level ministries play a key role in the design of the VET system: The Ministry of Education, University and Research sets the framework for VET in national programs for technical and vocational schools, and the Ministry of Labor and Social Policies sets the overall framework for VET (Savelli, 2014: 324). The regions and autonomous provinces are in charge of planning, organizing and providing VET.

The most important VET programs are higher technical education and training programs and programs at the higher technical institutes (Istituti Tecnici Superiori, ITS). Both programs were reorganized in 2008 by the administration of Romano Prodi, and provide professional specializations at the post-secondary level in order to meet the requirements of the labor market in the public and private sectors. The two main program types are planned and organized by the regions and autonomous provinces in the context of the territorial plans adopted every three years and their provision varies across the regions (Cedefop 2014: 30). ITS are set up as foundations, which include higher secondary education institutions belonging to a technical or vocational association, training providers accredited by the region, enterprises in one of the sectors covered by the ITS, university departments, and local authorities (Cedefop, 2014: 33).

Another factor that complicates the provision of ITS is that at least half of the training in ITS must be delivered by providers from companies. Therefore, companies must invest in ITS, which increases their VET costs. When looking at the enrolment numbers, the system does not perform well. Between 2010 and 2016, 5,702 students completed training and 4,166 of them obtained a diploma (INAPP, 2016). Thus, the return on the investment in terms of trained workforce is relatively low.

The German way of doing things can only be implemented if there is an ITS in close proximity to the German companies' facilities. This regional restriction results in 'islands' of DVET surrounded by a 'sea' of undiversified secondary education. One example of such an island is the Dual Education System Italy (DESI), which is a DVET project run by Lamborghini and Ducati. It should be noted that these two companies are owned by the German car manufacturer Audi. DESI offers 48 students two years of VET in an ITS as well as a job at the facilities of Ducati and Lamborghini. The two companies built new training facilities for this purpose and hired German tutors to teach the apprentices. The project aims to establish DVET locally and to enhance the capacities of Lamborghini and Ducati for providing DVET themselves in the long run.

DVET in Italy is similar to the system in place in Germany since it comprises both on-the-job and classroom training. The apprenticeship contract defines the roles and responsibilities of all parties, as well as the terms and conditions of the apprenticeship and the qualification to be obtained. The training program is an integral part of DVET. However, the training aspect is associated with a complication, as indicated by the interview with the CET: the lack of differentiation between the curricula for different types of secondary education. In other words, the skills that the students receiving secondary education acquire are the same despite the different school types (Interview with Jacopo Mancabelli, CET, November 8, 2018; see also Polesel, 2006). However, DVET is based on the principle of only teaching specific vocational contents, since otherwise the companies' investment in the skill formation would be too high. Furthermore, a non-differential curriculum may hinder the alleviation of the initial problem underlying the companies' drive to establish DVET: the mismatch between skills. Therefore, there are functional and monetary reasons as to why curricula should fit with the specific form of training.

Since the Italian government reformed their VET program, companies willing to offer DVET have been able to benefit from several incentives, such as the reduction in social security contributions (Cedefop, 2014: 35–36). However, due to the structure of Italy's economy, the responsiveness to the introduction of DVET is limited. The CET tried to develop a network committed to the promotion of apprenticeships, but it faced difficulties when trying to expand it: "In Italy we often find small, fragmented businesses. They lack money, time and know-how. In Italy, there aren't that many big businesses like here in Germany" (Interview with Jacopo Mancabelli, CET, November 8, 2018). Another important factor that needs to be taken into account is the political volatility concerning the design of (higher) education policy, which poses a significant challenge to businesses: "Every government wants to undo what the previous government had [sic] implemented" (Interview with Jacopo Mancabelli, CET, November 8, 2018).

Thus, even though recent policy approaches to DVET have been dynamic (see Kottaridi et al, 2019), they have not produced a stable framework for promoting apprenticeships. This combination of economic, educational and political factors appears to be the reason for the lack of strong networks promoting DVET. Although there are some local DVET projects in Italy, there is no initiative that compares to the multidimensional approach employed by the AFP in Spain. The CET has engaged in communication and training, but its activities have been limited with regard to improving the collaboration between schools and businesses for establishing internships, and it did not directly affect the design of apprenticeship programs.

In fact, the CET and other networks do not have access to policy makers; it would be relatively easily for them to approach policy makers at the local or regional levels, but it is challenging to bring about changes in laws and regulations that are relevant for DVET as they are defined by the national ministries in Rome (see Savelli, 2014). Consequently, German companies have attempted to implement a standardized approach to DVET, yet many were still forced to localize their approaches to DVET across their different sites of operation. However, it should also be noted that, according to Jacopo Mancabelli, the subsidiaries of German companies have invested too little in the development of strong networks and in the cooperation with Italian companies and other relevant organizations: "of course, we were ready to talk to them, but as German companies they thought: 'As a German company, we don't have to learn anything about DVET - thanks! We like to do this on our own'" (Interview with Jacopo Mancabelli, CET, November 8, 2018).

To summarize, German companies operating in Italy predominantly practice a localization strategy. Restrictions concerning access to vocational schools and high costs, due to the need to comply with the legal requirements for apprenticeships, hamper the transfer of DVET. However, in regions with ITS, German companies can practice a country-of-origin-strategy. Therefore, for Italy we can contend that both standardization and localization can be observed concerning the companies' approach to DVET.

Comparison of the two cases

Italy and Spain are two EU member states with similar problems. They have experienced high levels of youth unemployment, which can inter alia be traced back to a skills mismatch and skills shortages (Berlingieri et al, 2014; Mühlemann et al, 2018). Policy makers in both countries have realized that DVET and apprenticeships can help to alleviate this problem. Furthermore, the subsidiaries of certain German companies have attempted to transfer DVET from Germany to Italy and Spain. Thus, the German companies in both countries prefer to standardize the procedures for training their workforce.

The interviews conducted showed that the companies have chosen different strategies in the two countries. The German companies in Italy have launched a networked approach on the basis of the CET, with Robert Bosch GmbH and the Robert Bosch Foundation leading the way. In Spain, under the leadership of the Fundación Bertelsmann, German companies have formed the AFP network.

According to our interviewees, German companies are more successful in facilitating the transfer of the German-style DVET to Spain than to Italy. One of the reasons for this success is revealed by the AFP, which has more than a thousand members representing different institutions and therefore the preferences of the various stakeholders involved in VET in Spain. One of the members of the AFP is the CET, which is also involved in supporting the attempts of German companies like Robert Bosch GmbH to transfer apprenticeship models to Italy. While the CET is an active member of the large and diverse network in the Spanish context, it is less embedded in the network structures in Italy. Therefore, one of the reasons why many German companies have no choice but to practice localization is revealed by their participation in less well-developed and influential networks.

In addition to the descriptive characteristics of the networks in which the companies participate, the strategies of the networks, and the ability to make changes to it, are important. For example, in the beginning, the Fundación Bertelsmann, as a central organization within the AFP network, advised individual companies and schools, but later decided to change its strategy. It has moved from internal consultants to external consultants, who no longer advise individual companies and education institutions but instead turn directly to business associations, with the objective of developing attractive DVET options for their members. By choosing to approach business associations, the AFP has gained influence among small and medium-sized enterprises (SMEs). This approach has two advantages: First, it supports SMEs' participation in DVET. Without the support from an umbrella organization, that manages bureaucratic issues as well as the training of tutors and the rotation of apprentices, many SMEs would not have the capacity to take part in a dual VET project. Second, addressing the business associations directly guarantees more impact through the scaling effect, since this approach reaches more companies.

Both countries are still in the process of changing their VET institutions and schemes, and existing research highlights problematic aspects of the Spanish approach (see, for example, Marhuenda-Fluixá et al, 2019). In fact, what our analysis has concentrated on is not the overall success in introducing DVET but whether the subsidiaries of multinational companies can practice standardization concerning their apprenticeship models or must opt for localization. In this context, the comparative analysis showed that German companies can play an important role in introducing apprenticeships. For the companies to be successful as transfer agents, not only the national context matters but also the strategies they pursue for promoting DVET as well as their ability to adapt their strategies to new insights.

Discussion

A prolific strand of research has assessed the question of whether apprenticeship programs in German companies are the same abroad as in the country of origin. Having done extensive research on the process of how DVET programs are transferred to other countries, Pilz (2019: 37) contends that 'local factors in the host country exert such a strong influence that it is not possible completely to transfer the

German VET system to another country'. Our analysis of the attempts of German companies to transfer DVET to Italy and Spain resonate with this finding. However, by virtue of the theoretical underpinning of this study, which brings together VoC, policy transfer research and organization theories, our analysis can also provide insights that go beyond existing research.

First, we can state that the subsidiaries of multinational companies are willing to act as transfer agents concerning VET programs. The literature on policy transfer has paid limited attention to the important role of companies. On the one hand, this is plausible since companies seek to promote company policies and not public policies, whereas the concept of transfer agents originates from the literature on public policy (see Stone, 2004). On the other, companies have an interest in creating a level playing field that corresponds to their own standards and procedures. Hence, the subsidiaries of multinational companies do not only seek to introduce their VET models to production sites but attempt to diffuse their preferred approach to VET more broadly, aiming to spread it across the local and regional levels and, if possible, even the national level. Therefore, even if VET programs are predominantly firm-level policies, they can affect national policies on VET systems (see Culpepper, 2010). From this perspective, this exploratory study demonstrates the value of studying the strategic interests and behavior of companies for furthering research on policy transfer (see Marsh and Evans, 2012).

Related to this point is the second insight, namely that the presence of organizational networks increases the possibility of an individual subsidiary implementing a country-of-origin approach to VET and influencing the approach of other companies to VET, as well as the very design of the pertinent policies and institutions. The case study on Italy has shown that despite political commitment to strengthen DVET, German companies face difficulties in implementing their preferred DVET model, due to limited access to the necessary vocational schools and design issues. The policy responses in Spain to alleviating the skills mismatch can still be improved, but the emergence of the AFP as a broad and powerful network allows companies to bypass the policy arrangements and to establish an apprenticeship model implemented by local-level actors. Existing research on networks either adopts the perspective of VoC (see, for example, Marques and Hörisch, 2019) or concentrates on the implementation of public policies, such as the delivery of the Youth Guarantee (see, for example, Trein and Tosun, 2019). This analysis showed that it is worth conceiving of networks in a different fashion, namely as facilitators of cooperation that are initiated by private actors.

The third insight refers to the importance of coordination. As the example of the AFP showed, organizational networks can only function if they are coordinated appropriately. In this context, the Fundación Bertelsmann plays an important role in the direction of that particular network. However, this finding alludes to a more general point about the importance of governance arrangements for making networks work. It appears promising for future research on VET systems to concentrate not only on the role of networks but also to pay attention to how the networks are governed. In this regard, social network theory could offer guidance for a corresponding empirical analysis.

The fourth insight is an observation that was not mentioned in the earlier analysis, though it is still worth noting. German companies such as the Robert Bosch GmbH have recruited apprentices in Italy and Spain and then decided to train them in their facilities in Germany, since they could not implement their preferred DVET scheme in the host countries. Once the apprentices had completed their training, they were employed by the subsidiaries in Italy and Spain (Interview with Gabriela Martinez, CET, September 25, 2018; Interview with Jacopo Mancabelli, CET, November 8, 2018). This example shows how important an appropriately trained workforce is for these companies, and that they are willing to invest substantial resources in order to address skills mismatch and skills shortage. This finding questions the assumption of some studies that emphasize the cost of apprenticeships for companies (see, for example, Mühlemann et al, 2018). As far as we can infer on the basis of our interview material, companies value skilled labor more highly than an increase in training costs. This finding also contributes to the literature on policy transfer, since it shows that multinational companies can bypass national policy arrangements in the host country and make recourse to the policy and institutional arrangements in their home countries in order to attain their goal of generating a sufficiently skilled workforce.

The fifth point to be raised is a question, and concerns the implicit assumption of this and similar studies that concentrate on the transferability of VET systems originating from other countries. How much standardization of VET systems is necessary and how much adaptation to local conditions is desirable? This question probably needs to be addressed from the perspective of the individual companies, but it is still worth posing it since research in policy transfer has also shown that a direct copy of policy solutions originating from other countries can perform poorly under certain circumstances. This also entails the question of whether a model in all its components should be transferred from one country, or whether it is more effective to transfer certain components from different countries. Combining the best of different worlds may produce positive effects, but it can also result in poor performance. To get a better sense of what combinations of policy elements work under what circumstances, the literature on policy design (see, for example, Howlett et al, 2015) and policy mixes (see, for example, Bosch, 2011 and Eichhorst, 2015) could provide some helpful insights.

Conclusion

Policy makers across Europe now share the view that VET systems can smoothen the entry of young people into the labor market. An important driver for placing the issue of VET high on the political agenda was the economic and financial crisis that unfolded in 2007–2008 and which resulted in an increase in youth unemployment. The increase was particularly marked in the Southern European countries that have traditionally faced difficulties in integrating young people into their labor markets (see, for example, Berlingieri, 2014). For VET systems to be effective, they need to be tailored to the needs of employers and the labor market (Eichhorst, 2015). Since a mismatch between the skills of young job-seekers and the skills demanded by the employers has been found to be a major impediment to increasing youth employment, DVET as practiced for years in Germany has been considered as a model to be transferred to Southern European countries.

In this chapter, we showed that German companies have attempted to act as transfer agents and to establish apprenticeship systems in Italy and Spain. In both countries, the companies' attempts have been affected by the existing policy and institutional arrangements. Therefore, while German companies are, in principle, willing to invest in a system of DVET that corresponds to the model in place in Germany, they have to adopt an approach that corresponds to the local context and therefore deviates from the German apprenticeship model.

If networks can be formed and developed, German companies can induce other companies to join their efforts and jointly they can negotiate with vocational schools curricula and learning conditions that fit their needs. Therefore, German companies can have an impact on VET systems in their host countries, even if the conditions are unfavorable. The effects will be most visible and sustainable when the companies do not act by themselves but engage in well-managed networks.

Notes

[1]   Information retrieved from: https://www.bmbf.de/de/duales-ausbildungssystem-weltweit-gefragt-328.html.

[2]   Evidently, the data presented in Figure 7.3 are not very recent. However, the UNCTAD data are the best data available on bilateral investment and are used by other recent publications, too (see, for example, Camarero et al, 2019).

[3]   The VoC approach assumes that countries display distinct characteristics which do not change over time. As Ahlquist and Breunig (2012), for example, have shown, the concept of country clusters developed by VoC scholars does not hold true when applying advanced clustering techniques. However, for the purpose of this analysis, the country clusters posited by the VoC approach are of little relevance. We refer to this particular approach, since it provides a plausible theoretical connection between the characteristics of national economies and their VET systems.

[4]   The Open Method of Coordination has allowed European Union (EU) member states to share experiences and learn from policy experimentation. Through a governance mechanism of annual policy and national reports, the Open Method of Coordination seeks to promote convergence towards best practice and 'what works' among member states (Tosun et al, 2019).

[5]   The core determinants for the initial net formation as well as the internal dynamics continue to be the subject of a lively academic discussion. For an extensive review of the debate on the initial start-up phase, see, for example, Schepker et al (2014); for a review of the internal dynamics debate, see, for example, Majchrzak et al (2015); and for a review of the debate on alliance capabilities, see, for example, Möller and Halinen (2017).

[6]   Research on environmental management systems has shown that these are prone to diffuse because they help companies to save resources. Therefore, there is a 'business case' for adopting these (see, for example, Burritt et al, 2019).

References

Ahlquist, J.S. and Breunig, C. (2012) Model-based clustering and typologies in the social sciences, *Political Analysis*, 20(1): 92–112.

Antonakakis, N. and Tondl, G. (2015) Robust determinants of OECD FDI in developing countries: insights from Bayesian model averaging, *Cogent Economics & Finance*, 3(1): 1–25.

Baron, D.P. (2013) *Business and its Environment*, London: Pearson.

Bassols, C. and Salvans, G. (2016) *High-Quality Dual Vocational Learning in Spain: the Alliance for Dual Vocational Training, European Case Study*, Barcelona: Fundación Bertelsmann.

Berlingieri, F., Bonin, H. and Sprietsma, M. (2014) *Youth unemployment in Europe: Appraisal and Policy Options*, Stuttgart: Bosch Foundation.

BOE (Boletin Oficial del Estado) (2012) Legislación consolidada, Real Decreto 1529/2012, https://www.boe.es/buscar/pdf/2012/BOE-A-2012-13846-consolidado.pdf

Bonoli, G. and Wilson, A. (2019) Bringing firms on board, inclusiveness of the dual apprenticeship systems in Germany, Switzerland and Denmark, *International Journal of Social Welfare*, 28(4): 369–79.

Bosch, G. (2011) The German labor market after the financial crisis: miracle or just a good policy mix, in D. Vaughan-Whitehead (ed) *Work Inequalities in the Crisis: Evidence from Europe*, Cheltenham: Edward Elgar.

Burritt, R.L., Herzig, C., Schaltegger, S. and Viere, T. (2019) Diffusion of environmental management accounting for cleaner production: evidence from some case studies, *Journal of Cleaner Production*, 224: 479–91.

Busemeyer, M.R. (2016) The political economy of education and vocational training reforms in Western Europe from a historical perspective, in E. Berner and P. Gonon (eds) *History of Vocational Education and Training in Europe: Cases, Concepts and Challenges*, Bern: Peter Lang.

Busemeyer, M.R. and Trampusch, C. (2012) Introduction: The comparative political economy of collective skill formation, in M.R. Busemeyer and C. Trampusch (eds) *The political Economy of Collective Skill Formation*, Oxford: Oxford University Press.

Busemeyer, M.R. and Vossiek, J. (2016) Mission impossible? Aufbau dualer Berufsausbildung in England und Irland, *WSI Mitteilungen*, 69(4): 254–63.

Cainarca, G.C. and Sgobbi, F. (2012) The return to education and skills in Italy, *International Journal of Manpower*, 33: 187–205.

Camarero, M., Montolio, L. and Tamarit, C. (2019) What drives German foreign direct investment? New evidence using Bayesian statistical techniques, *Economic Modelling*, 83: 326–45.

Cantwell, J.A., Dunning, J.H. and Lundan, S.M. (2010) An evolutionary approach to understanding international business activity: the co-evolution of MNEs and the institutional environment, *Journal of International Business Studies*, 41: 567–86.

Cedefop (European Centre for the Development of Vocational Training) (2014) Vocational education and training in Italy: short description, https://www.cedefop.europa.eu/files/4132_en.pdf

Cedefop (2017) Apprenticeship review: Italy: building education and training opportunities through apprenticeships, http://www.cedefop.europa.eu/files/4159_en.pdf

Chabanet, D. (2014) Between youth policy and employment policy: the rise, limits and ambiguities of a corporatist system of youth representation within the EU, *Journal of Common Market Studies*, 52(3): 479–94.

Christ, C. and Dobbins, M. (2016) Increasing school autonomy in Western Europe: a comparative analysis of its causes and forms, *European Societies*, 18(4): 359–88.

Culpepper, P.D. (2010) *Quiet Politics and Business Power: Corporate Control in Europe and Japan*, New York: Cambridge University Press.

De La Porte, C. and Heins, E. (2015) The sovereign debt crisis, the EU and welfare state reform, *Comparative European Politics*, 13(1): 1–7.

Dilli, S., Elert, N. and Herrmann, A.M. (2018) Varieties of entrepreneurship: exploring the institutional foundations of different entrepreneurship types through 'Varieties-of-Capitalism' arguments, *Small Business Economics*, 51(2): 293–320.

DiMaggio, P.J. and Powell, W.W. (1991) *The New Institutionalism in Organizational Analysis*, Chicago, IL: University of Chicago Press.

Dirección General de Industria y de la Pequeña y Mediana Empresa (2018) Retrato de la PYME, http://www.ipyme.org/Publicaciones/ Retrato-PYME-DIRCE-1-enero-2018.pdf

Dolado, J.J., Jansen, M., Felgueroso, F., Fuentes, A. and Wölfl, A. (2013) Youth labour market performance in Spain and its determinants: a micro-level perspective, *OECD Economics Department Working Papers*, 1039.

Dolowitz, D.P. and Marsh, D. (2000) Learning from abroad: the role of policy transfer in contemporary policy making, *Governance*, 13(1): 5–23.

Drahokoupil, J. and Myant, M. (2015) Putting comparative capitalism's research in its place: varieties of capitalism in transition economies, in M. Ebenau, I. Bruff and C. May (eds) *New Directions in Comparative Capitalisms Research*, London: Palgrave Macmillan.

Eichhorst, W. (2015) Does vocational training help young people find a (good) job? *IZA World of Labor*, 112: 1–10.

Eichhorst, W., Rodríguez-Planas, N., Schmidl, R. and Zimmermann, K.F. (2015) A road map to vocational education and training in industrialized countries, *ILR Review*, 68: 314–37.

Forés, B. and Camisón, C. (2016) Does incremental and radical innovation performance depend on different types of knowledge accumulation capabilities and organizational size? *Journal of Business Research*, 69(2): 831–48.

Fortwengel, J. and Jackson, G. (2016) Legitimizing the apprenticeship practice in a distant environment: institutional entrepreneurship through inter-organizational networks, *Journal of World Business*, 51: 895–909.

Gonon, P. (2017) Quality doubts as a driver for vocational education and training (VET) reforms: Switzerland's way to a highly regarded apprenticeship system, in M. Pilz (ed) *Vocational Education and Training in Times of Economic Crisis: Lessons from Around the World*, Cham: Springer.

Hall, P. and Gingerich, D. (2004) Varieties of capitalism and institutional complementarities in the macroeconomy: an empirical analysis, discussion paper, Max-Planck Institute for the Study of Societies, 04/5.

Hall, P. and Soskice, D. (2001) *Varieties of Capitalism: The Institutional Foundations of Comparative Advantage*, New York: Oxford University Press.

Hermann, A.M. and Peine, A. (2011) When 'national innovation system' meets 'varieties of capitalism' arguments on labour qualifications: on the skill types and scientific knowledge needed for radical and incremental product innovations, *Research Policy*, 40(5): 687–701.

Hörisch, F., Tosun, J., Erhardt, J. and Maloney, W. (2020) Varieties of Capitalism and labour market opportunities for the youth, *European Journal of Government and Economics*, 9(3): 232–51.

Howlett, M., Mukherjee, I. and Woo, J.J. (2015) From tools to toolkits in policy design studies: the new design orientation towards policy formulation research, *Policy & Politics*, 43(2): 291–311.

INAPP (2016) Vocational education and training in Europe: Italy, Cedefop ReferNet VET in Europe reports, http://libserver.cedefop. europa.eu/vetelib/2016/2016_cr_it.pdf

Karamessini, M. (2008) Continuity and change in the Southern European social model, *International Labour Review*, 147(1): 43–70.

Knill, C. (2005) Introduction: cross-national policy convergence: concepts, approaches and explanatory factors, *Journal of European Public Policy*, 12(5): 764–74.

Kottaridi, C., Louloudi, K. and Karkalakos, S. (2019) Human capital, skills and competencies: varying effects on inward FDI in the EU context, *International Business Review*, 28(2): 375–90.

Lahusen, C., Schulz, N. and Graziano, P.R. (2013) Promoting social Europe? The development of European youth unemployment policies, *International Journal of Social Welfare*, 22(3): 300–9.

Li, J., Wiemann, K., Shi, W., Wang, Y. and Pilz, M. (2019) Vocational education and training in Chinese and German companies in China: a 'home international' comparison, *International Journal of Training and Development*, 23(2): 153–68.

Maggetti, M. and Gilardi, F. (2016) Problems (and solutions) in the measurement of policy diffusion mechanisms, *Journal of Public Policy*, 36(1): 87–107.

Majchrzak, A., Jarvenpaa, S.L. and Bagherzadeh, M. (2015) A review of interorganizational collaboration dynamics, *Journal of Management*, 41: 1338–60.

Majumdar, S. (2017) Foreword: technical and vocational education and training (TVET) and skills at the center stage, in M. Pilz (ed) *Vocational Education and Training in Times of Economic Crisis: Lessons from Around the World*, Cham: Springer.

Manuti, A., Pastore, S., Scardigno, A.F., Giancaspro, M.L. and Morciano, D. (2015) Formal and informal learning in the workplace, *International Journal of Training and Development*, 19: 1–17.

Marhuenda-Fluixá, F., Chisvert-Tarazona, M. and Palomares-Montero, D. (2019) The implementation of dual VET in Spain: an empirical analysis, in F. Marhuenda-Fluixá (ed) *The School-Based Vocational Education and Training System in Spain: Technical and Vocational Education and Training: Issues, Concerns and Prospects*, Singapore: Springer.

Marques, P. and Hörisch F. (2019) Promoting workplace-based training to fight youth unemployment in three EU countries: different strategies, different results? *International Journal of Social Welfare*, 28(4): 380–93.

Marsh, D. and Evans, M. (2012) Policy transfer: coming of age and learning from the experience, *Policy Studies*, 33(6): 477–81.

Ministerio de Educación, C.Y.D. (2019) Datos y cifras, Curso escolar 2017/2018, https://sede.educacion.gob.es/publiventa/descarga.action?f_codigo_agc=18727

Molina, O. and Rhodes, M. (2007) The political economy of adjustment in mixed market economies: a study of Spain and Italy, in B. Hancké, M. Rhodes and M. Thatcher (eds) *Beyond Varieties of Capitalism: Conflict, Contradictions, and Complementarities in European Economy*, New York: Oxford University Press.

Möller, K. and Halinen, A. (2017) Managing business and innovation networks: from strategic nets to business fields and ecosystems, *Industrial Marketing Management*, 67: 5–22.

Möller, K., Rajala, A. and Svahn, S. (2005) Strategic business nets: their type and management, *Journal of Business Research*, 58: 1274–84.

Mühlemann, S., Wolter, S.C. and Joho, E. (2018) *Apprenticeship Training in Italy: A Cost-Effective Model for Firms?* Gütersloh: Bertelsmann Stiftung.

OECD (2019) FDI in figures, http//www.oecd.org/investment/fdi-in-figures-october-2019.pdf

Pilz, M. and Li, J. (2014) Tracing Teutonic footprints in VET around the world? *European Journal of Training and Development*, 38: 745–63.

Pilz, M. (2019) The same procedure everywhere? (Apprenticeship) training in German companies in India, China and Mexico, in T. Deissinger, U. Hauschildt, P. Gonon and S. Fischer (eds) *Contemporary Apprenticeship Reforms and Reconfigurations*, Wien: Lit Verlag.

Polesel, J. (2006) Reform and reaction: creating new education and training structures in Italy, *Comparative Education*, 42: 549–62.

Pudelko, M. and Harzing, A.W. (2007) Country-of-origin, localization, or dominance effect? An empirical investigation of HRM practices in foreign subsidiaries, *Human Resource Management*, 46: 535–59.

Rangone, M. and Solari, S. (2012) From the Southern-European model to nowhere: the evolution of Italian capitalism, 1976–2011, *Journal of European Public Policy*, 19: 1188–206.

Royo, S. (2008) *Varieties of Capitalism in Spain: Remaking the Spanish Economy for the New Century*, New York: Palgrave Macmillan.

Savelli, S. (2014) Education and training in Italy: status and transitions, *Education Journal*, 3(6): 323–39.

Šćepanović, V. and Martín-Artiles, A. (2020) Dual training in Europe: a policy fad or a policy turn? *Transfer: European Review of Labour and Research*, 26(1): 15–26.

Schepker, D.J., Oh, W.Y., Martynov, A. and Poppo, L. (2014) The many futures of contracts: moving beyond structure and safeguarding to coordination and adaptation, *Journal of Management*, 40: 193–225.

Schippers, S. (2009) *Systemberatung zwischen Anspruch und Wirklichkeit: eine wirkungsorientierte Analyse der Mubarak-Kohl-Initiative in Ägypten*, Marburg: University of Konstanz.

Schröder, M. (2014) *Varianten des Kapitalismus: Die Unterschiede liberaler und koordinierter Marktwirtschaften*, Wiesbaden: Springer.

Shore, J. and Tosun, J. (2019a) Assessing youth labor market services: young people's perceptions and evaluations of service delivery in Germany, *Public Policy and Administration*, 34(1): 22–41.

Shore, J. and Tosun, J. (2019b) Personally affected, politically disaffected? How experiences with public employment services impact young people's political efficacy, *Social Policy & Administration*, 53(7): 958–73.

Stockmann, R. (1999) The implementation of dual vocational training structures in developing countries: an evaluation of 'Dual Projects' assisted by the German agency for technical cooperation, *International Journal of Sociology*, 29: 29–65.

Stockmann, R. and Silvestrini, S. (2013) *Metaevaluierung Der Berufsbildung: Ziele, Wirkungen und Erfolgsfaktoren Der Deutschen Berufsbildungszusammenarbeit*, Muenster: Waxman.

Stone, D. (2004) Transfer agents and global networks in the 'transnationalization' of policy, *Journal of European Public Policy*, 11(3): 545–66.

Stone, D. (2012) Transfer and translation of policy, *Policy Studies*, 33(6): 483–99.

Thelen, K. (2008) Skill formation and training, in J. Geoffrey and J. Zeitlin (eds) *The Oxford Handbook of Business History*, Oxford: Oxford University Press.

Tosun, J. (2017) Promoting youth employment through multi-organizational governance, *Public Money & Management*, 37(1): 39–46.

Tosun, J., Arco-Tirado, J.L., Caserta, M., Cemalcilar, Z., Freitag, M., Hörisch, F and Malony, W.A. (2019b) Perceived economic self-sufficiency: a country-and generation-comparative approach, *European Political Science*, 18(3): 510–31.

Tosun, J., Hörisch, F. and Marques, P. (2019a) Youth employment in Europe: coordination as a crucial dimension, *International Journal of Social Welfare*, 28(4): 350–7.

Tosun, J., Unt, M. and Wadensjö, E. (2017) Youth-oriented active labor market policies: explaining policy effort in the Nordic and the Baltic states, *Social Policy & Administration*, 51(4): 598–616.

Trein, P. and Tosun, J. (2019) Varieties of public–private policy coordination: how the political economy affects multi-actor implementation, *Public Policy & Administration*, https://doi.org/10.1177/0952076719889099

Trigilia, C. and Burroni, L. (2009) Italy: rise, decline and restructuring of a regionalized capitalism, *Economy and Society,* 38: 630–53.

Wiemann, J. and Fuchs, M. (2018) The export of Germany's 'secret of success' dual technical VET: MNCs and multiscalar stakeholders changing the skill formation system in Mexico, *Cambridge Journal of Regions, Economy and Society*, 11: 373–86.

Wrana, J. and Revilla Diez, J. (2016) Can multinational enterprises introduce new institutions to host countries? An explorative study about MNEs' training programs with educational institutes and their potential influence on Vietnam's vocational education sector, *Geographische Zeitschrift*, 104: 158–82.

8

US Style Entrepreneurship as a Pathway to Youth Employment: Exporting the Promise

Radha Jagannathan and Michael J. Camasso

Introduction

Often celebrated as the 'richest country in the world', the US generates wealth through various means, the most prominent engine of this economic growth being innovation. From condensed milk to suspension bridges, Americans have been active inventors in either filling a niche or addressing a need. Many world rankings on entrepreneurial capacity, inclination, and behavior put Americans in the forefront, and there is little debate that Americans 'play for keeps', with high propensity for risk and even higher expectations of rewards.

Automation and computerization in the labor market have the increased potential for displacing many of today's youth from traditional jobs. The American response to this has been one of energizing youth to engage in small business start-ups and other entrepreneurial activities. While entrepreneurship is considered as an eminently reasonable pathway to solving the youth unemployment problem in the US, given its deep-seated, cultural proclivity for taking risks, can this approach work in other cultures/countries where risk taking is not so readily built into their culture?

This chapter will describe the work ethos of Americans, how this ethos manifests itself in the demand and supply sides of the labor market, and the extent to which the US has pursued an 'entrepreneurship as a solution to youth unemployment' model. We also explore the feasibility of exporting this model to the Mediterranean countries that exhibit substantial problems with youth employment.

The American work ethos

Legendary works by Adam Smith and Alexis de Tocqueville speak quite eloquently to American economic and political individualism. The right to make a living as one chooses, own property, make economic decisions in one's self-interest, practice self-reliance, and to have access to free markets and competition – all characteristics of economic individualism described by Adam Smith in his *Wealth of Nations* (1776) – are firmly embedded in the American psyche. Beginning with Alexis de Tocqueville's (1840, 1945) masterpiece, *Democracy in America*, the US has been judged to be the exceptional capitalist democracy founded on the values of egalitarianism, liberty, individualism and laissez-faire economics (Lipset, 1979). De Tocqueville traces this exceptionalism to its 'Puritanical origin', its good fortune to exploit a European knowledge base without 'laboring to amass this treasure', and a geographical location and natural resources which facilitated boundless economic expansion (de Tocqueville, 1840: 37–40, and Chapter XIX on What Causes almost all Americans to Follow Industrial Callings). De Tocqueville also heaped praise on Americans for their pragmatism, their orientation toward action, values that limited the appetite for intellectualism as an end in itself, and their honor for labor and making money, noting that even the President of the US works for pay (de Tocqueville, 1840:161–62).

A component of America's value orientation which held special intrigue for de Tocqueville, and which continues to puzzle many even today, is how a nation of individuals can function as a cohesive society. He identifies the secret as 'The Principle of Self-Interest Rightly Understood' (de Tocqueville, 1840: Chapter VIII), much like the workings of the 'invisible hand' resulting in the common good. Referred to also as the altruism of self-interest, de Tocqueville's principle guides Americans by stressing the utility, indeed the virtue, of 'an enlightened regard for themselves' as the motivation for helping others. De Tocqueville contrasts this approach to ensuring the public welfare with that of the European elites who are facile with the idea of self-sacrifice, 'incessantly talking of the beauties of virtue' given without expectation of reward, but whose actions belie such abnegations (de Tocqueville, 1840: 130). The principle in all likelihood accounts for some of the stark differences in civilian terror that distinguished the American Revolution from the exceedingly bloody events that took place in France and elsewhere in Europe (Lefebvre, 1962; Brinton, 1965; Lipset, 1979).

David McClelland (1961; 1964), in his deep dive into American's culture and psyche, a little more than a century after De Tocqueville, describes a set of values that had changed very little. He describes the 'American Value Formula' as a combination of: (1) free choice according to one's wishes and desire; (2) action over contemplation; and (3) the need for achievement and other-directedness (McClelland, 1961: 73). Much like Adam Smith and De Tocqueville, McClelland too identified the principle of obligation to self as the necessary condition for obligation to society.

The resilient spirit Americans possess has helped weather many a political, social or economic storm – be it slavery, the great depression or presidential sex scandals dating back to Grover Cleveland. The American labor market is itself an exemplar of this seemingly boundless capacity to bounce back from adversities. In the pages that follow, we take a look at how this principle of 'self-interest rightly understood' translates to the American youth labor market from both a supply and demand perspective.

Youth unemployment in the US stood at 7.7% in December 2019, quite low in comparison to the European average of 14.2%, and only behind Germany which had a slightly lower rate of 5.6%, according to the most recent data from the International Labor Organization (ILO). There is, however, much racial diversity in the extent of youth unemployment – the US Bureau of Labor Statistics reports youth unemployment among African-Americans to be the highest, at 14.6%, followed by Hispanics at 11.3%, with Whites and Asians having low rates of around 8%. But what has the US done to prepare youth for productive employment and how effective has this been? How effective were the demand-side interventions that the US has historically tried to curb (youth) unemployment? And how have these attempts been guided by the principle of self-interest rightly understood? What about the potential of entrepreneurship as a response to youth unemployment? We now turn to answering these questions.

Considerations on the supply side of the labor market: getting ready for employment

Generally speaking, employment preparation and labor supply decisions of youth are intrinsically tied to the idea of human capital development in its various forms – basic schooling, vocational training or career and technical education (CTE). Understanding the other side of the equation, that is, the specific types of human capital that employers demand, and how this is influenced by opportunities for apprenticeships, on-the-job training, traditional job training programs, and other active labor market policies such as wage subsidies and minimum wage legislation, is equally important. We first review the theory and empirical record on human capital acquisition that relate to labor supply in the US.

In formulating his ideas about human capital development, Becker (1993; 1996) makes the distinction between two approaches or investment strategies. The first strategy is to provide broad 'general education', what in the US is termed liberal education. The focus here, in essence, is its lack of focus: students are exposed to a broad spectrum of knowledge culled from the arts, sciences and humanities. The goal is to create individuals capable of critical thinking, the capacity to 'learn how to learn', appreciate the arts and, perhaps most importantly, purvey the national culture to future generations. The second educational strategy is to stress specific knowledge and training which, in principle, limits individuals – who have been socialized in this fashion – in the knowledge and skills necessary for negotiating an increasingly complex and diverse world.

The specific skill strategy does appear to have important advantages in capitalist labor markets, however, since workers with specific and specialized skills are less likely to quit their jobs, and their skills are more likely to compel company loyalty. And as Becker (1996) points out, workers with specific skills are more likely to receive promotions and are among the last to be laid off during business downturns (Becker, 1996: 147). Bench or line workers can, with additional training, become managers, but the reverse is not feasible if the manager lacks specific technical skills when he/she entered the firm.

The selection of a general or specific educational path to human capital growth is a choice rooted in cultural values and preferences. In his study of democracy in America, de Tocqueville (1840; 1945) observes that Americans show less aptitude and taste for general ideas than the French. He goes on to comment that the:

> habit and taste for general ideas will always be greatest among a people of ancient culture and extensive knowledge. This is not to say the French approach to creating human capital is superior, on the contrary general ideas are no proof of the strength, but rather of the insufficiency of the human

intellect; for there are in nature no beings exactly alike, no things precisely identified, no rules indiscriminately and alike applicable to several objects at once. The chief merit of general ideas is that they enable the human mind to pass rapid judgment on a many great objects at once; but, on the other hand, the notions they convey are never other than incomplete, and they always cause the mind to lose as much in accuracy as it gains in comprehensiveness. (de Tocqueville, 1840 [1945]: 14)

The French commitment to general ideas remains steadfast and is reflected in the French conceptions of *métier* (job) (d'Iribarne, 2009); and *dirigisme* (managed capitalism) (Bourdieu, 2005; Murphy, 2017; Peet, 2012); preference for income redistribution (Guillaud, 2013); disdain for entrepreneurship (Ulijn and Fayolle, 2004; Bosma and Kelly, 2018); and the centrality of les Grandes Écoles (Bourdieu, 1998). It may also have contributed to the highly segmented labor market in the country and the neglect of specific knowledge initiatives like vocational education (OECD, 1984; OECD, 2016). The US has witnessed a steady growth in general education, with a college baccalaureate degree seen as the best ticket to insure economic success.

We depict the structure of the educational system in the US in Figure 8.1. After completing eight years of compulsory education in elementary and lower secondary school (middle or junior high schools), students enter four-year comprehensive high schools, and can choose a general pathway leading to a four-year college or career, or a technical education (CTE) track hopefully leading to training and a job. Most of this technical training takes place in comprehensive high schools rather than in separate vocational career centers, in response to concerns that physical separation of students will set up segregation along racial grouping, in violation of the Equal Education Opportunity Act of 1974 (Kuczera and Field, 2013: 21). Successful completion of high school/upper secondary school results in a general education diploma, or a diploma and certificate in the case of vocational students. In principle, the American vocational student has both a general education and basic skills in a subject area that includes agriculture, business office operations, marketing, home health and economics, computer maintenance and operation, trade or financial literacy. Critics however maintain that the typical US vocational student has neither the general literacy or numeracy nor the basic technical skills to get a job that pays more than minimum wage.

Figure 8.1: Education system in the United States

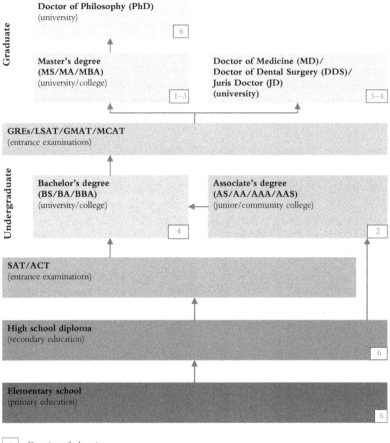

Unlike Spain and Italy, which continue to struggle to improve their upper secondary vocational systems, the US has attempted to find redemption at the lower tertiary level in the form of community colleges. President Obama said as much in his speech to a joint session of Congress in 2009:

> I ask every American to commit to at least one year or more of higher education or career training. This can be community college or a four-year school, vocational training or an apprenticeship. But whatever the training may be, every American will need to get more than a high school diploma. (Kuczera and Field, 2013: 17)

Two major weaknesses of vocational and technical education at the upper secondary level in the US are low-quality training curricula and instruction delivered: (1) without programmatic and financial oversight; and (2) without the input and/or active involvement of actual/prospective employers (Zimmermann et al, 2013; Zirkle, 2017; Eichhorst et al, 2015). In their review of CTE obtained through community college, Kuczera and Field (2013) warn that dysfunction at the high-school level could be repeated at the lower tertiary level with substantial financial cost to students if accountability is not improved. Vocational education had, in fact, become so unpopular that during the 2006 reauthorization of the Perkins Act – the Act that mandated an alternative to generation education – the term 'vocational' was replaced with the expression 'career and technical' education or CTE. Notwithstanding the name change, vocational education continues to suffer from issues of quality, financial support, business commitment and public acceptance (Kincheloe, 2018; Kuczera and Field, 2013; Zimmermann et al, 2013).

Considerations on the demand side of the labor market: getting employed

It might appear puzzling to some as to why Americans, and particularly American businessmen, do not see value in an alternative school-work schema or long-term apprenticeships, when other countries like Germany and Switzerland with strong economies, apparently do. The rationale apparently stems from a literal and cultural application of Becker's (1993) human capital theory. As Lerman (2017) observes, in a perfectly competitive labor market firms will provide specific training which enhances productivity, but not general training which will not be cost-effective, since the benefits will not offset training costs before other firms hire away the trained workers. Hence the only way to finance general training is to lower the wages of full-time workers (Lerman, 2017: 306) or, possibly as Ryan (2016) remarks, to allow the work-based learning to be financed entirely by the student-trainee, primarily through foregone earnings. Trainees will be paid the value of their marginal product, net of the direct cost to the employer training them (Ryan, 2016: 15). When viewed through the prism of 'self-interest rightly understood' and the American value formula, however, this strategy makes perfect economic sense in America's 'free-wheeling' arena of largely unregulated capitalism – at least in the short run. If, on the other hand, one assumes a labor market for skilled employers with imperfect competition among employers, where the contest for employees is less intense, and where wage differences do not cause large-scale quitting, then worker training would not affect the firm's profit margin. Such a market is consistent with what McClelland (1964) has called the 'German value formula – I must believe and do what I should for the good of the whole' (McClelland, 1964: 80). The preferred method of vocational education in the US, in contrast, continues to be on-the-job training (Zimmermann et al, 2013; Eichhorst et al, 2015), an approach that does not require the close collaboration of government, employers and unions, and clearly signals low confidence in school-based CTE.

The Trump administration did undertake some efforts to breathe new life into industry-education partnerships through apprenticeship programs, and to boost CTE. In 2017 President Trump issued an executive order expanding apprenticeships, noting that 'many colleges and universities fail to help students graduate with the skills necessary to secure high paying jobs in today's workforce' (White House, Office of Press Secretary, 2017). A key component of this order is the establishment of 'Industry-Recognized Apprenticeships' where third-parties, that is, business and industry trade groups, unions and joint labor-management organizations, receive expedited review and registration in the US Department of Labor. Working on the model of apprenticeship widely employed in the building/construction trades, the Trump measure promised to extend the model to retail, hospitality and manufacturing (Scheiber, 2017). If the program is to be successful it will require several fundamental changes in the way America conducts its school-to-work transition. First, students would need to be convinced that vocational education and training does not preclude further generic/cognitive development and career mobility (Valiente and Scandurra, 2017). Second, employers need to be convinced that the investment in dual programs and apprenticeships will lead to the creation of loyal future employees (Ryan, 2016). And third, full-time employees and unions must be convinced that participation in these programs will not yield lower wages for full-time workers. In short, nothing less than a broad cultural change would seems to be in order, a change all the more difficult considering that real wage increases of American workers have been substantially higher than most Scandinavian and all Southern Mediterranean countries over the past decade (Economist Intelligence Unit, 2014).

The Trump administration has also shown its commitment to reviving CTE in July 2019, when President Trump signed into law the Strengthening Career and Technical Education for the 21st Century Act, which effectively restored Perkins funding for CTE through 2024.

With bipartisan support, this Act reauthorized the languishing Carl D. Perkins Career and Technical Education Act of 2006, and provides about $1.2 billion annually to CTE programs, which now include any work-place based learning opportunities such as internships (Evans, 2019). To align education and training investments across agencies and facilitate cross-agency coordination and communication, the Act also brought definitions of key concepts of CTE into conformity with other related Acts, such as the Every Student Succeeds Act and the Workforce Innovation and Opportunity Act.

Historically, though, the US has had a strong tradition of implementing what are now widely recognized as government job training programs. The US, more than any other nation, has sought to increase youth and adult employment and labor force participation through the use of subsidized public sector jobs and training programs. In each of the several iterations of the country's principal (federal) employment/jobs training legislation, for example, the Comprehensive Employment and Training Act (1973), the Job Training Partnership Act (1982), the Workforce Investment Act (1998) and the Workforce Innovation and Opportunity Act (2013), sizeable proportions of funds have been earmarked or have found their way to public sector employment. The results have been underwhelming and in many cases quite costly as well.

Numerous evaluations of the Comprehensive Employment and Training Act (CETA) programs indicated that many of the funds were used by governments to supplant local efforts. When new public-sector jobs were created, and this apparently did not happen often, the employment benefits were more often than not quite modest and benefitted women and not men (Maynard, 1995; LaLonde, 1995). Assessments of the Job Training Partnership Act (JTPA) show that while discounted benefits for adults over seven years averaged about $3,000, the returns to public sector employment for youth amounted to a net cost for males of $6,000 and $1,200 for females (Carneiro and Heckman, 2003). An evaluation of the residential Job Corps program, directed at unemployed youth, also demonstrated very little employment impact (Burghardt and Schochet, 2001). Finally, evaluations of the Workforce Investment Act (WIA) and the Workforce Innovation and Opportunity Act (WIOA), have produced mixed and at times confusing estimates of program benefit. Both WIA and WIOA have announced concerted efforts to insure that more subsidies target employers in the private sector. If this is true, then findings by Hollenbeck (2009), indicating a negative benefit of $8,000 for dislocated workers, are especially disheartening. One can encapsulate the generally disappointing performance of American job training programs in a pithy statement that Heckman made in response to a question on how much he thought training schemes in the US help their clientele: 'zero is not a bad number' (*The Economist*, April 6, 1996).

Stimulated perhaps by the Trump administration's renewed efforts to revitalize worker training and apprenticeship in a rapidly expanding economy, the popular press in the US has once again brought the failures of worker training in America (Fadulu, 2018; Thrush, 2018; Scheiber, 2017) to the public's attention. Fadulu (2018), for example, rails against 'Reagan's JTPA', but neglects to recount the shortcoming of Clinton's WIA or Obama's WIOA. Job Corps, a political staple since 1964, continues to underperform badly, as Thrush (2018) points out, with participants' average yearly earnings at $12,486, barely above the poverty level for a single individual. Notwithstanding these public sector employment failures, this form of active labor market policy (ALMP) in America continues to be promulgated by sizeable numbers of academics, public policy makers, politicians and members of the press. Cynically, opponents in the business community and in government appear to acquiesce, treating such advocacy as a cost of doing business – this despite a call from President Obama himself to change course! In a 2014 press conference, then President Barack Obama told reporters: "We got to move away from what our Labor Secretary, Tom Perez, calls our 'train and pray' approach. We train them and we pray that they can get a job" (White House Office of the Press Secretary, 2014).

Other active labor market policies, such as increases in minimum wage and wage subsidies to employers, have also garnered their share of attention in recent years. The conventional wisdom, supported by many labor economists and businessmen, is that the former reduces the demand for workers by disincentivizing employers to pay lower entry wages for new workers with skills and experience deficits. The latter, on the other hand, have been viewed favorably as a means of bridging the gap between oftentimes low entry-level wages and wages that incentivize work over inactivity.

Government subsidies to private sector employers have been used in the US to fund transitional jobs to increase short-term employment, but have proven less successful over the long term (Dutta-Gupta et al, 2016). Returns to subsidies in the public sector have not been nearly as noteworthy; in point of fact, they have often been negative. Card et al (2017), using a meta-analysis of 207 evaluations of active labor market policies, report medium-term impacts of -1.1% and long-term impacts of zero.

The payment of a minimum wage is another way of providing a wage subsidy to employees, except in this instance the subsidy originates directly from the employer, potentially reducing the firm's profits and/or investment/expansion capital. The principal arguments for enacting a minimum wage are rarely based on criteria such as economic efficiency, labor market flexibility, or business growth; rather, they proceed from the tenets of social justice. The Economic Policy Institute (2019), an American think tank based in Washington, DC, for example, argues that a $15.00 per hour federal minimum wage is necessary to lift pay for nearly 40 million workers, reverse decades of growing pay inequality between the lowest-paid workers and the middle class, and help significantly level the wages of white Americans and American 'workers of color'. The Economic Policy Institute also cites the importance of this minimum wage for spurring business activity and job growth; however, this contention has been challenged by a broad spectrum of business and economic organizations, including the US Chamber of Commerce, the National Federation of Independent Businesses (NFIB), and the National Association of Manufacturers. If economic theory is correct and if the empirical record is to be taken seriously, proscriptions against using a minimum wage as an economic growth tool would appear to have a great deal of merit.

In the US and in Europe the controversy over the minimum wage rages on in a more nuanced form, with advocates opining that economic consequences are conditioned upon the size of the increase as well as the base wage from which the increase has been calculated (Card and Krueger, 1995; Borjas, 2008). It would be expected, for example, that raising the minimum wage in a state or city that has a high wage already in place would see very little employment impact, compared to a low-wage state or city. A recent high-profile experiment in Seattle, Washington – an American city with one of the nation's highest minimum wages at $9.47 – calls even these assumptions into question. The city increased its minimum wage to $11.00 in 2015 and $13.00 in 2016. Using administrative data spanning all industries in the city, Jardim et al (2017) report that the 2015 increase produced disemployment effects that offset the wage increases (an elasticity of less than -1). The subsequent 2016 increase to $13.00 yielded much more pronounced reductions in employer payroll expenses and by extension employee earnings, with a net elasticity of -3. Thus, it would appear that even in circumstances where increases proceed from a high wage base, the net results are reductions in employee hours and fewer employees.

Entrepreneurship as an employment strategy in the United States

Entrepreneurship, the dynamic process of creating incremental wealth, is at the very soul of the American capitalist economic system (Schumpeter, 1962; Casson, 2003; Baumol, 2010). Given the labor supply and demand issues confronting youth, increasing entrepreneurship is seen as a means for bringing disadvantaged and unemployed youth into the labor market (OECD, 2016; Vogel, 2015; Stam and Van Stel, 2011). As we have emphasized throughout, Americans inherently are risk takers, and do not easily 'shelter-in-place' economically speaking. The US is placed at the very top in the Hofstede ranking of countries on individualism, self-interest and self-determination, all intrinsic components that comprise the entrepreneurial spirit (Hofstede et al, 2010).

Nowhere else is the principle of 'self-interest rightly understood' more evident than in the American entrepreneurial spirit. Unlike rigid labor markets that are characterized by employee protectionism in much of Europe, American workers exhibit greater job mobility in a fairly flexible marketplace. If the American worker is not treated right by the employer, she is savvy enough to take any on-the-job training from the employer and move on to other employers in search of better prospects and working conditions, or even start her own business.

While entrepreneurial skills like creative thinking, calculated risk taking, irreverence for consensual views, rule-challenging behavior, and so on, are not necessarily popular qualities for new employees in established businesses, they are extremely important for the creation of small businesses built around breakthrough ideas and innovations. Innovative technologies created by small US firms in the 20th century include air conditioning, the assembly line, fracking, the electronic spreadsheet, CAT scanner, microprocessor, human growth hormone, and hundreds of others (Baumol, 2010; Vogel, 2015).

The obstacles to the development of entrepreneurial activity and small business formation are formidable and include attracting sufficient financing, obtaining necessary mentoring and consultation, and building a technical skill set containing human capital tools like negotiating ability, financial literacy, and presentation competence, among others. It is also paramount that the prospective entrepreneur be permitted to function within a social context that fosters bridging capital and network building. Svendsen and Svendsen (2004), for example, discuss how social capital in the form of network associations help break down market barriers by reducing the skepticism of customers around the quality and reliability of new product. Lack of supportive networks are also viewed by OECD (2016) as a major barrier to entrepreneurship for disadvantaged youth.

The US, of course, has a long history of supporting innovative small and medium-sized businesses (SMEs). Through its Small Business Administration, Offices of Entrepreneurial Development, National Federation of Independent Business (NFIB) Young Entrepreneur Foundation, Women's Business Ownership, HUB Zone Program, and the Department of Commerce, the government has sought to encourage business creation and innovation through financing, education and training, regulation and tax waivers and management services (Reamer, 2017). Some of the more nascent efforts to encourage youth entrepreneurship include The Youth Entrepreneur Institute, The Kauffman Center for Entrepreneurial Leadership, The National Consortium for Entrepreneurship Education, YoungBiz, BizWorld, Education, Training & Enterprise Center, The National Foundation for Teaching Entrepreneurship, and Operation Hope. These and other efforts have no doubt helped the US retain its title as the country with the highest early-stage entrepreneurial activity (TEA) rates among developed countries (Stam and Val Stel, 2011; Bosma and Kelley, 2018).

What is more, many of these entrepreneurship programs are focused on developing an entrepreneurial mindset in individuals from a very early age – one serial entrepreneur (Zamary, 2017a) believes that first grade is not too soon to start! A 2017 *Huffington Post* article entitled 'Young Entrepreneurs – Coolest Youth Startups in the United States', highlights a number of inspirational innovations by grade schoolers, some of which include: (1) EvanTube, started by 10-year-old Evan, which reviews toys and builds Lego sets online, has nearly 2 billion views by more than 2 million subscribers, and makes an estimated $1.3 million a year; (2) Mo's Bows, a home-made bow-tie business, started by Moziah Bridges when he was 9 years old, now worth over $1 million – Mo Bridges, now 16, is one of the youngest American CEOs and the youngest contender on the popular American reality show Shark Tank, a show where young entrepreneurs get the opportunity to turn 'their ideas into lucrative empires'; and (3) Herban Movement, winner of 2015 Microsoft's Innovation Award, a student-run company started by high school senior Joseph Fortuna, that designs and sells educational products such as cookbooks and environment-friendly bags (Zamary, 2017b).

Each year Babson College (US) and several collaborating institutions publish a report entitled the Global Entrepreneurship Monitor (GEM). The report combines data on entrepreneurial behavior and attitudes collected from a sample of about 2,000 adults in each participating country, as well as data on entrepreneurial context gathered from at least 36 'carefully chosen' national experts in each country, called The National Experts Survey, or NES. In Tables 8.1 and 8.2 we present comparative information from the GEM report on the countries included in this book[1] (Bosma et al, 2020).

Table 8.1 shows that the US has the highest percentage of youth entrepreneurship among our study countries, at 37.9%, with Italy, France and Spain registering rates at the lower end of the spectrum. The highest levels of entrepreneurial activities of any country, as measured by the Total Entrepreneurial Activity (TEA) and Established Business Ownership (EBO) rate, are also in the US, at 17.4% and 10.6% respectively. Lowest TEAs are found in Italy, and EBOs in France. Spain and the US show a much more equitable distribution of entrepreneurial activities by gender.

With respect to attitudes and perceptions of entrepreneurial activities, the US again has the highest percentages of people who believe that there are good opportunities to start a business in their area (67.2%) and those who are confident that they have the personal knowledge, skills, and experience to start a new business (65.5%). Surprisingly, the Italians (27.6%) and the Germans (29.7%) report the lowest levels of fear of failure in starting a new business, as opposed to the US where this number is at 35.1%, closer to the French level.[2] The Portuguese report the greatest fear of failure at 52.6%, with the Spanish and Greeks representing the middle of the spectrum.

Americans' motivation in starting a new business is to 'make a difference', while Italians are motivated by 'building great wealth' or 'to earn a living'. The Americans also top the list of countries where entrepreneurs believe they will create six or more jobs in the next five years, and that their business idea has national and global scope, indicative of high potential of high-impact entrepreneurship.

In Table 8.2, we summarize the data gleaned from national experts in each country on the entrepreneurial framework, that is, conditions that are important by their presence (for example, access to finance) or absence (for example, burdensome regulations) in stimulating and nurturing entrepreneurship. Each expert is asked to weigh in on each of 12 indicators of the entrepreneurial ecosystem, and a National Entrepreneurship Context Index (NECI) is constructed as a weighted average of the expert ratings on the 12 indicators. The US is ranked

Table 8.1: Entrepreneurship – a comparison of perception, motivation and action across study countries

Characteristic	France[1]	Germany	Greece	Italy	Portugal	Spain	USA
Youth entrepreneurship (%)							
Age group 18–24	3.2	10.10	13.20	1.90	16.70	5.00	15.80
Age group 25–34	8.1	11.80	6.30	7.60	18.70	8.50	22.10
Total	11.3	21.90	19.50	9.50	35.40	13.50	**37.90**[2]
Self-perceptions (%)							
Easy to start a business	—	47.60	46.90	74.60	41.10	38.50	71.20
Perceived opportunities	35.00	52.20	49.90	45.10	53.50	36.10	**67.20**
Perceived capabilities	37.50	45.80	51.60	48.10	61.40	50.80	**65.50**
Fear of failure	37.10	29.70	40.60	27.60	52.60	48.20	35.10
Entrepreneurial intention	18.60	9.10	12.40	5.40	19.80	7.40	13.70
Motivation (%)							
Make a difference	—	44.40	32.30	11.00	41.70	49.40	**66.40**
Build great wealth	—	32.00	48.20	95.50	43.60	59.50	69.00
Continue family tradition	—	68.70	35.30	26.70	31.40	13.40	30.60
Earn a living	—	42.60	51.60	89.50	54.40	42.30	41.40
Activity (%)							
Total Entrepreneurial Activity (TEA)	6.1	7.60	8.20	2.80	12.90	6.20	**17.40**
Established business ownership rate	2.5	5.20	12.30	4.70	11.00	6.30	10.60
Gender equality (Ratio)							
Female/male TEA ratio	0.75	0.60	0.86	0.60	0.60	0.95	0.91
Impact (%)							
Job creation (6+ jobs) in 5 years	—	1.90	1.20	0.30	2.20	0.60	**5.70**
Business has national scope	—	2.00	1.30	0.20	2.10	0.90	**2.60**
Business has global scope	—	0.90	0.50	0.10	0.50	0.20	**1.00**

Notes: [1]France did not participate in the 2018–19 study; these data are from 2018–19.
[2]Bolded numbers indicate highest ranking for USA.
Source: GEM Global Report 2019–20

10th among the 54 developed and developing countries ranked.[3] One important dimension of NECI is the level of complementarity between societal values and preferences and the norms of entrepreneurship. Not surprisingly, and quite consistent with the principle of 'self-interest rightly understood', and a cultural backdrop that encourages risk taking and individual achievement, the US ranks at the very top on this measure. We note that the Mediterranean countries' rank on this measure ranges from 29 out of 54 in Spain to 50 out of 54 in Portugal, with Greece at 40, Italy at 37, and France at 31. There is also one external factor that the US ranks at the very top, and it is availability of sufficient funds to new startups, ranging from informal investment and bank loans to government grants and venture capital.

The two other summary measures found at the bottom of the table report the World Bank's rating on a scale of 1–100 of how easy it is to do business in a country (Bosma et al, 2020), and a global competitiveness rank designed by the World Economic Forum to assess how efficiently factors of production are combined to achieve economic growth (Schwab, 2019). The US comes out on top on both of these measures, with Greece faring the worst on both.

Exporting the promise of entrepreneurship to the Mediterranean countries

It is not easy to export deep-seated cultural traits from one country to another. The comparative data shown in Tables 8.1 and 8.2 drive home two of the most significant differences between the US and comparison countries: levels of confidence in one's ability to succeed, and the cultural/social norms that are conducive to entrepreneurship.[4] Schumpeter's observation regarding the potential transfer problems of 'Swedish socialism' to America: 'it is absurd for other nations to copy Swedish examples; the only effective way to do so would be to import the Swedes and to put them in charge' (Schumpeter, 1962: 335) may provide a parallel here. So is it reasonably safe to conclude that it's really the external components of the entrepreneurial ecosystem that may lend themselves to manipulation by the government or society to create a more entrepreneurship-friendly environment? What might the Mediterranean countries do to emulate the US to create flourishing entrepreneurship, especially among the young, short of importing Americans?

As shown in Table 8.2, all of the Mediterranean countries rank quite low with respect to access to capital for new startups. Most of them have adopted, to a smaller or larger extent, a reasonable set of strategies to promote youth entrepreneurship. For each country of

Table 8.2: Entrepreneurial framework conditions – a comparison across study countries

Characteristic	France[1]	Germany	Greece	Italy	Portugal	Spain	USA
Entrepreneurial eco-system							
Expert ratings on a scale of 1–10							
Cultural and social norms	4.71	4.78	4.35	4.43	3.61	4.82	**7.68**[2]
Entrepreneurship finance	4.68	5.31	3.88	4.50	4.85	4.87	**6.04**
Government policies							
Support and relevance	5.86	4.07	3.56	3.57	4.26	5.33	4.37
Taxes and bureaucracy	5.34	4.15	2.43	3.03	2.42	5.17	4.90
Entrepreneurship programs	5.64	6.21	3.50	4.13	4.41	5.96	4.21
Entrepreneurship education at school age	2.88	2.71	2.62	2.87	2.63	2.65	**3.92**
Entrepreneurship education post school age	5.64	4.80	4.45	4.94	4.64	5.45	5.42
R & D transfer	4.79	4.78	4.30	4.64	3.69	5.26	4.48
Commercial/legal infrastructure	5.34	6.29	4.92	4.81	5.00	6.04	5.79
Physical infrastructure	7.65	6.45	6.06	5.40	7.12	6.95	**7.50**
Internal market burdens/entry regulations	3.92	5.13	4.00	4.51	3.74	5.05	4.38
Internal market dynamics	4.29	5.79	5.15	4.89	4.17	5.31	4.99
Entrepreneurial eco-system – overall scores							
NECI Rating (Rank/ 54)	5.62 (10)	5.04 (16)	4.10 (40)	4.31 (33)	4.21 (38)	5.24 (12)	**5.31 (10)**
World Bank ease of doing business rating: 0–100	77.29	79.70	68.40	72.90	76.50	77.90	**84.00**
World Economic Forum global competitiveness rank	17/140	7/141	59/141	30/141	34/141	23/141	**2/141**

Notes: [1]France did not participate in the 2018–19 study; these data are from 2018–19.

[2]Bolded numbers indicate highest ranking for USA.

Source: GEM Global Report 2019–20

interest here, we provide a brief profile of where it stands in regard to youth entrepreneurship, and reprise the 'policy roadmap' it has chosen to follow.

Greece

A recent OECD publication entitled *The Missing Entrepreneurs 2019: Policies for Inclusive Entrepreneurship* shows that there is very little change in self-employment or TEA rates among youth between 2009–2013 and 2014–2018, but outlines an important step undertaken by the Ministry of Economy, Development and Tourism in 2017 to support recent college graduates to create businesses with grants of €5,000 to €25,000 (OECD/European Union, 2019). The NES-GEM data for Greece show that: (a) credit expansion in the country is negative, with the banking sector not currently working effectively; and (b) the results that merit the most attention pertain to funding mechanisms, such as crowdfunding, informal investors, digital platforms and business angel funding. In addition, corporate tax rates remain a significant obstacle to entrepreneurs, even though Greece recently lowered its tax rate from 29% to 24% (Bosma et al, 2020).

France

The self-employment rates among youth increased from 3.9% in 2009 to 5.5% in 2018, and promoting entrepreneurial spirit has become a central policy priority in France (OECD/European Union, 2019). A new law, entitled the New Action Plan for Business Growth and Transformation (Le plan d'action pour la croissance et la transformation des entreprises) was enacted in 2019, with the objective of enabling business startups and expansion of existing businesses by revamping burdensome regulations (for example, simplifying administrative requirements, allowing online business registration, and more straightforward bankruptcy procedures). The 2019 GEM report finds that as a result of many government policies enacted during the last decade favoring business creation, the entrepreneurial dynamism has increased substantially in France – for example, the number of new startups increased by 12% between 2016 and 2017, resulting in more than 55,000 jobs. An important component of the suite of policies the country adopted includes one that started in 2018 which aligned the rights of entrepreneurs with wageworkers, enabling the former to be subject to the same benefits regarding maternity leaves, unemployment allocations and pension contributions as the latter. It is expected that this policy especially will narrow the gap between entrepreneurial intention and action in France (Bosma and Kelley, 2019).

Italy

With the lowest levels of TEA, the Italian entrepreneurship landscape continues to appear gloomy. Bosma et al (2020) report that Italy has not implemented any significant legislative measures to promote entrepreneurship since the Start-up Act introduced in 2012. Macro-economic trends, burdensome administrative procedures, difficulties in raising capital, high levels of risk aversion, and lack of entrepreneurial competencies, all continue to contribute to a non-fertile breeding ground for new enterprises. Despite widespread dissemination of GEM findings, Italy appears to have little appetite for new policies encouraging youth self-employment (Bosma et al, 2020). However, a recent OECD publication reports some good news, at least regionally speaking. According to this report (OECD/European Union, 2019), there are some recent efforts in Southern Italy aimed at strengthening support for youth entrepreneurs. In 2017, a measure called Resto al Sud ('I remain in the South') was introduced in Abruzzo, Basilicata, Calabria, Campania, Molise, Puglia, Sardinia and Sicily to aid 18–35-year-olds with new startups. This is an incentive program that offers consulting services to potential young entrepreneurs and up to €40,000 in funding, only 65% of which is repayable at a subsidized interest rate.

Portugal

As we saw from Tables 8.1 and 8.2, Portugal has high levels of TEA and youth entrepreneurship that closely rivals the US. In addition, their entrepreneurial ecosystem shows quite a favorable picture, scoring high on supportive government policies and good physical and commercial infrastructure. The Portuguese also rank high in their perceived entrepreneurial capabilities; however, they exhibit a strong fear of failure in capitalizing on opportunities, with cultural and societal norms that do not counter this fear. According to the 2019 GEM survey results (Bosma et al, 2020), 'entrepreneurship has become deeply ingrained in the vocabulary of Portuguese policy makers as a way of solving unemployment issues, promoting innovation and driving SME development' (Bosma et al, 2020: 157). The Portuguese government has definitely been moving in the direction of creating an entrepreneurship-friendly environment, with a number of measures implemented to directly support enterprises with funding and market development (for example, the 2016 StartUp Portugal Program, the 2018 StartUp Portugal + Program). However, other barriers remain, especially with recurring bureaucratic and tax inefficiencies. According to the OECD report, the government continues to be supportive especially of youth entrepreneurship, as evidenced by significant investments in entrepreneurship education and in programs such as Program of Support for Entrepreneurship and Self-employment Creation (Programa de Apoio ao Empreendedorismo e à Criação do Próprio Emprego – PAECPE) and the Youth Investment Program (Programa Investe Jovem) (OECD/European Union, 2019).

Spain

With a fairly high NECI rating of 12/54, and a relatively good entrepreneurial ecosystem (for example, supportive government policies, low taxes/bureaucracy, entrepreneurship programs, favorable physical and commercial infrastructure, and so on, it is quite puzzling that Spain registers such low levels of TEA and youth entrepreneurship. Just like neighboring Portugal, the Spanish score highly on their perceived entrepreneurial capabilities and highly on fear of failure, again begging the question of whether externally conducive conditions can compensate for an inherent thirst for adventure the Americans possess. By all accounts, the Spanish government is quite committed to growing SMEs, and the topic of youth entrepreneurship continues to take center stage in policy discussions, with the government launching the Youth Employment Plan 2019–2021, a follow-up to its Entrepreneurship and Youth Employment Strategy 2013–2016 (OECD/European Union, 2019), and with a goal of reducing youth unemployment by 10% by 2021. The 2019 GEM survey of national experts finds that uncertainties in the international as well as domestic political environments represent significant challenges to Spanish entrepreneurs, and recommends that Spain devotes its attention to high-potential entrepreneurship, especially among youth, by improving the country's educational system and facilitating innovation and knowledge transfers (Bosma et al, 2020).

Concluding thoughts and recommendations

It is clear that for youth entrepreneurship to put down deep roots, three foundational components need to be conspicuously present in a country: (1) cultural and societal norms that are promotive and supportive of risk taking; (2) a system of human capital development that enables early age and continuous exposure to essential knowledge/ opportunities and skills acquisition to become an entrepreneur; and (3) a policy framework and an entrepreneurial ecosystem that result in a fertile breeding ground for innovation and self-employment.

As the preceding country-specific profile on entrepreneurship efforts makes clear, countries with a strong entrepreneurial framework alone (for example, Spain) do not post impressive gains. Perhaps what is needed to boost youth entrepreneurship, and to overcome deficits in the intrinsic entrepreneurial spirit in these countries, is a combination of a strong human capital foundation which includes the creation of an entrepreneurial mindset – a blend of success-oriented attitudes of initiative, intelligent risk taking, collaboration, and opportunity recognition – and a friendly ecosystem.

In the US, the country derives its status as an economic powerhouse primarily from small businesses that comprise 99.9% of its 30 million firms, and account for about 45% of its GDP (US Small Business Administration, 2019). Based on the relatively more successful US model of entrepreneurship, we offer the following recommendations for the Mediterranean countries of Greece, Italy, Spain, Portugal, and France:

Enhancement of human capital: entrepreneurship education

Introduce and/or strengthen youth entrepreneurship education starting at a very early age and provide opportunities to explore individuals' entrepreneurship potential. The most recent GEM findings indicate that this aspect of entrepreneurship promotion is universally the weakest (Bosma et al, 2020). The importance of this human capital development strategy is exemplified eminently by Switzerland, the top NECI-ranked country in Europe, with the highest marks for offering entrepreneurship education throughout the students' lifecycle.

The education strategy would include: (1) instilling an entrepreneurial mindset, that is, a blend of success-oriented attitudes of initiative, intelligent risk taking, collaboration, and opportunity recognition; (2) exposing students to practicums/internships/apprenticeships during summers while in upper primary and secondary schools, and continuing this education at tertiary levels; (3) providing the knowledge, skills, and tools students will need to try their hand at new ventures; and (4) integrating entrepreneurship education with the school curriculum, and adopting region-wide or national standards to increase consistency.

It goes without saying that implementing this strategy would require an unflinching commitment from the local, regional and central governments with respect to funding, coordination, and evaluation of outcomes. Instead of the 'one and done' approach that is often seen among the various ALMPs in these countries, this approach would entail delineating a clear structure, standards for implementation, and a careful measurement and assessment of whether this form of entrepreneurship education has borne its intended fruits, along with an identification of best practices. Public-private partnerships in which the US has had a long tradition (although Europe is now catching up at least in the area of digital initiatives, climate change, and so on) can be an important source of funding support for education initiatives. We recall the amazement with which our presentation on one such public-private partnership called the Nurture thru Nature (NtN) program was received by an education-labor group in Marseilles, France. We tried to convince the audience that such a thing was eminently possible, and that it has worked to the benefit of all entities involved for over a decade. These public-private partnerships can consist of corporations, philanthropic foundations, government agencies, nonprofit organizations, and other organizations in the public domain such as community groups. The unifying principle that undergirds this type of 'coming together' is the search for a solution to a pressing problem, and can prove to be an effective solution to resource-strapped local governments. And curbing high rates of youth unemployment certainly qualifies as a pressing social problem.

Enhancement of entrepreneurship ecosystem

Much like the creation of entrepreneurs, we can ask whether the entrepreneurship ecosystem evolves naturally or if it is intelligently designed? Isenberg (2011) points out that it is typically: 'the result of intelligent evolution, a process that blends the invisible hand of markets and deliberate helping hand of public leadership that is enlightened enough to know when and how to lead as well as let go the grip in order to cultivate and ensure (relative) self-sustainability'. This interpretation allows for an active role for policy makers at the local, regional and national governments in the creation of a favorable terrain for innovators to birth and grow their ideas – after all, even the best idea for a product or service is doomed to die an early death without the proper nurturing it requires.

In the preceding pages, we reprised information on each study country on what's being done regionally and nationally to improve the entrepreneurial context, using data culled from the GEM-NES 2019 interviews and *The Missing Entrepreneurs* (OECD/European Union, 2019). The broad spectrum of recommendations provided by international bodies, such as the EU, the World Economic Forum or the OECD, includes: (1) adopting policies that attract, promote and nurture entrepreneurship (for example, StartUp Portugal+ Program, the SpanishYouth Employment Plan 2019–2021, Resto al Sud in Southern Italy, and the New Action Plan for Business Growth and Transformation in France); (2) providing an inviting physical and commercial infrastructure; (3) increasing access to capital; and (4) reducing bureaucratic red-tape. In addition, we recommend that governments or other sponsoring entities: (1) undertake these policy/ regulatory efforts in conjunction with the human capital development strategy already discussed; (2) insist on a system of accountability for funds expended; and (3) as part of the accountability framework, make a deliberate effort to assess how the initiatives fare. To identify the best combination of policy and regulatory framework, we recommend that governments adopt a design framework that enables them to study policy impacts, either through randomized experiments or strong quasi-experiments, conducted at local or regional levels before scaling up to the national level.

In the US, in addition to the SBA and the Department of Commerce, the National Science Foundation (NSF) has taken on an active role in promoting and providing seed funding to innovators (without expecting any equity in return) whose ideas have potential commercial and societal impact. Fund recipients come from diverse fields ranging from advanced manufacturing, the Internet of Things and artificial intelligence to semiconductors and wireless technologies. The NSF awards about $190 million each year to startups and small businesses through the Small Business Innovation Research (SBIR)/ Small Business Technology Transfer (STTR) program. The National Institute of Health (NIH) invests over a billion dollars through the SBIR/STTR initiative also, and provides funding for innovations and startups in the biomedical/health industry. In addition to funding, the SBIR/STTR program includes a good measure of social capital in the form of connections to other entrepreneurs, technical leaders and industry experts. And all NSF and NIH funding requirements have a built-in component of accountability of funds as well as performance.

There are no parallel organizations like the NSF or the NIH that devote considerable energies to entrepreneurship in Europe overall or in individual European countries. The European Science Foundation (ESF) headquartered in Strasbourg, France, is a non-governmental non-profit association of selected European countries (Belgium, Bulgaria, France, Hungary, Romania, Serbia, and Turkey) and provides assistance to members and partners in coordinating/managing EU-funded grants, and general research and evaluation. Science Europe, a similar organization but with broader representation in Europe with 26 member countries, provides services that facilitate, coordinate and synthesize research across Europe. Neither of these organizations plays a supportive role for entrepreneurs, and neither even remotely comes close to what the NSF and NIH do in the US.

Absent such organizations at the continental level, countries have to rely on assistance at their own national level. Organizations at this level are not plentiful; for example the Spanish Foundation for Science and Technology that functions under the auspices of the Ministry of Science, Innovation and Universities, or The Foundation for Science and Technology under the Ministry of Science, Technology and Higher Education in Portugal, provide support for general scientific research, but nothing specific as it relates to entrepreneurship. A final suggestion we have is to expand the mandate of these national institutions to include specific support for inspiring, encouraging and supporting entrepreneurial activities.

Notes

[1]   France was not a participant country in GEM's 2019–2020 data collection effort. The data that are shown in the table are from the 2018–2019 GEM report (Bosma and Kelley, 2018).

[2]   The following quote from Peter Sims, a best-selling author and head of the BLK SHP Foundation that provides entrepreneurial support to startups, provides a counter to these GEM survey results, and reflects the more prototypical sentiment about Americans' risk seeking and risk tolerance:

> But after working as a venture capital investor in the US, then in Europe, I realized one day – while riding on a train through the English countryside – that when it came to risk taking, there really isn't anything like the culture of entrepreneurship in America. In England, you're considered an entrepreneur if you buy a small company and try to grow it. In Germany, most of the economy is driven by the *Mittelstand*, large, privately held companies that grow 5% to 10% a year. In France, Italy, and Spain, government regulations and high capital costs hamper start-ups. Yet in many parts of America, especially the valleys and universities, almost everyone is an entrepreneur, willing to tinker, toil, and enthuse about ideas late into the night, perfectly aware that failure is probable, even likely. Our cultural idols are the people who are willing to take enormous personal risk and toil through troughs of defeat. They emerge somehow as stronger human beings, perhaps wildly wealthy, or at

the very least wiser and more original versions of themselves. (*Time Magazine*, 2015)

See also the study cited earlier by Hofstede et al (2010).

[3] Although France is also shown to be ranked number 10, this ranking is from the 2018 GEM survey year, when the US was ranking number 6.

[4] These differences also hold for the three other western countries that have a higher NECI ranking than the US (Switzerland, Netherlands and Norway).

References

Baumol, W.J. (2010) *The Microtheory of Innovative Entrepreneurship*, Princeton, NJ: Princeton University Press.

Becker, G. (1993) *Human Capital: A Theoretical and Empirical Analysis with Special Reference to Education*, Chicago, IL: University of Chicago Press.

Becker, G. (1996) *Accounting for Tastes*, Cambridge, MA: Harvard University Press.

Borjas, G. (2008) *Labor Economics*, New York: McGraw Hill.

Bosma, N. and Kelley, D. (2019) *Global Entrepreneurship Monitor 2018/19 Global Report*, Global Entrepreneurship Research Association, London: London Business School.

Bosma, N., Hill, S., Ionescu-Somers, A., Kelley, D., Levie, J. and Tarnawa, A. (2020) *Global Entrepreneurship Monitor: 2019/2020 Global Report*, Global Entrepreneurship Research Association, London: London Business School.

Bourdieu, P. (1998) *Practical Reason: On the Theory of Action*, Stanford, CA: Stanford University Press.

Bourdieu, P. (2005) *The Social Structure of the Economy*, Cambridge: Polity Press.

Brinton, C. (1965) *The Anatomy of Revolution*, New York: Vintage Books.

Burghardt, J. and Schochet, P. (2001) *National Job Corps Study: Impacts by Center Characteristics*, Princeton, NJ: Mathematica Policy Research, Inc.

Card, D. and Krueger, A.B. (1995) *Myth and Measurement: The New Economics of the Minimum Wage*, Princeton, NJ: Princeton University Press.

Card, D., Kluve, J. and Weber, A. (2017) What works? A meta-analysis of recent active labor market program evaluations, *Journal of the European Economic Association*, 16: 894–931.

Carneiro, P.M. and Heckman, J.J. (2003) Human Capital Policy, IZA Discussion Paper 821, https://ssrn.com/abstract=434544

Casson, M. (2003) *The Entrepreneur: An Economic Theory* (second edition), Northampton, MA: Edward Elgar Publishing.

De Tocqueville, A. (1840, 1945) *Democracy in America*, vol 2, New York: Vintage Books.

D'Iribarne, P. (2009) National cultures and organisations in search of a theory: an interpretative approach, *International Journal of Cross Cultural Management*, 9: 309–21.

Dutta-Gupta, I., Grant, K., Eckel, M. and Edelman, P. (2016) *Lessons Learned from 40 Years of Subsidized Employment Programs*, Washington, DC: Georgetown Center on Poverty and Inequality, https://www. georgetownpoverty.org/wp-content/uploads/2016/07/gcpi-Subsidized-Employment-Paper-20160413.pdf

Economic Policy Institute (2019) Why America needs a $15 minimum wage, https://www.epi.org/publication/why-america-needs-a-15-minimum-wage/

Economist Intelligence Unit (2014) What's next: future global trends affecting your organization: evolution of work and the worker, https://www.shrm.org/foundation/ourwork/initiatives/preparing-for-future-hr-trends/publishingimages/pages/evolution-of-work/2-14%20theme%201%20paper-final%20for%20web.pdf

Eichhorst, W., Rodríguez-Planas, N., Schmidl, R. and Zimmermann, K.F. (2015) A road map to vocational education and training in industrialized countries, *ILR Review*, 68(2): 314–37, https://doi.org/10.1177/0019793914564963

Evans, E. (2019) Rejoice! Perkins funding is back on track, http://grantsoffice.com/efunded/tabid/867/entryid/206/rejoice-perkins-funding-is-back-on-track.aspx

Fadulu, L. (2018) Why is the US so bad at worker retraining? *The Atlantic*, January 4, https://www.theatlantic.com/education/archive/2018/01/why-is-the-us-so-bad-at-protecting-workers-from-automation/549185/

Guillaud, E. (2013) Preferences for redistribution: an empirical analysis over 33 countries, *Journal of Economic Inequality*, 11: 57–78.

Hofstede, G.H., Hofstede, G.J. and Minkov, M. (2010) *Cultures and organizations: Software of the Mind*, 3rd edn, New York: McGraw-Hill.

Hollenbeck, K. (2009) Workforce investment act (WIA) net impact estimates and rates of return: what the European social fund can learn from the WIA experience, paper presented to European Commission, Washington, DC, https://research.upjohn.org/confpapers/2/

Isenberg, D. (2011) Introducing the entrepreneurship ecosystem: four defining characteristics, *Forbes*, May 25, https://www.forbes.com/sites/danisenberg/2011/05/25/introducing-the-entrepreneurship-ecosystem-four-defining-characteristics/#441fa3075fe8

Jardim, E., Long, M.C., Plotnick, R., van Inwegn, E., Vigdor, J. and Wething, H. (2017*) Minimum Wage Increases, Wages, and Low-income Employment: Evidence from Seattle*, NBER working paper series, 23532, Cambridge, MA: National Bureau of Economic Research.

Kincheloe, J.L. (2018) *How Do We Tell the Workers*, New York: Routledge.

Kuczera, M. and Field, S. (2013) *A Skills Beyond School Review of the United States*, OECD Reviews of Vocational Education and Training, Paris: OECD Publishing, http://dx.doi.org/10.1787/9789264202153-en

LaLonde, R.J. (1995) The promise of public sector sponsored training programs, *Journal of Economic Perspectives*, 9(2): 149–68.

Lefebvre, G. (1962) *The Coming of the French Revolution, 1789*, London: Routledge and Kegan Paul.

Lerman, R. (2017) Why firms do and don't offer apprenticeships, in M. Pilz (ed) *Vocational Education and Training in Times of Economic Crisis*, Cham: Springer Nature, pp 305–20.

Lipset, S.M. (1979) *The First New Nation: The United States in Historical and Comparative Perspective*, New York: Anchor Books.

Maynard, R. (1995) Subsidized employment and non-labor market alternatives for welfare recipients, in D.S. Nightengale and R.H. Haveman (eds) *The Work Alternative: Welfare Reform and the Realities of the Job Market*, Washington, DC: The Urban Institute, pp 109–36.

McClelland, D.C. (1961) *The Achieving Society*, Princeton, NJ: Van Nostrand.

McClelland, D.C. (1964) *The Roots of Consciousness*, Princeton, NJ: Van Nostrand.

Murphy, J. (2017) *Yearning to Labor: Youth, Unemployment, and Social Destiny in Urban France*, Lincoln, NE: University of Nebraska Press.

OECD (1984) Policies for post-compulsory education and training, unpublished manuscript.

OECD (2016) *Job Creation and Local Economic Development 2016*, Paris: OECD Publishing.

OECD/European Union (2019) *The Missing Entrepreneurs 2019: Policies for Inclusive Entrepreneurship*, Paris: OECD Publishing.

Peet, J.R. (2012) Special report: France: so much to do, so little time, *The Economist,* November 17, 1–16, https://www.economist.com/special-report/2012/11/17/so-much-to-do-so-little-time

Reamer, A. (2017) Federal efforts in support of entrepreneurship: a reference guide, George Washington University Institute of Public Policy, https://gwipp.gwu.edu/federal-efforts-support-entrepreneurship-reference-guide-working-draft

Ryan, P. (2016) Monopsony power and work-based training, in G. Coppola and N. O'Higgins (eds) *Youth and the Crisis: Unemployment, Education and Health in Europe*, London: Routledge, pp 13–35.

Scheiber, N. (2017) Trump move on job training brings 'skills gap' debate to the fore, *New York Times*, June 15, https://www.nytimes.com/2017/06/15/business/economy/trump-job-training-skills-gap.html

Schumpeter, J.A. (1962) *Capitalism, Socialism, and Democracy*, New York: Harper & Row.

Schwab, K. (2019) *The Global Competitiveness Report 2019*, Geneva: The World Economic Forum.

Smith, A. (1776) *The Wealth of Nations*, reprint edn, E. Cannan (ed), New York: Modern Library.

Stam, E. and van Stel, A. (2011) Types of entrepreneurship and economic growth, in A. Szimai, W. Naude and M. Goedhuys (eds) *Entrepreneurship, Innovation, and Economic Development*, New York: Oxford University Press, pp 78–95.

Svendsen, G.L. and Svendsen, G.T. (2004) *The Creation and Destruction of Social Capital: Entrepreneurship, Co-operative Movements and Institutions*, Cheltenham: Edward Elgar.

The Economist (1996) Training and jobs, April 6.

Thrush, G. (2018) $1.7 billion federal job training programs 'failing the students', *New York Times*, August 26, https://www.nytimes.com/2018/08/26/us/politics/job-corps-training-program.html

Time Magazine (2015) Is America still the home of the brave? March 28, https://time.com/3761744/america-home-of-the-brave/

Ulijn, J. and Fayolle, A. (2004) Towards cooperation between European start-ups: the position of the French, Dutch, and German entrepreneurial and innovative engineer, in T.E. Brown and J. Ulijn (eds), *Innovation, Entrepreneurship and Culture: The Interaction Between Technology, Progress and Economic Growth*, Cheltenham, England: Edward Elgar, pp 204–32.

US Small Business Administration (2019) *United States Small Business Profile 2019*, Washington, DC: Office of Advocacy.

Valiente, O. and Scandurra, R. (2017) Challenges to the implementation of dual apprenticeships in OECD countries: a literature review, in M. Pilz (ed) *Vocational Education and Training in Times of Economic Crisis*, Cham: Springer Nature, pp 41–58.

Vogel, P. (2015) *Generation Jobless?* London: Palgrave Macmillan.

White House, Office of the Press Secretary (2014) Remarks by the President and Vice President on skills training, https://obamawhitehouse.archives.gov/the-press-office/2014/04/16/remarks-president-and-vice-president-skills-training

White House, Office of the Press Secretary (2017) Presidential executive order expanding apprenticeships in America, June 2015, https://www.whitehouse.gov/presidential-actions/3245/

Zamary, C. (2017a) Why entrepreneurship should be taught in first grade, *Huffington Post*, December 6.

Zamary, C. (2017b) Young entrepreneurs: coolest youth startups in the United States, *Huffington Post*, December 6.

Zimmermann, K.F., Biavaschi, C., Eichhorst, W., Giulietti, C., Kendzia, M.J., Muravyev, A., Pieters, J., Rodriguez-Planas, N. and Schmidl, R. (2013) Youth unemployment and vocational training, *Foundations and Trends in Microeconomics*, 9(1–2): 1–157.

Zirkle, C. (2017) A qualitative analysis of high school level vocational education in the United States: three decades of positive change, in M. Pilz (ed) *Vocational Education and Training in Times of Economic Crisis*, Cham: Springer Nature, pp 321–37.

9

Grading the Implementation Prospects: Where Do We Go from Here?

Radha Jagannathan

Many books, journal articles and opinion pieces have been written about the youth unemployment issue, and it is certain that a great many more will be written in the future. Economists and other social scientists have done an adequate job in pointing out the causes and consequences of the problem, and they have often helped politicians, governmental officials and the business community with the design of policies and programs that try to address it. Yet as we have seen throughout these chapters, knowledge and data do not appear to be compelling enough reasons to motivate the implementation of actions that could dramatically reduce the youth unemployment rates in Southern Mediterranean countries. This, of course, begs the question of why the apparent disconnect, if the proposed interventions do not require a complete reorientation of a nation's basic cultural values? Five hypotheses are offered, recognizing that they are not entirely mutually exclusive.

Good policy advice often goes unheeded

There are two policies, that is, minimum wages and government-subsidized, public sector jobs and job training, that not only fail to reduce unemployment but actually may contribute to its increase. Economic theory suggests that if you raise the price of any commodity, including labor, the demand will decrease. A recent high-profile experiment conducted in Seattle, Washington, provided an example of what usually occurs when the minimum wage is raised in a local labor market (Jardim et al, 2017). In 2015 the city raised its minimum wage from $9.47 an hour to $11.00. In 2016 the wage was raised again to $13.00. Spanning data from all industries in Seattle, these economists report that in 2015 the disemployment effect produced an elasticity of less than -1, and in 2016 reductions in employee earnings in the low wage market produced a staggering elasticity of -3. You will find the same sort of negative relationship acknowledged in any standard labor economics text (for example, Borjas, 2008).

Public sector 'make work' and job training have also been widely studied. Caliendo and Schmidl (2016) undertook a study of 37 evaluations of active labor market policies directed at youth in Europe, and reported that public sector work program had 'zero effect' on subsequent job quality or stability. Card et al (2017) come to much the same conclusion in their meta-analysis, noting medium term impacts of -1.1% and long-term effects of zero. An evaluation of one of America's newest federal jobs training programs, the Workforce Innovation and Opportunity Act (WIOA), conducted by Hollenbeck (2009), indicated a negative benefit of $8,000 for dislocated workers.

Notwithstanding the accumulated evidence to show that neither of these policies are remedies for youth employment, they continue to be pursued. This leads us to our second hypothesis.

Policy makers listen to the wrong social scientists

There is an old joke in the program evaluation literature that says some people use research the same way a drunk uses a lamp-post: not for illumination but for support (Greenberg and Schroder, 1997). From the world of epidemiology and public health, some readers may recall government officials in Great Britain citing research in the late 1990s that Mad Cow disease could not spread to humans, or very recent pronouncements from the World Health Organization (WHO) in January 2020 that COVID-19 could not spread between people (Corcoran, 2020). In the social sciences, for reasons that will become more apparent when stating the third hypothesis, it is much easier to receive advice from the wrong economist, political scientist or sociologist, because they occur in higher densities. From a list of examples much too numerous to enumerate I provide one – it is however one of great significance. Leading to the financial collapse of 2008 we have at least two Nobel Laureates in economics offering 'data-driven opinion' that the high-risk loan strategies, implemented by the US government-supported Fannie Mae and Freddie Mac mortgage-backed securities agencies, posed little or no risk to the American taxpayer. In 2002, Joseph Stiglitz penned an important and influential article stating that the new risk-based standards would greatly expand home ownership, increase the stake of poor Americans in the American Dream, and expand the middle class (Morgenson and Rosner, 2011). Also in 2002, Paul Krugman's offered the following advice in a *New York Times* column to fight a 2001 recession (Krugman, 2002): 'the Fed needs more than a snapback; it needs soaring household spending to offset moribund business investment'. Krugman's prescription was to create a housing bubble to replace the Nasdaq bubble. It, of course, was advice that wreaked havoc on the US and many other national economies for nearly a decade, and ended up substantially shrinking the home ownership it promised to create. More recently, Krugman (Hirsh, 2019) admitted that he and other mainstream economists were wrong about the positive effects of globalization on the US labor market, particularly on the loss of higher wage jobs.

Policy makers rely too much on social sciences with poor forecasting records

In arguments before the US Supreme Court in 2017 on partisan redistricting (gerrymandering) in the state of Wisconsin, the plaintiffs used evidence amassed by political scientists, called 'the efficiency gap', to argue for a more scientifically-based process. Chief Justice John G. Roberts, after hearing this argument, stated that he was wary of taking the issue of redistricting 'away from democracy' and throwing it into the courts to make decisions, using what he termed 'sociological gobbledygook' (Rocco, 2017). The responses from professional associations that represent many social scientists were immediate. Eduardo Bonilla-Silva, president of the American Sociological Association (ASA), responded, remarking sociological research is rigorous and empirical, and gave ten examples, including modern public opinion polling (Bonilla-Silva, 2017). Given the fragility of scientific polling – the election of Donald Trump, Trump amassing over 74 million votes in the 2020 election, the 2016 Brexit referendum, and polls leading up to it – to give only three recent major failures of polling, one would think another example would better bolster the ASA position.

In an extraordinary effort at mass collaboration, social science researchers at Princeton and Columbia universities issued the Fragile

Families Challenge (FFC). The challenge was open to researchers irrespective of scientific discipline from around the world, and a money prize was awarded to the applicant (457 submissions were received) who, using the Fragile Families longitudinal dataset comprising thousands of families measured on 12,000 covariates, was best able to predict six important child and family outcomes: grade point average of child (GPA), grit of child, material hardship, eviction of household, job layoff of caregiver, and job training of caregiver. The predictions ranged from around 23% accuracy in the case of material hardship, to 3% in the case of job layoff. The researchers at Princeton and Columbia conclude that:

> social scientists studying the life course must find a way to reconcile a widespread belief that understanding has been generated by these data – as demonstrated by more than 750 published journal articles using Fragile Families data – with the fact that the very same data could not yield accurate predictions of these important outcomes. (Salganik et al, 2020: 8402)

It is difficult to identify an area in the social sciences (for example, criminal justice, welfare policy, child welfare) where such a paradox does not exist.

Lack of social science consensus is seen as an obstacle to successful interventions

Low levels of predictive accuracy, failures to forecast calamitous or catastrophic events, and promulgating programs that do not work, have engendered a healthy skepticism around the contributions that much of social science has to offer. Responding to the skepticism, social science has increasingly resorted to the use of consensus as a way of establishing legitimacy. To use an example from the Fragile Families Challenge, let us take the example of 'grit', that is, perseverance in the face of formidable obstacles. There is a broad consensus among social psychologists and sociologists that grit is essential for individuals and families living in poverty conditions to successfully escape those conditions. In the FFC, grit could be predicted on average 6% of the time from a validation dataset, leaving anyone inclined to find individuals with this quality very little guidance.

In a now famous lecture given at Caltech in 2003, the author and Harvard-trained physician, Michael Crichton, had this to say about consensus:

> Let's be clear: the work of science has nothing whatever to do with consensus. Consensus is the business of politics. Science, on the contrary, requires only one investigator who happens to be right, which means that he or she has results that are verifiable by reference to the real world. What is relevant is reproducible results. The greatest scientists in history are great precisely because they broke the consensus. (Crichton, 2003: 7)

In the area of youth unemployment social science has yet to reach a consensus on best practices, but I do not see this as an obstacle to the development of effective policies and counter-measures. If one follows Crichton's thinking, disarray and disagreement more readily open up debate and inquiry which, in turn, facilitates innovation and opportunity. I have embraced this strategy of open debate here in this final chapter by asking each of our authors to assess the prospects of implementing the German dual model and American-style entrepreneurship in their respective countries. Jagannathan and Tosun, the authors of the American and German chapters, also made assessments of the feasibility of successful adoption of these models in Italy, Spain, Portugal, Greece, and France. Authors ranked feasibility on a scale of 1 to 10, with 1 indicating no chance of successful implementation and 10 designating no chance of failure. Authors were asked to use the data and arguments they presented in the preceding chapters as a basis for their rankings, and to summarize their reasoning in a short description. I present these ratings in Table 9.1, followed by each author's justification.

It is clear from Table 9.1 that the Jagannathan-Tosun assessments, and those of the Mediterranean country chapter authors, do not reflect consensus as often as they reflect difference. The differences between the Tosun and country authors' assessments were Italy (5–7), Spain (6–8), Portugal (6–2), Greece (4–6) and France (8–5); the Jagannathan-country author differences were Italy (4–4), Spain (5–4), Portugal (6–6), Greece (5–7) and France (4–4). Overall, in only three instances – all in feasibility ranking of American entrepreneurship – was there consensus, and this consensus coalesced around equal likelihood of success (in the case of Portugal) or failure (in the cases of France and Italy).

Table 9.1: Scorecard on feasibility of German dual model and American entrepreneurship model (out of 10)

Scorer	France	Greece	Italy	Portugal	Spain
Tosun					
German model	8	4	5	6	6
Jagannathan					
American model	4	5	4	6	5
Caserta – Italy					
German model			7		
American model			4		
Arco Tirado – Spain					
German model					8
American model					4
Marques – Portugal					
German model				2	
American model				6	
Tsoulou – Greece					
German model		6			
American model		7			
Camasso – France					
German model	5				
American model	4				

Let's examine the reasons the authors used to reach their final rankings, produced here verbatim.

Box 9.1: Caserta – Italy

The German dual education model The recent training and apprenticeship programs in Italy were both intended to integrate the education system with the labor market, in an attempt to reduce the mismatch between supply and demand of labor, particularly noticeable in the youth section of that market. Although it is difficult to evaluate the impact of such recent reforms on the performance of the labor market, a number of critical comments can be made. In fact, the intended integration of the two systems, education and production, has not been achieved. The apprenticeship program has remained too much work-based, while the Alternanza Scuola-Lavoro program has remained too much school-based. Firms have adopted the apprenticeship program mainly to take advantage of the associated subsidies; schools have maintained full control of the Alternanza Scuola-Lavoro program, with the result that even the time spent at the productive site is not working time, but a continuation of the time spent at school. Hence, the road to a proper dual system, along the lines of the German one, is still a long one.

However, there is no valid alternative to that system. So it is worth investigating why it has so far failed to deliver the expected results. No doubt, the system is under-financed and needs some organizational adjustments, but the main reason for its failure lies in some distinctively Italian (especially southern Italian) cultural traits. When it comes to judging education, popular opinion puts high school on a standard superior to technical and vocational school. It is not long ago that humanities were considered disciplines of a higher standard than hard or soft sciences. Work and business values are not usually taught at school. Business culture has been considered for a long time a culture of a lower standing. All this has kept the world of education apart from the world of production and business. Such popular feelings are hard to disappear. Still, it cannot now be denied that they have had an effect on legislation and actual behaviours. It looks as if there is no shared language between the world of education and the world of business. If there is no shared language, it comes as no surprise that it is difficult to match supply and demand in the labor market.

American entrepreneurship model Young Italian southerners may have to wait a long time before finding a job, so that many of them choose to leave for the north of the country, lured by the supposedly higher wages and better opportunities in the north. Hence, it looks as if the price system is working. More jobs are available in the north; this relative abundance is signalled through the price system, and young people plan to move north. This is consistent with the fact that southern universities are reporting lower and lower student enrolment in the last 20 years. What typically happens is that young people perceive that job opportunities are in greater number in the northern regions. And based on that perception they decide to move even before completing their higher education; in many cases they move right after high school. In that case the connection between the education system and the labor market seems to be working. Young people perceive that it is enough to get a degree from a northern university to find a job. Thus, combining data on youth unemployment in the northern regions with the outflow of young students from the south, the picture emerging is one of an effective redistribution system and an efficient labor market, where excess supply is driven to the regions where there is excess demand.

However, there is an inconsistency in this picture. One would expect that, precisely because of this outflow of young people, youth unemployment should decrease. Unfortunately, this has not happened. Youth unemployment in the south of the country does not seem to be getting any lower. The main reason for this is that the outflow of young people concerns fundamentally the skilled ones, that is, those who have followed the track leading to higher education. Those who have followed the technical or vocational track do not seem to be that much attracted by job opportunities in the northern regions. Hence, the price system appears to be working for the skilled young people, but not for the unskilled ones. It must be said, in passing, that even if the price system worked for all, we would still have a problem, that is, the fate of a region that is deprived entirely of its young labor force. Surely, no one could stop people from relocating within or across countries, but no one could ignore that there is a strong preference to stay close to where one was born. It follows from this that any free market approach to the labor market, especially with respect to the education-work link, is bound to lead, in the best possible world, to the desertification of one part of the country.

Box 9.2: Arco Tirado – Spain

The German dual VET model aligns more with traditional VET in Spain, and is perceived more favorably in the last five years approximately, since the diffusion by mass media of the benefits of the German model for youth employability, particularly for the age group 16–18 after the 2008 crisis. However, this model does not resolve the main problem of Spain, which is concentrated in the age group 14–16 years, since in Spain basic compulsory education ends at 16. Before current levels of sympathy for the German model many intellectuals in Spain were very critical of the German model, since it began to segregate kids for 'blue collar' or 'white collar' professions at the early age of 12.

During the dictatorship the way for youth to access labor market was through 'apprenticeship', and apparently the German model for that resonates with Spanish people.

Geographical proximity, and the fact that both countries are partners in the EU, is a very influential factor because of the tendency to increase and extend collaboration beyond financial and economic products. Another underlying factor is the substantial demographic decline of the labor force in Germany and the need to plan immigration to mediate the negative impact on employment and growth. In this regard, Spanish workers have a high reputation of being hard workers in Germany, gained during the 1960s and 1970s when 600,000 Spaniards migrated to Germany.

The Spanish government needs to reform or recycle or readapt the important parallel network of school-based VET centers, in order to rescue and strengthen the fragile connections and collaboration with the industry sector. And this process has more possibilities of being successful if the dual VET model works. So, the governments at the national and regional levels are multiplying their efforts and investment with German partners who have the experience. However, as I mention in the chapter, more transparency on how those programs are being conducted is absolutely necessary in order to ensure the sustainability of the model in the medium and long term. Tables with descriptive evaluation data at the end of the program are not enough in Spain, particularly with small and medium enterprises.

In spite of the important efforts made by the government to develop an entrepreneurship mindset, particularly among youth in and out of schools, entrepreneurial activity in Spain takes place in a social context that does not fully endorse that model, along with insufficient financing, mentoring, or financial literacy. American 'self-interest rightly understood, it seems to me, is not understood the same way in Spain.

Frequent news in Europe accusing American multinationals (for example, Google, Twitter, Facebook) of tax evasion does not help at all, either, to change people's perception and knowledge to realize the fact that those world corporations were brought here for particular reasons.

Box 9.3: Camasso and Moissonier – France

In our description and assessment of the French vocational and technical education system, we attempted to make the point that the undeveloped state of the country's VET and apprenticeship programs has less to do with motivations, technical expertise, corruption and some of the other obstacles found in the Southern Mediterranean (where France has only one foot in the water), and much more to do with a cultural preference set that prizes 'the talent for abstraction; the ability to simplify complex problems while leaving room for their complexities and an overall knowledge of French history, philosophy and culture' (Camasso and Jagannathan, 2021). This value orientation, we believe, is of critical importance when issues of system transfer and adoption are involved. The German and American systems of organizing their economies are very different, as other chapters in this book clearly point out; however, they do share one common feature, that is, the necessity of converting theoretical knowledge into practical applications. We believe this commonality places both in contrast to France, especially in the case of America.

American capitalism has never been popular in France. This unpopularity, moreover, is grafted upon a type of one-way rivalry that dates back to America's founding. When, arguably, France's most cherished cultural icon, its wine industry, was destroyed by phylloxera vastatrix it was the US that came to France's aid with disease-resistant vines. In World Wars I and II, America was twice again back on French soil.

The German-French relationship has deep cultural and historical underpinnings that we feel also mitigate French adoption of a system that is built upon a strong respect for technical expertise. We have described the substantial role that German workers play in the German production process, and the much more limited role played by French workers. The dismantling of a centralized, state-controlled capitalism by the people who are the central, state-controlling capitalists, does not strike us as very likely, and without such a change we do not see the French VET system changing dramatically, short of a crisis.

The American historian, Will Durant (1939) famously wrote 'around every Rome hover the Gauls; around every Athens some Macedon'. In today's France, the one Lefebvre identified as the direct descendant of classical Roman and Greek civilizations, it might appear to those directly involved in the education system that a new generation of Gauls and Macedonians are circling the city.

Box 9.4: Tsoulou – Greece

Traditionally, the vocational high-school path in Greece is more attractive to students from lower educational and socioeconomic backgrounds, compared to those who attend general high schools. EPAL and EPAS could provide future employment options for young adults, who would likely fail to obtain a high school certificate or enter the market as unskilled workers, since they would not have the means to support private tutoring, a standard for those attending general high school to improve their scores in the Pan-Hellenic exams. Therefore, the vocational path can be valuable for this share of youth, assuming that EPAL and EPAS significantly update their curriculum to reflect current market needs (aligned with the private sector) and ensure continuous education of their students for resilience. On the other hand, employment opportunities that arise through the vocational path are usually low-wage, while related education is limited in its ability to promote the students' intellectual growth. This can be critical in offering opportunities for future personal development, and also restrictive in the sense that students are called to decide about their future at such an early age. Therefore, while there is potential in the dual education model, investing in general education combined with support on research and development can be more beneficial in the long term, as it can provide multiple choices and pathways for students.

Greeks are characterized by an entrepreneurial spirit, and the country's landscape offers opportunities for starting a new business in sectors such as tourism, leisure and sustainable agriculture. However, existing cultural and governmental mechanisms and the debt crisis that are discussed at length in Chapter 5 present significant obstacles against youth entrepreneurship. Therefore, related incentives are needed that can support small businesses and target improvements in insurance, taxation, initial capital and bureaucratic processes. Educated youth could further benefit from efforts to promote the high-tech sector and the software industry, in parallel to establishing connections to the international market. Lastly, incorporating entrepreneurship into education and providing consulting services to young adults can also inspire venture spirit.

Box 9.5: Marques – Portugal

It is difficult to implement the German model in Portugal for several reasons. As regards coordination in the industrial relations system, which according to the comparative political economy literature is crucial to boost this kind of training, there is poor coordination and thus it is difficult to involve employers and unions in the provision of workplace training. In terms of labor law, which is also seen as important, although employees with permanent contracts have high job security, the opposite happens for workers with temporary contracts. As temporary workers cover mainly young labor market participants, it therefore also becomes problematic to encourage students to enroll in dual-VET programmes. Reforms recently implemented during the sovereign debt crisis further aggravated this problem because they further deregulated labor legislation, reducing even more the incentives to invest in specific skills. This is important because workers tend to invest less in specific skills if they do not have job stability. Finally, the dual-VET system in Germany is connected with a large manufacturing sector, which hires a large number of workers with this kind of training. The Portuguese manufacturing sector is shrinking and is much less competitive. Some companies may be interested in this type of training, but they represent a low proportion of jobs.

As for the American entrepreneurial model, there are also some difficulties when trying to import it to address youth unemployment in Portugal. A number of conditions are necessary to implement this model, namely access to risk capital, the existence of top-level universities, and the labor market. Portugal faces difficulties in meeting these conditions for several reasons. First, compared with Liberal Market Economies (LMEs) where entrepreneurship is more successful, Portugal lacks access to risk capital. Access to this kind of capital was not abundant before the crisis and the situation was further aggravated during the sovereign debt crisis, when Portugal lost access to international financial markets. Equally, although there has been a massive investment in higher education over recent years, Portugal does not have top-level universities as LMEs do. As for the degree of flexibility, although reforms have been made to labor legislation since 2011, the degree of protection is still higher than in LMEs.

Notwithstanding, it is possible that entrepreneurship and policies focused on graduates will deserve more attention in the future. This may happen for three reasons. First, high unemployment among graduates is a pressing problem in Portugal, and thus entrepreneurship can be part of the solution. Second, the Portuguese government has recently announced new policies to boost entrepreneurship, including the attraction of big international conferences like the Web Summit, which has taken place in Lisbon since 2016. Besides the fact that these events may provide Portuguese start-ups with access to venture capital, the Portuguese government has, very recently, launched new programmes to facilitate access to risk capital (StartUP Portugal). Although this does not solve all the problems, it can provide better conditions to boost entrepreneurship. Third, empirical studies evaluating public programmes conclude that programmes promoting entrepreneurship show good results.

Box 9.6: Tosun – Germany

Generally speaking, countries with considerable German foreign direct investment have a good chance of adopting the German VET model. Our own research, but also the existing literature, has clearly shown that German companies seek to transfer the German VET system to the various sites where they are operate. The production processes rely on adequately skilled workforce and therefore companies are willing to invest in their training. However, the existence of Germany companies is a necessary but not a sufficient condition for adopting the German apprenticeship model. National or local-level factors can impede the companies' attempts to establish the German model. Most importantly, the apprenticeship model can only work if there exist good-quality and accessible education and training institutions. Without such an infrastructure, it is difficult to transfer the German model, even if the companies are committed to it. Since Greece has comparatively weak education institutions, the score given to that country is 4. Italy has a slightly better infrastructure concerning VET, but the educational landscape varies strongly across regions and communities. The situation is a bit better in Spain and Portugal and therefore they received a score of 6. France has an education system that resembles that of Germany and therefore, it received the highest score of 8.

Box 9.7: Jagannathan and Camasso – United States

Chapter 8 describes in detail the American work ethos and the entrepreneurial spirit that undergirds it within the larger framework of free-market capitalism. As I note in the chapter, paraphrasing de Tocqueville, Americans are known for their pragmatism and their orientation toward action, values that limit their appetite for intellectualism as an end in itself, and their honor for labor and making money. I recall a conversation I had with a friend in France some years ago, one I believe perfectly captures the American ethos which is quite at variance with the work culture in some other countries. He said that "we [French] think and we think and we think some more – but you Americans – you think and you think, and then you *do*".

The US has a long and rich history of the entrepreneurial spirit that has resulted in economic success for many of its youth and adults. Qualities such as creative thinking, calculated risk taking, irreverence for consensual views, and rule-challenging behavior – qualities that are extremely important for the creation of small businesses built around breakthrough ideas and innovations – have a fertile ground in America. Business failures are worn proudly as a rite of passage, valued for the lessons learned, and seen more as an opportunity to pivot rather than as terminal points. The entrepreneurial support system also includes risk-embracing venture capitalists, incubators for ideas provided by institutions such as the National Science Foundation, a general educational curriculum that incorporates entrepreneurship at an early grade, and a relatively less bureaucratic burden.

It is clear that for youth entrepreneurship to put down deep roots, three foundational components need to be conspicuously present in a country: (1) cultural and societal norms that are promotive of opportunities and supportive of risk taking; (2) a system of human capital development that enables early age and continuous exposure to essential knowledge/opportunities, and skills acquisition to become an entrepreneur; and (3) a policy framework, financial support and an entrepreneurial ecosystem that result in a fertile breeding ground for innovation and self-employment. Greece, Spain, Portugal and Italy fall far shorter (relative to the US' top ranking) on supportive cultural or societal norms according to recent GEM data; and the overall score on the entrepreneurial ecosystem places Greece (40/54), Italy (33/54), and Portugal (38/54) at a much lower rank than the US (10/54). While Portugal may show a relatively high total entrepreneurial activity, fear of business failure reigns there; and while Spain appears to have a favorable ecosystem, it doesn't post impressive gains on entrepreneurial activities. A culture of clientelism and nepotism in Greece may preclude entrepreneurship as a pathway to success; and despite a high perception of opportunities, intentionality toward business startups is quite low in Italy. What is needed to boost youth entrepreneurship and to overcome deficits in the intrinsic entrepreneurial spirit in these countries is a combination of a strong human capital foundation which includes the creation of an entrepreneurial mindset – a blend of success-oriented attitudes of initiative, intelligent risk taking, collaboration, and opportunity recognition – and a friendly ecosystem.

Rather than presenting a barrier to advancing the science necessary to ameliorate youth unemployment, I believe this type of discourse is an essential step in the process of developing social science–based policies and programs that actually work.

If this method of rating appears too crude for some readers, I ask them to examine the alternative. Consensus in the social science, notwithstanding low levels of prediction accuracy as measured by R^2, MSE or some variant, continues to flourish. It is achieved by what Hofman et al (2017) refer to as the 'widespread adoption within the social and behavioral sciences of a particular style of thinking that emphasizes unbiased estimation of model parameters over predictive accuracy' (Hofman et al, 2017: 486). The focus is on whether or not a regression parameter estimate is statistically significant. They point out that this approach has come under a torrent of recent criticism out of concern that an 'unthinking search for statistical significance has resulted in a proliferation of nonreplicable findings' (Hofman et al, 2017: 486; see also Gigerenzer, 2004). I should note that much of this torrent is from outside the social sciences in the fields of computational sciences and machine learning.

My hope is that this presentation of a feasibility scorecard will motivate continuing debate in an area of public policy (youth unemployment) where ostensive consensus has been achieved by social scientists through quantitative analyses with low prediction accuracy and therefore little accountability. As Tetlock and colleagues suggest (Tetlock et al, 2017; Tetlock et al, 1989), pre-decisional accountability is engendered by an awareness of how relevant audiences will react to a policy prescription. For example, the congruency or lack of it, between the forecasts of dual system success in Portugal (stipulating, of course, that both assessments are empirically based) by analysts from Germany and Portugal, increase cognitive complexity, which Tetlock et al (2017) claim causes analysts to contemplate a greater number of germane factors and modify their predictions based on (broader) audience data.

Useful social science has broad application

The idea that research can be generalized and transferred is an obvious goal of all science, including social science. An investigation into the history of science, however, shows that it is as often the case as not that causal relationships are contingent on such factors as historical time, cultural values, and geographical location. Shadish et al (2002) use as an example the proposition that threat from an out-group of superior strength causes in-group cohesion. There are many instances from ancient Greece and Rome, Denmark in World War II, Vietnam in French Indo-China, American wars, and so on, where this cohesion became manifest; there are also numerous instances where this did not happen. Shadish et al (2002: 15) give this account: 'In 1492 the King of Granada had to watch as his Moorish subjects left the city to go to their ancestral homes in North Africa, being unwilling to fight against the numerically superior troops of the Catholic Kings of Spain'.

Transferability and generalizability dovetail very nicely with the perspective of globalism, modernism, and post-nationalism. Examples of the new global order of economic and political associations seem everywhere: the World Trade Organization, the WHO, the EU, and so on. It may be wishful thinking, however, to believe that nation states, their unique cultures and histories, have simply been woven into some cosmopolitan quilt. The chapters in this book reflect the experiences and expertise of the authors; they also resonate the cultural value orientations that give rise to the German dual system, American-style entrepreneurship, the penchant for general education, the avoidance of risk, and other beliefs and preferences that can influence strategies to reduce youth unemployment.

During the 2016 US presidential campaign, many of the candidates in the Democratic Party called for an economic system that was more like the capitalist model used in Sweden. This has happened, once again, in the 2020 campaign for the US presidency. It has apparently been a clarion call for a great many social scientists and politicians for many decades. And, as I noted in the first chapter, it is a call that is likely to yield only frustration.

Good social science can still be useful, even with limited generalizability and narrow transferability. Understanding the conditions that maximize the probability of implementation can save resources, circumvent false expectations and help strike a balance between economic efficiency and national pride, where required. The German dual system operationalizes an approach to human capital formation that reflects a balance between general (conceptual) and specific knowledge and skills. But, as McClelland (1964) observed, this system also resonates with a deeper cultural structure which he referred to as the 'German value formula', that is, 'I must be able to believe and do what I should do for the good of the whole' (McClelland, 1964: 80). A balanced economy requires both strong knowledge and technical components that produce both manufactured goods and professional services for export. The American version of free-wheeling capitalism is also more than a commitment to unregulated markets. It is a value orientation that flows from its Puritan ancestry and an 'American value formula' that has and continues to emphasize free choice, action over contemplation, and the need for individual achievement (McClelland, 1964: 23).

I believe that without the recognition of a nation's basic value orientation, transferability and generalizability of any technology, including human capital development strategies, could fall short of intended objectives and can lead to unexpected consequences. The probabilities of the latter occurring would be expected to increase dramatically if the 'value formulae' in the donor and recipient cases are inconsistent.

References
Bonilla-Silva, E. (2017) ASA President Eduardo Bonilla-Silva responds to Chief Justice Roberts, *American Sociological Association*, https://www.asanet.org/news-events/asa-news
Borjas, G. (2008) *Labor Economics*, New York: McGraw Hill.
Bosma, N. and Kelley, D. (2018) *Global Entrepreneurship Monitor 2018/2019*, Global Report, London: Global Entrepreneurship Research Association.
Caliendo, M. and Schmidl, R. (2016) Youth unemployment and active labor market policies in Europe, *IZA Journal of Labor Policy*, 5(1): 1–30.

Camasso, M.J. and Jagannathan, R. (2021) *Caught in the Cultural Preference Net: Three Generations of Employment Choices in Six Capitalist Democracies*, New York: Oxford University Press.

Card, D., Kluve, J. and Weber, A. (2017) What works? A meta-analysis of recent active labor market program evaluations, *Journal of the European Economic Association*, 16(3): 894–931.

Corcoran, K. (2020) An infamous WHO tweet saying there is no clear evidence, *Business Insider*, April 18.

Crichton, M. (2003) Aliens cause global warming, Caltech Michelin Lecture, January 17, http://www.sepp.org/newsepp/gw-aliens-crichton.htm

Durant, W. (1939) *The Life of Greece: The Story of Civilization (#2)*, New York: Simon & Schuster.

Gigerenzer, G. (2004) Mindless statistics, *Journal of Socio-Economics*, 33: 587–606.

Greenberg, D. and Schroder, M. (1997) *The Digest of Experiments*, 2nd edn, Washington, DC: The Urban Institute.

Hirsch, M. (2019) Economists on the run, https://foreignpolicy.com/2019/10/22/economists-globalization-trade-paul-krugman-china/

Hofman, J.M., Sharma, A. and Watts, D.J. (2017) Prediction and explanation in social systems, *Science*, 355: 486–8.

Hollenbeck, K. (2009) Workforce investment act (WIA) net impact estimates and rates of return: what the European social fund can learn from the WIA experience, paper presented at European Commission, Washington, DC, https://research.upjohn.org/confpapers/2/

Jardim, E., Long, M.C., Plotnick, R., van Inwegn, E., Vigdor, J. and Wething, H. (2017) *Minimum Wage Increases, Wages, and Low-income Employment: Evidence from Seattle*, NBER working paper series, 23532, Cambridge MA: National Bureau of Economic Research.

Krugman, P. (2002) Dubya's double dip? *New York Times*, August 2, Section A, p 21.

McClelland, D.C. (1964) *The Roots of Consciousness*, Princeton, NJ: Van Nostrand.

Morgenson, G. and Rosner, J. (2011) *Reckless Endangerment*, New York: Henry Holt and Co.

Rocco, P. (2017) Justice Roberts said political science is sociological gobbledygook: here's why he said it and why he's mistaken, *Washington Post*, http://www.washingtonpost.com/news/monkey-cage/wp2017/10/04/

Salganik, M. et al (2020) Measuring the predictability of life outcomes with a scientific mass collaboration, *Proceedings of the National Academy of Sciences*, 117(15): 8398–403.

Shadish, W.R., Cook, T.D. and Campbell, D.T. (2002) *Experimental and Quasi-Experimental Design*, Boston: Houghton Mifflin.

Tetlock, P.E., Mellers, B.A. and Scoblic, J.P. (2017) Bringing probability judgments into policy debates via forecasting tournaments, *Science*, 107: 481–3.

Tetlock, P.E., Skitka, L. and Boettger, R. (1989) Social and cognitive strategies for coping with accountability, *Journal of Personality and Social Psychology*, 57: 632–40.

Time Magazine (2015) Is America still the home of the brave? March 28.

Index

References to figures appear in *italic* type; those in **bold** type refer to tables.

A

active labor market policies (ALMPs) *see* ALMPs (active labor market policies)
Afonso, A. 135
AFP (Alianza para la Formación Profesional Dual), Spain 184–5, 186–7, 189, 191, 192, 193, 194
African-Americans, youth unemployment rate 205
Aldieri, L. 30
Alianza para la Formación Profesional Dual (AFP), Spain 184–5, 186–7, 189, 191, 192, 193, 194
Alianza para la FP Dual (Alliance for Dual Vocational Education), Spain 64
Alianzafpdual, Spain 64, 65
ALMPs (active labor market policies) 6, 7–8, 110, 139–40, 141, 224, 234
  France 95–6
  Greece 110–11, 119
  Portugal 128, 140, 141–52, **143**, **150**, **153**, 154, 156
  Spain 67, **68**, 69–71
  Sweden 95
Alternanza Scuola-Lavoro, Italy 34–5, 37, 238–9
America *see* US (United States)
American Sociological Association (ASA) 235
American Value Formula 205, 209, 248
apprenticeships 128
  France 88–9
  Portugal 128
  Spain 71–2
  see also Germany, dual education model; VET (vocational education and training)
Aravani, E. 119
ASA (American Sociological Association) 235

Asian Americans, youth unemployment rate 205
ASPETE (schools of pedagogical and technological education), Greece 108
Audi 189
Austria 3, 167
Azkenazy, P. 91

B

Babson College 216
Baccalauréat général, France 87–8
Baccalauréat professionel, France 86, 88
Baccalauréat technologique, France 86
Banfield, E.C. 43
bankruptcy policies 12
Basic Vocational Education and Training (VET/Básica), Spain 63
Bassols, C. 66–7
Becker, G. 86, 206, 209
BEP (Brevet d'Études Professionnelle), France 86, 87, 88
Bernal-Verdugo, L.E. 27
Bertelsmann Foundation 64, 67, 71
Berufsfachschulen, Germany 9
Bisin, A. 5
BizWorld, US 215
Bonilla-Silva, Eduardo 235
Borjas, G.J. 30
Bosma, N. 90, 114, 221
Bourdieu, P. 81, 82, 89
Brada, J.C. 27
'brain drain' 24, 105
Brazil 11
Brevet de Technicien Supérieur (BTS), France 88
Brevet d'Études Professionnelle (BEP), France 86, 87, 88
Bridges, Mo 215
bridging capital 44

BTS (Brevet de Technicien Supérieur), France 88
Burroni, L. 176
Busemeyer, M.R. 177
Butkus, M. 56

C

Cahuc, P. 87–8, 91
Cainarca, G.C. 179
Caliendo, M. 69, 110, 234
Cámara de Comercio (Chamber of Commerce), Spain 64, 65, 184
Camasso, Michael J. 1, 5
Canada 11
CAP (Certificat d'aptitude professionnelle), France 86, 87, 88
Card, D. 212–13, 234
'career and technical' education (CTE), US 209, 210–11
Carl Perkins Career and Technical Education Act (Perkins Act) (2006), US 209, 210–11
Cart, B. 89
Cedefop (European Center for the Development of Vocational Training) 34, 64, 88, 171
  ESI (European Skill Index) 32–3, 56, 108–9
  Skills Forecast: Trends and Challenges to 2030 109
Center for European Trainees (CET) 184, 185, 189, 191
Centre for Knowledge and Innovation from Dualiza Bankia, Spain 65
CEOE (Confederation of Employers' Organisations), Spain 64, 184
CEPYME (Confederation of Small and Medium-Sized Enterprises), Spain 64
Certificat d'aptitude professionnelle (CAP), France 86, 87, 88
CET (Center for European Trainees) 184, 185, 189, 191
CETA (Comprehensive Employment and Training Act) programs, US 211
Chamber of Commerce (Cámara de Comercio), Spain 64, 65, 184
Chambers of Crafts and Commerce, Germany 10
China, accession to WTO 129, 130
Chrichton, Michael 237
Classes préparatoire aux grandes écoles (CPGE), France 89
clientelism, in Greece 14, 105, 246
CMEs (coordinated market economies) 5, 6, 7, 15, 83, 134, 136, 137, 140, 174, 177, 178, 179

Common Quality Assurance Framework (CQAF), Spain 66
community colleges, US 208, 209
Comprehensive Employment and Training Act (CETA) programs, US 211
Comprehensive Employment and Training Act (1973), US 16, 211
Compulsory Secondary Education (ESO), Spain 63
Confederation of Employers' Organisations (CEOE), Spain 64, 184
Confederation of Small and Medium-Sized Enterprises (CEPYME), Spain 64
consensus, lack of in social sciences 236–47, **238**
Continental European counties 6
Contract-Employment, Portugal 146
cooperation 43, 183
coordinated market economies (CMEs) 5, 6, 7, 15, 83, 134, 136, 137, 140, 174, 177, 178, 179
corruption, in Greece 14, 15, 118, 120
Costa Dias, M. 154
COVID-19 pandemic, economic consequences of 2–3
CPGE (Classes préparatoire aux grandes écoles), France 89
CQAF (Common Quality Assurance Framework), Spain 66
CTE ('career and technical' education), US 209, 210–11
culture, and economies 4–5, 7
CUPESSE (Cultural Pathways to Economic Self-sufficiency and Entrepreneurship) project, EU 12–13, 38, **39–40**, 41, 171
Czech Republic 25

D

Dalla, E. 105
de Tocqueville, Alexis 1, 16, 82, 204–5, 206–7, 245
debt crisis 130, 131, 138, 150, **150**, 151–2, 156
Denmark 6–7, 57
Department of Commerce, US 215, 226
Department of Labor, US 210
DESI (Dual Education System Italy) 189
Didaktorika (PhDs), Greece 108
diffusion studies 180
DiMaggio, P.J. 181
Diplôme Universitaire de Technologie (DUT), France 88, 97
d'Iribarne, Philippe 83, 89

dirigisme, France 13, 14, 81–3, 91, 94
  and labor supply 86–90, *87*
D'Isanto, E. 29
divergence 182
Dixon, R. 56
Dolowitz, D.P. 180–1
Dual Education System Italy (DESI) 189
'Dualiza Bankia,' Spain 64–5
Ducati 189
Durant, Will 242
DUT (Diplôme Universitaire de
  Technologie), France 88, 97

E

EAFA (European Alliance for
  Apprenticeship) 64
École des Hautes Études Commerciales,
  France 82
École Nationale d'Administration,
  France 82
École Normal Superieure, France 82
École Polytechnique, France 82
economic cycle, impact on youth
  unemployment 24, 29–30
Economic Policy Institute 213
economies, typologies of 103
  Esping-Anderson 6–7, 83
  VoC (varieties of capitalism) 5–6, 7, 15,
    128, 134, 167, 173–80, 181–2, 193
Education, Training & Enterprise Center,
  US 215
Eichhorst, W. 179
elites, in France 81–2
emigration, from Greece 105
Employment Contract program,
  Portugal 148, 149
Employment Initiative, Portugal 145,
  146, 151
Employment Passport, Portugal 146, 151
EMU (Economic and Monetary
  Union) process
  impact on Portugal 129–30, 150, **150**
entrepreneurship
  Europe 10–12, *11*
  France 11, 90, 94, 220–1, 223–6
  Germany 11, 94
  Greece 15, 114–15, 118, 120, 220,
    223–6, 246
  Italy 114, 221, 223–6, 246
  Portugal 114, 128, 140, 141, 142, 148,
    155, 157, 158, 221–2, 223–6, 246
  Sweden 94
  US (United States) 1–2, 10–12, *11*,
    94, 248
  see also US (United States),
    entrepreneurship model

Entrepreneurship and Youth Employment
  Strategy 2013–2016, Spain 222
Equal Education Opportunity Act (1974),
  US 207
Erasmus Plus 171
ESF (European Science
  Foundation) 225–6
ESF (European Social Fund) 112
ESO (Compulsory Secondary Education),
  Spain 63
Esping-Anderson, G. 6–7, 83
Étatisme, France 13, 84
  and labor supply 86–90, *87*
EU (European Union) 225
  CUPESSE (Cultural Pathways to
    Economic Self-sufficiency and
    Entrepreneurship) project 12–13,
    38, **39–40**, 41, 171
  Eastern enlargement, 2003 129, 130
  impact of EMU (Economic and
    Monetary Union) process on
    Portugal 129–30, 150, **150**
  youth unemployment 24–5, **26–7**
Europe
  entrepreneurship 10–12, *11*
  youth unemployment rates 10
European Alliance for Apprenticeship
  (EAFA) 64
European Center for the Development
  of Vocational Training *see*
    Cedefop (European Center for the
    Development of Vocational Training)
European Central Bank 110
European Commission 110, 112
European Network of Public
  Employment Services (SPE-UE) 69
European Research Network on
  Vocational Education and Training
  (VETNET) 64–5
European Science Foundation
  (ESF) 225–6
European Social Fund (ESF) 112
European Values Survey 43
Evaluation Institute of the Education
  (INEE), Spain 65
Every Student Succeeds Act, US 211
experimentalism, in Portugal 15, 128–9,
  155, 156–7

F

Fachoberschule, Germany 9
Fachschulen, Germany 9
Fadulu, L. 212
Fasano, L.F. 43
Fayolle, A. 8, 90
Featherstone, K. 102, 103

Federal Institute for Vocational Education
and Training, Germany 10
Fernández, R. 5
FFC (Fragile Families Challenge) 235–6
Field, S. 209
Fordism 138, 139
Fortuna, Joseph 215
Foundation for Science and Technology,
Portugal 226
FPEmpres, Spain 64
Fragile Families Challenge (FFC)
235–6
France 13–14, 206–7
ALMPs (active labor market
policies) 95–6
and the American entrepreneurship
model 16, 237, **238**, 241–2
apprenticeships 88–9
business culture 90
capitalism and labor market
demand 83–6
as a CME (coordinated market
economy) 83, 84
as a conservative/capitalist economy 83
cultural *dirigisme* 81–93
demography, economy and labor force
participation statistics **92–5**
economic growth 91
education and VET (vocational
education and training) system
79–80, 82, 86–9, *87*
elites 81–2, 83
entrepreneurship 11, 90, 94, 220–1
recommendations for 223–6
ethnographic studies 96–7
firm-level institutions 85–6
GEM (Global Entrepreneurship
Monitor) entrepreneurship
rating 59, 216, 220–1
and the German dual education
model 95, 237, **238**, 241–2
Index of Economic Freedom 2020
ranking 84
industrialisation 81
labor market change 91, **92–4**,
94–6, **95**
over-education 85
risk avoidance score 90
self-employment 91
social issues 2
VET (vocational education and
training) 23, 79–81
work culture 8, 89
youth unemployment rates 3, 81, 91
Freeman, R.B. 30
Fundación Bankia 64

Fundación Bertelsmann 184, 191,
192, 194
Fundación de las Cajas de Ahorro,
Spain 70
Fundae 66–7

G

Gannon, M.J. 83
GEM (Global Entrepreneurship
Monitor) 11, 13, 42–3, 59, 72, 114,
120, 216, **217**, 218, **219**, 223, 225
German Value Formula 8, 210, 248
Germany 247
as a CME (coordinated market
economy) 83
as a conservative/capitalist economy 83
dual education model 2, 4, 8–10, 9–10,
17, 23, 31, 88, 89, 136, 165–6, 167,
177, 237, **238**, 244–5, 247, 248
and France 95, 237, **238**, 241–2
German multinationals as transfer
agents 167, 179–84, 186–8, 189–96,
193, 194, 195–6
and Greece 14–15, 103, 112–13,
117–18, 119–20, 167
and Italy 15–16, 24, 34, 41, 44, 167,
171–2, *172*, 182, 188–92, 237,
238, 238–9
and Mediterranean countries 15–16
and Portugal 127–8, 136–7, 140, 141,
142, 149, 150, 151, 155, 156, 158,
167, 237, **238**, 243
and Southern European countries
15–16, 136
and Spain 15–16, 71–2, 167, 169–70,
171–2, *172*, 182, 186–8, 191, 192,
237, **238**, 240–1
economic growth 91
elite universities 83
entrepreneurship 11, 94
FDI (Foreign Direct Investment)
172–3, *173*
firm-level institutions 85–6
GEM (Global Entrepreneurship
Monitor) entrepreneurship
rating 216
Index of Economic Freedom 2020
ranking 84
PISA data 57
work cultures 8
youth unemployment rates 3, 10, 25,
91, 168, *168*, 205
Getting Skills Right: France
(OECD) 80–1
Global Entrepreneurship Monitor
(GEM) 11, 13, 42–3, 59, 72, 114,
120, 216, **217**, 218, **219**, 223, 225

global financial crisis 2007–2008
166, 234–5
Goyer, Michael 85
Grandes Écoles, France 14, 79–80, 82,
83, 89, 207
Great Depression 2, 3
Great Recession 2008
impact on youth unemployment 24–5,
27, 29, 52
Greece
ALMPs (active labor market
policies) 110–11, 119
and the American entrepreneurship
model 16
Cedefop ESI ranking 32, 109
corruption 14–15
economic background and
context 101–3, 111
economic consequences of the
COVID-19 pandemic 3
education system 107, 107–9,
118–19
entrepreneurship 15, 114–15, 118, 120,
220, 246
recommendations for 223–6
GEM (Global Entrepreneurship
Monitor) entrepreneurship
rating 114, 220, 246
and the German dual education model
14–15, 103, 112–13, 117–18,
119–20, 167
graduates 104
labour market institutions, over-
education and skills 106–9
NEET rate 25, 104
over-education 14, 15, 108
sovereign debt crisis 14, 101,
110–11
VET 108–9
Youth Guarantee scheme 112
youth unemployment 103–6, 171
rates 3, 25, 101, 103
youth voices studies 115, **116–17**,
117–20
Grollman, P. 71–2
Guillaud, E. 84
Guiso, L. 5
Gutiérrez, S. 69

H

Hall, P.A. 5, 6, 7, 83, 134, 175
Hancké, B. 5, 84, 85
Hauptschule, Germany 9
Heckman, J.J. 30
Hispanic Americans, youth
unemployment rate 205
Hofman, J.M. 246

Hofstede, Geert 90, 214
Hollande, François 2
Hollenbeck, K. 211, 234
Hörisch, F. 66, 140
HUB Zone Program, US 215
human capital 86, 205–6, 209

I

I remain in the South (Resto al Sud),
Italy 221, 226
ICT (information and communication
technologies) 138
IeFP (Sistems di Istruzione e Formazione
Professionale), Italy 34
IEK (vocational training institute),
Greece 108
ILO (International Labor
Organization) 10, 205
IMF (International Monetary Fund) 110
Index of Economic Freedom 2020
(Heritage Foundation) 84
'Industry-Recognized Apprenticeships,'
US 210
INE (Spanish Statistics Institute) 60
INEE (Evaluation Institute of the
Education), Spain 65
INEE (National Institute of Evaluation in
Education), Spain 66
INE-GSEE (Labour Institute of the
Greek General Confederation of
Labour) 113
information and communication
technologies (ICT) 138
INJUVE (Public Institute of Youth),
Spain 59
INOV program, Portugal 146–7, 149,
151, 152
institutional isomorphism 181
integration 182
Intermediate VET, Spain 63
International Labor Organization
(ILO) 10, 205
International Monetary Fund (IMF) 110
internships, in Portugal 145–6, 148, 155
Isenberg, D. 224
Istituti Tecnici Superiori (ITS), Italy 188–9
Italy
and the American entrepreneurship
model 16, 41–2, 237, **238**, 239–40
as an MME 7, 176
Cedefop ESI ranking 32–3
cultural factors and work values 37–8,
39–40, 41, 42–5
economic consequences of the
COVID-19 pandemic 3
educational system 34–5
entrepreneurship 114, 221, 246

recommendations for 223–6
GEM (Global Entrepreneurship
    Monitor) entrepreneurship
    rating 11, 42–3, 59, 114, 216,
    221, 246
and the German dual education
    model 15–16, 24, 41, 44, 167,
    171–2, *172*, 182, 188–92, 237,
    238, 238–9
labor market 25, 35
NEET rate 25
regional economic variations 25
risk avoidance score 90
segmented economy and regional
    variations 35–6
VET (vocational education and
    training) 31–5, 36–8, 170–1, 171–2,
    172, 173, 179, 188–91, 193
policy prescriptions 41–5, *42*
Youth Guarantee scheme 171
youth unemployment 3, 12–13, 22–3,
    24–5, **26–7**, 168–9, 172
causes of 27, 29–34
rates 104, 168, *168*
ITS (Istituti Tecnici Superiori),
    Italy 188–9
IUT (University Institute of Technology),
    France 88
Ivy League universities, US 82, 83

J

Jansen, M. 70
Job Corps, US 212
Job Creation and Local Economic
    Development (OECD) 84–5
'Jobs Act,' Italy 35
JTPA (Job Training Partnership Act),
    US 16, 211, 212

K

Kauffman Center for Entrepreneurial
    Leadership, US 215
Kelley, D. 90
Kennedy, Paul 81
Knill, C. 181
knowledge-based economies 138–9
knowledge-based economy, Portugal's
    transition to 128, 138, 141
Kottaridi, C. 173
Kougias, K.G. 111
Krugman, Paul 235
Kuczera, M. 209

L

La Buona Scuola, Italy 36–7
Labour Institute of the Greek General
    Confederation of Labour
    (INE-GSEE) 113

LABREF database (European
    Commission) 128, 142
Lamborghini 189
Latvia 167
Le plan d'action pour la croissance et la
    transformation des entreprises (New
    Action Plan for Business Growth and
    Transformation), France 220, 226
Lerman, R. 209
liberal education, US 206
liberal market economies (LMEs) 5, 6, 7,
    15, 134, 136, 137, 140, 174, 177–8,
    179, 244
Lisbon Strategy 147, 149, 152
LMEs (liberal market economies) 5, 6, 7,
    15, 134, 136, 137, 140, 174, 177–8,
    179, 244
localization 182, 184, 194–5
Italy 188–91, 192
López, A. 67

M

Machiavelli, N. 43
Macron, E. 81, 82, 96–7
Madeo, K. 102
Malkoutzis, N. 105
Marques, P. 66, 140
Marseilles, France 14
Marsh, D. 180–1
material capital 82
McClelland, David 8, 205, 210, 248
Mediterranean countries 7–9
and the American entrepreneurship
    model 218, **219**, 220–2
and German dual education
    model 15–16
impact of Great Recession 2008 on
    youth unemployment 24–5
mental health, and youth unemployment
    in Greece 105–6
Metaptycjiaka (Master's programmes),
    Greece 108
Mills, C, Wright 82
minimum wage policies 4, 233, 234
Italy 27
Spain 59, 70
US (United States) 212, 213–14
Ministry of Economy, Development and
    Tourism, Greece 220
Ministry of Education and Religious
    Affairs, Greece 107
Ministry of Education, Culture and Sport
    (Ministerio de Educació, Cultura
    y Deporte/MECD), Spain 60–1,
    65, 66
Ministry of Education, University and
    Research, Italy 188
Ministry of Labor, Spain 176

Ministry of Labor and Social Policies, Italy 188
Ministry of Science, Innovation and Universities, Spain 226
Ministry of Science, Technology and Higher Education, Portugal 226
Mitrakos, T. 118
MMEs (mixed-market economies) 7, 175
Mokyr, J. 5
Moldes, R. 69
Möller, K. 183
Mosca, Gaetano 43
Mroz, T.A. 30
Mumbai, India 11
Murphy, J.P. 80, 95–7
Murray, Charles 82

N

National Association of Manufacturers, US 213
National Consortium for Entrepreneurship Education, US 215
National Entrepreneurial Context Index (NECI) 90, 114, 216, 218, **219**
National Federation of Independent Businesses (NFIB), US 213, 215
National Foundation for Teaching Entrepreneurship, US 215
National Institute for Educational Evaluation, Spain 65
National Institute of Evaluation in Education (INEE), Spain 66
National Institute of Health (NIH), US 225
National Reform Programme, Spain 69
National Science Foundation (NSF), US 226, 245
National System of Qualifications, Portugal 144
NECI (National Entrepreneurial Context Index) 90, 114, 216, 218, **219**
NEET (Not in Employment, Education or Training) young people 2, 109
  Greece 25, 104
  impact of COVID-19 pandemic on 3
  international comparative data 25, **28–9**
  Italy 25
  Portugal 146, 148
  Spain 25, 52, 69
nepotism, in Greece 14, 105, 118, 120, 246
Netherlands 3, 8, 23, 25
networks 193–4, 195–6
  strategic business nets 183

New Action Plan for Business Growth and Transformation (Le plan d'action pour la croissance et la transformation des entreprises), France 220, 226
NFIB (National Federation of Independent Businesses), US 213, 215
Nice, France 14
NIH (National Institute of Health), US 225
NLFET (Not in Labor Force, Education or Training) young people 2
non-meritocracy, in Greece 14, 105
Nordic countries 3, 6, 7–8
Norway 6–7
NSF (National Science Foundation), US 226, 245
NtN *(Nurture thru Nature)* program 1, 224
nuclear power, public attitudes towards 82–3

O

Obama, Barack 208, 212
OECD 225
  Getting Skills Right: France 80–1
  Job Creation and Local Economic Development 84–5
  Youth Unemployment in France: Recent Strategies 79–80
  youth unemployment rates 24
Offices of Entrepreneurial Development, US 215
O'Higgins, N. 27
Okun's coefficient 55
Open Method of Coordination 181
Operation Hope, US 215
output gap
  Italy 29
  Spain 56
over-education 134
  France 85
  Greece 14, 15, 108
  Portugal 134
  Spain 178–9

P

Pan-Hellenic exams (Panellinies), Greece 108, 242
Papadimitriou, D. 102
Pareto, Vilfredo 43
Paris, France 14
Passport Entrepreneurship, Portugal 148
Pastore, F. 9

Perkins Act (Carl Perkins Career and
    Technical Education Act) (2006),
    US 209, 210–11
Pillai, R.K. 83
Pilz, M. 192–3
PIRLS (Progress in International Reading
    Literacy Study) 106
PISA (Programme for International
    Student Assessment),
    OECD 57, 106
Plan for Youth Employment 2019–2021,
    Spain 70–1, 72
policy convergence 181
policy diffusion 180
policy transfer 167, 180–1, 193, 194–6
Polytechneia (research or technical
    universities), Greece 108
Portugal
    access to risk capital 137, 155, 158
    ALMPs (active labor market
        policies) 128, 140, 141–52, **143**,
        150, **153**, 154, 156
    and the American entrepreneurship
        model 15, 16, 127–8, 137, 140,
        141, 142, 149, 150, 151, 155, 156,
        237, **238**, 244
    apprenticeships 128
    economic crisis 111, 130, 138, 139,
        150, **150**, 151, 156
    entrepreneurship 114, 128, 140, 141,
        142, 148, 155, 157, 158, 221–2,
        223–6, 246
    EPL (employment protection legislation)
        reform 131, 140, 156
    experimentalism 15, 128–9, 155,
        156–7
    GEM (Global Entrepreneurship
        Monitor) entrepreneurship
        rating 59, 114, 216, 221, 246
    and the German dual education
        model 127–8, 136–7, 140, 141, 142,
        149, 150, 151, 155, 156, 158, 167,
        237, **238**, 243
    graduate policies 140, 141, 145–6, 149,
        155, 157
    impact of EMU (Economic and
        Monetary Union) process on
        129–30, 150, **150**
    industrial relations 135
    internships 145–6, 148, 155
    manufacturing sector 130, 136–7
    NEET rate 146, 148
    skill mismatches 131, 132, *133*, 134
    sovereign debt crisis 130, 131, 138, 150,
        150, 151–2, 156
    statism/state role 127–8, 134, 135,
        149–50, 155, 157

temporary contracts 131–2, *132*,
    136, 156
transition to knowledge-based
    economy 128, 138, 141
VET (vocational education and
    training) 135, 144, 158
Youth Guarantee scheme 145, 146,
    151, 152, **153**
youth unemployment 127–9, 157
    context and nature of *129*, 129–32,
        132, *133*, 134
    rates 127, 129, *129*, 140, 157
Powell, W.W. 181
'practice to theory' model 8
precarity
    Greece 14, 104
    Italy 31
    Spain 60
price system 21, 23, 33, 35, 36, 239, 240
Princess Foundation of Girona 64, 184
Program of Support for Entrepreneurship
    and Self-Employment Creation
    (Programa de Apoio ao
    Empreendedorismo e à Criação
    do Próprio Emprego - PAECPE),
    Portugal 222
Programa Investe Jovem (Youth
    Investment Program), Portugal 222
Programme for International Student
    Assessment (PISA), OECD 57, 106
Progress in International Reading Literacy
    Study (PIRLS) 106
PS (Socialist Party), Portugal 139
Ptychia (professional education degrees),
    Greece 108
Public Institute of Youth (INJUVE),
    Spain 59
public sector employment 233, 234
    Greece 104
    US 211
Public Service of State Employment,
    Spain 66
public-private partnerships 224
Putnam, R.D. 43–4

Q

QANRP (quality assurance national
    reference), Spain 66

R

Realschule, Germany 9
responsiveness 182
Resto al Sud (I remain in the South),
    Italy 221, 226
Robert Bosch Foundation 184, 186, 191
Robert Bosch GmbH 186, 187, 191, 194
Roberts, Chief Justice John G. 235

Royo, S. 178–9
Ryan, P. 209

S

Salganik, M. 236
Salvans, G. 66–7
San Francisco, US 11
Sancha, I. 69
Sapienza, P. 5
Savage, T.H. 30
SBIR (Small Business Innovation
    Research) /STTR (Small Business
    Technology Transfer) program,
    US 225
scarring effects of unemployment 30–1
Schmidl, R. 110, 234
Schmillen, A. 30
Schumpeter, J.A. 8, 90, 138, 139, 218
scientific research 225–6
Seattle, Washington, US 213–14, 234
Seputiene, J. 56
Sgobbi, F. 179
Shadish, W.R. 247
Shanghai, China 11
Sistems di Istruzione e Formazione
    Professionale (IeFP), Italy 34
Skills Forecast: Trends and Challenges to
    2030 (Cedefop) 109
Slovakia 167
Slovic, P. 82, 84
Small Business Administration, US 215
Small Business Innovation Research
    (SBIR) /STTR (Small Business
    Technology Transfer) program,
    US 225
Smith, Adam 204
social capital 215
social sciences
    broad application of 247–8
    lack of consensus in 236–47, **238**
    and policy makers 234–6
Socialist Party (PS), Portugal 139
Sombart, W. 4
Soskice, D. 5, 6, 7, 83, 134, 175
Southern European countries 6, 134
    and the German dual education
        model 15–16, 136
    and the US entrepreneurial model 136
    VET (vocational education and
        training) 135, 166–7
Southern Italy see Italy
sovereign debt crisis 166
    Greece 14, 101, 110–11
    Portugal 130, 131, 138, 150, **150**,
        151–2, 156
    Spain 13

ALMPs (active labor market
    policies) 67, **68**, 69–71
and American entrepreneurship
    model 16, 72
as an MME 7, 175–6
apprenticeships 71–2
Cedefop ESI ranking 32, 56
economic growth rates 55–6
education system 56–7
    general education reforms 60–1, 65–6
educational spending 56–7, 66
entrepreneurship 13, 114, 222,
    223–6, 246
    recommendations for 223–6
GEM (Global Entrepreneurship
    Monitor) entrepreneurship
    rating 59, 72, 114, 216, 222, 246
and the German dual education
    model 15–16, 71–2, 167, 169–70,
    171–2, 172, 182, 186–8, 191, 192,
    237, **238**, 240–1
impact of economic cycles 58
impact of the COVID-19 pandemic 3
minimum wage 70
NEET rate 25, 52, 69
over-education 178–9
PISA data 57
poor wages 59–60
risk avoidance score 90
self-employment 59
teaching profession 65
temporary contracts and
    underemployment 58–9
VET (vocational education and
    training) 60–7, 61, **62–3**, 63–5, **67**,
    169–70, 171–2, 172, 173, 178–9,
    184–5, 186–8, 193
Youth Guarantee scheme 13, 69, 70,
    71, 176
youth unemployment 52, **53–4**,
    168–9, 172
    causal factors 55–60
    impact of Great Recession on 52, 55
    legislative and regulatory
        measures 60–1, **61**, **62–3**, 63–7, **67**,
        68, 69–71
    rates 3, 25, **53**, 54, 104, 168, 168
    regional variations 51, 52, **54**, 57
Spanish Confederation of Small and
    Medium-Sized Enterprises 184
Spanish Foundation for Science and
    Technology 226
Spanish Statistics Institute (INE) 60
SPE-UE (European Network of Public
    Employment Services) 69
standardization 167, 182, 183, 184, 194–5
    Spain 186–8

Standing, G. 104
Start-Up Act (2012), Italy 221
StartUp Portugal Program 2016 222, 244
StartUp Portugal + Program
    2018 222, 226
State Education Inspectorate, Spain 65
State Foundation for Training and
    Employment (Fundación Estatal para
    la Formación en el Empleo/Fundae),
    Spain 66
statism, in Portugal 127–8, 134, 135,
    149–50, 155, 157
statism/state role 127–8, 134, 135,
    149–50, 155, 157
Stiglitz, Joseph 235
strategic business nets 183
Strategy for Entrepreneurship and
    Youth Employment 2013–2016,
    Spain 69, 72
Strengthening Career and Technical
    Education for the 21st Century Act
    (2019), US 210–11
STS (Higher Technician's Section),
    France 88
Svendsen, G.L. 215
Svendsen, G.T. 215
Sweden 218
    ALMPs (active labor market policies) 95
    democratic capitalism 6–7
    economic growth 91
    entrepreneurship 94
    Index of Economic Freedom 2020
        ranking 84
    risk avoidance score 90
    youth employment 7–8
    youth unemployment 91
Switzerland 223
symbolic capital 82, 83

T

Tawney, R.H. 4
teaching profession, in Spain 65
TEI (technical education institutes),
    Greece 108
temporary employment 58–9, 131–2,
    132, 136, 156
terrorism, France 2
Tetlock, P.E. 247
Themelis, S. 104
'theory to practice' model 8
third way policies 139, 155–6
Thrush, G. 212
TIMSS (Trends in International
    Mathematics and Science
    Study) 106
Topel, R.H. 30
Tosun, J. 142

transfer studies *see* policy transfer
Trends in International Mathematics and
    Science Study (TIMSS) 106
Triantafyllidou, D. 106–7
Trigilia, C. 176
Troncoso-Ponce, D. 70
Trump, Donald 210–11, 212, 235
trust 43
    in governments 82–3
Tsekeris, C. 115

U

UK 71, 83
Ulijn, J. 8, 90
Umkehrer, M. 30
unemployment
    as cause of future unemployment
        30–1
    scarring effects of 30–1
    see also youth unemployment
United Nations Sustainable Development
    Goal #4 3
University Institute of Technology (IUT),
    France 88
US (United States)
    ALMPs (active labor market
        policies) 212–13
    American Value Formula 205, 209, 248
    demand side of labor market 209–14
    economic consequences of the
        COVID-19 pandemic 2–3
    economic growth 91
    education system 207–9, *208*
    elite universities 82, 83
    entrepreneurship 1–2, 10–12, *11*,
        94, 248
    entrepreneurship model 2, 4, 10–12,
        11, 16, 17, 23, 203–4, 214–16, **217**,
        218, 222–6, 237, 247
        and France 16, 95, 237, **238**, 241–2
        and Greece 16
        and Italy 16, 41–2, 237, **238**, 239–40
        and Mediterranean countries 218,
            219, 220–2
        and Portugal 15, 16, 127–8, 137, 140,
            141, 142, 149, 150, 151, 155, 156,
            237, **238**, 244
        and Southern European countries
            136
        and Spain 16, 72
    GEM (Global Entrepreneurship
        Monitor) rating 42–3
    Index of Economic Freedom 2020
        ranking 84
    labor market supply side 205–9, *208*
    minimum wage policies 212, 213–14
    presidential campaign 2016 247

risk avoidance score 90
SMEs 215
VET (vocational education and
    training) 207–9, *208*
wage subsidies 212–13
work ethos 204–5, 245
youth unemployment
    racial diversity in 205
    rates 2–3, 10, 205
US Chamber of Commerce 213

V

Varajão, J. 154
Verdier, T. 5
VET (vocational education and
    training) 135, 144, 158
France 13–14, 23, 79–80, 79–81, 82,
    86–9, *87*
Greece 108–9
Italy 12–13, 31–5, 36–8, 170–1,
    171–2, *172*, 173, 179, 188–91,
    193
    policy prescriptions 41–5, *42*
    policy approaches 33–4
Portugal 135, 144, 158
purposes of 23
Southern European
    countries 135, 166–7
Spain 13, 60–7, 61, **62–3**, 63–5, **67**,
    169–70, 171–2, *172*, 173, 178–9,
    184–5, 186–8, 193
US (United States) 207–9, *208*
'youth experience gap' 31–2
see also Germany, dual education
    system; US (United States),
    entrepreneurship model
VET/Básica (Basic Vocational Education
    and Training), Spain 63
VETNET (European Research Network
    on Vocational Education and
    Training) 64–5
VoC (varieties of capitalism) typology
    5–6, 7, 15, 134
    critiques of 179–80
    Portugal 15, 128
    and VET systems 167, 173–9, 181–2,
    193
vocational education and training
    (VET) *see* VET (vocational
    education and training)
Vocational Training Act 1969
    (Germany) 166

W

wage subsidies
Portugal 147–8

Spain 70
US 212–13
Ward, M.P. 30
Weber, Max 4
welfare states 138–9
    and typology of national economies
    6–7, 83
White Americans, youth unemployment
    rate 205
WIA (Workforce Investment Act) (1998),
    US 16, 211, 212
WIOA (Workforce Innovation and
    Opportunity Act) (2013), US 16,
    211, 212, 234
Wise, D.A. 30
Women's Business Ownership, US 215
work attitudes and values
    CUPESSE (Cultural Pathways to
    Economic Self-sufficiency and
    Entrepreneurship) project, EU
    12–13, 38, **39–40**, 41
Workers' Commissions, Spain 66
Workforce Innovation and Opportunity
    Act (WIOA) (2013), US 16, 211,
    212, 234
Workforce Investment Act (WIA) (1998),
    US 16, 211, 212
World Bank 114
World Economic Forum 225
World Values Survey 43
WTO (World Trade Organization), and
    China 129, 130

Y

YEI (Youth Employment Initiative),
    Greece 112–13
Young Entrepreneur Foundation, US 215
YoungBiz, US 215
Youth Employment Initiative (YEI),
    Greece 112–13
Youth Employment Package, EU 110
Youth Employment Plan 2019–2021,
    Spain 222, 226
Youth Enterprise Institute, US 215
Youth Guarantee 110, 140–1, 166–7, 193
    Greece 112
    Italy 171
    Portugal 145, 146, 151, 152, **153**
    Spain 13, 69, 70, 71, 176
Youth Invest program, Portugal 148–9
Youth Investment Program (Programa
    Investe Jovem), Portugal 222
Youth Opportunities Initiative, EU 110
youth unemployment 22, 157
    causal factors 4, 22–3, 27, 29–34, 165
    impact of economic cycle on 24, 29–30

impact of Great Recession 2008 24–5,
    27, 29
impact of the COVID-19
    pandemic 2–3
international comparative data 25, **26–7**
negative impacts of 4

youth labour market overview 2–4
Youth Unemployment in France: Recent
    Strategies (OECD) 79–80

Z

Zingales, L. 5